LAWYERS CAN S … HEALTH

Under English law, … accident (on the roads, at work, in hospital, or wherever) is not entitled to compensation – however horrendous his injuries – unless he proves in a Court of law that his accident was caused by someone else's fault. He therefore employs a team of lawyers who will try to show that his accident was the fault of the other party, and the other party's (insurance company's) team of lawyers will try to show that it wasn't; and the Judge will decide which version he accepts. If the Judge decides that the injured person hasn't proved his case, not only does he get no compensation, but he has to pay all the legal costs – his own and those of the other party. The average time it takes for a personal injury case to come to Court is four years from the date of the accident, and in over a third of such cases it takes between four and eight years – as found by the Royal Commission on Legal Services.

What sort of justice is this, which gives a seriously injured person compensation for his injuries only after a four year war of attrition, if he wins his case; and if he loses (and does not qualify for legal aid), makes him pay some £20,000 in legal fees for the Court's decision that he is *not* entitled to any compensation?

This book is in four parts. The first examines how the lawyers have been able to foist such a ludicrous system on the British public. The second chronicles some actual case histories, and shows what this system can mean for those who inadvertently get caught up in it. The third shows how the system – particularly the division of lawyers into solicitors and barristers, and the fact that the injured person claiming compensation (plaintiff) is virtually powerless in the hands of his lawyers – makes for incompetence and corruption on their part. In fact about 97% of all personal injury cases, in respect of which writs are issued, never get to Court, but are either abandoned or settled out of Court by the plaintiff accepting whatever derisory or insubstantial sum the defendant's insurance company offers. The fourth suggests the solution.

MICHAEL JOSEPH got a law degree at Cambridge University, and qualified as a solicitor in 1962. In the Solicitors' Final examination he came in the first three out of some five hundred candidates. His first book, The Conveyancing Fraud, of which 50,000 copies have been sold, was published in 1976.

Lawyers can seriously damage your health

Michael Joseph M.A.
Solicitor of the Supreme Court

Michael Joseph
27 Occupation Lane
Woolwich
London S.E.18

FURTHER COPIES OF THIS BOOK ARE OBTAINABLE
FROM THE AUTHOR at
27 OCCUPATION LANE, WOOLWICH, LONDON S.E.18
Price £3.95 (post free)

ISBN 0 9505023 2 4

Cover design by Wendy Hoile

Text set by Jubal Multiwrite Ltd,
66 Loampit Vale, London S.E.13.
Printed and bound by Anchor Brendon Ltd,
of Tiptree, Essex

Contents

Introduction

The following is an extract from 'Person to Person', B.B.C. Radio 4 (June 18 1980):

DEREK ROBINSON: And now we have Michael Joseph on the line, which is a name which rings all sorts of bells with me and I'm sure it does with you, Lord Denning, when I tell you that Mr. Joseph is a — solicitor.
MICHAEL JOSEPH (for it is he): Thank you. Lord Denning, you said in answer to another questioner that if someone came forward with a better system for personal injury compensation we'd all be very pleased. Well I have a better system, and that is for accident victims to get compensation automatically without having to prove negligence. The present system is disastrous from the victim's point of view, who often has to wait five or six years for his case to come to Court, but it suits the lawyers very well. For instance Queen's Counsel *gets £1000 a day and the barrister who sits behind him saying nothing* — [the words in italics were uttered but not transmitted].
ROBINSON (sharply): Lord Denning is ready to answer your question.
LORD DENNING: You will know that there was a Royal Commission on this presided over by Lord Pearson,* and I would have liked them to have recommended a system of compensation without fault so as to save the community all the expense and delay of litigation, but after the Royal Commission reported they were against it. So I'm afraid we are landed with it as they made no radical suggestion. So I don't see any government altering it after a Royal Commission has reported, though I personally would sympathize with you. I think the remedy is to speed up these cases, and you've got to remember that insurance companies on the whole do settle cases quickly when they're good bona fide cases.
JOSEPH: But insurance companies will often offer derisory sums, and the plaintiffs are then pressured by their own solicitors

---

* Not to be confused with the Royal Commission on Legal Services, Chairman, Lord Benson.

to accept. The Royal Commission was set up because of public disquiet over the Thalidomide question, and when years later they come up with their damp and squalid findings everyone has forgotten about it.
DENNING: You're quite right. Very often that does happen with a Royal Commission. I've often thought that is the government's way of delaying things, but I'm afraid it's part of our system. I sympathize entirely with your view, but I don't know that we can do much more about it at the moment.
JOSEPH: Have you ever expressed concern?
DENNING: Yes, but people don't always listen to what I say. When we get cases which are long delayed we are very concerned, and we do our best to reprove those responsible for the delay. But I'm afraid the matter has been considered by the Royal Commission and I don't think we can do anything about it.
JOSEPH: But it's not just the delay or even cost, but the impossibility of proving how the accident happened if, for instance, there are no witnesses.
DENNING: You're quite right. I sympathize with you, Mr. Joseph, but it's part of our system at the moment and I don't see we can alter it at this stage.
ROBINSON: Mr. Joseph, thank you for calling. And, er, you know, life is not perfect I'm afraid.

* * * * * *

Quite so, Mr. B.B.C. interviewer. And some of life's little imperfections are more interesting than others. And this particular imperfection, and the reasons for it, strike me as being so interesting that I have decided to write a book about it.

* * * * * *

N.B.1. To avoid saying man *or woman*, men *or women*, his *or her*, a thousand times, I ask my readers to accept that when I use the male noun, as in 'professional man' or similar, I include the female.

N.B.2. When italics appear in a quotation they are *my* italics unless stated.

N.B.3. A glossary of legal and other possibly unfamiliar terms appears at the end of the book.

Part One

Why we have the legal system we do

1 *Tradesmen and professionals*

When you go into a pub and order two pints of bitter, half of Guinness, a lager and lime and oh, er, four of those sausages, you won't know whether the total should come to £2.80 or £3.65. The barman knows you don't know, and so in the case of a moderately elaborate order the chances are that he will add 10% or 20% to the correct price, which will find its way into his pocket before the night is out. This is one of the standard dodges by which barmen eke out their no doubt meagre earnings — connived at by brewers and publicans alike in that a price list is rarely, if ever, displayed. There are, of course, more sophisticated tricks in the business, and an alert barman will know which ruse to employ when. If the pub is noisy and crowded he'll probably settle for the straight overcharging. With a young couple hand in hand, he might decide the girl is sufficiently intoxicated with her companion as to be unlikely to notice any deficiency in the intoxicants which *he* dispenses. Thus he might stand the rim of the glass in a saucer of gin, so that the ultimate 'gin and orange', although smelling authentic, actually contains only the latter beverage. Another endearing habit is to supplement the beer in the cellar with the left-overs in every glass — having been either emptied surreptitiously into a tray or bucket under the counter during trading, or else collected after closing time.

The publican's trade is notorious for this type of swindling, but many trades offer similar opportunities. Sometimes the customer has virtually no means of knowing whether he is being duped. In the case of a major car repair, for instance, how does the customer know whether the big ends or whatever actually *have* been renewed? Unless he is himself an able mechanic, who is prepared to strip his engine down after the repair has been carried out (in which case he would probably do the job himself anyway), he doesn't. And if a mechanic, when asked to test a suspect clutch, drives the car up a hill whereupon the clutch slips, how does the customer know that the mechanic — by changing gear and simultaneously accelerating at an appropriate moment — has not deliberately *made* it slip? When your only daughter gets married, and you instruct a catering firm to lay on the reception — fifty bottles of wine will allow each guest three glasses each which *should* be enough — how do you know that the fifty bottles charged for were actually supplied? Unless you insist on pouring all the drinks yourself, and counting each bottle as it is emptied (a procedure hardly likely to enhance the conviviality of the proceedings), you don't.

How does the fruit and vegetable broker in London, who supplies a hundredweight of strawberries (which he's never seen) to a retailer in Stockport, know whether that gentleman is telling the truth when he says that the fruit arrived over-ripe and had to be sold at half price, or whether he is 'pulling a stroke'? A London broker once told me of some of the 'strokes' he pulled, and which in turn had been pulled on him. Once he offered a French lorry driver, who had delivered a load of apples he had ordered from France, a £10 note with a bit of paper bearing a Midlands address — i.e. he was offering the driver a tip in order to get his goods transported to their ultimate destination otherwise free of charge. To his amazement (for £10 was the going rate for this service) the driver started jumping up and down apparently incoherent with rage. Neither having any understanding of the other's language, it was several noisy minutes before the broker realized what had happened. The lorry driver was in fact the *owner* of the French haulage firm, who had decided to drive one of his lorries over to try and discover why his drivers were taking so long on their overseas deliveries — an anecdote which may help explain the furore which greeted the proposals to make the tachograph (spy in the cab) compulsory. Lorry drivers, it seems, have their perks as well as businessmen.

I remember meeting the representative of a reputable dry rot control and wood preservation firm, on behalf of the owner of a block of shops. A slight attack of dry rot had been discovered in one of the shops, and the owner had instructed this specialist firm to make a 'free' survey of the rest of his property. The specialist duly went round all the shops, plugging his damp meter into all the skirting boards, which duly registered excess moisture 'sufficient to support a growth of *merulius lacrymans* or other fungal decay'. In due course the firm submitted its report and recommendations together with neat little plans attached to big stiff prospectuses. Although no further outbreak of dry rot had been discovered, and the building was only thirty years old, apparently *all* the damp-proof courses in *all* the shops had unaccountably broken down, and the firm recommended new chemical damp-proof courses throughout, at a cost of several thousand pounds. One of the shops had a wood block floor. This, according to the report, being laid on concrete was *not* good practice; and for another £*x* hundred the firm recommended ripping up the (perfectly sound) wood block floor and replacing it with another layer of concrete. Happily the owner consulted another firm, which decided that only in one small area had the damp-proof course broken down. For the rest, the damp meter had been picking up condensation. And so on, and so on.

The BBC Checkpoint programme, presented each week by Roger Cook, chronicles the various ways man finds to swindle man. My favourite episode was on cowboy plumbers (June 12 1980). A workman employed by a certain company recounted how, when called in to repair a boiler, he would remove its vital parts – even though he could see at a glance that the fault was trivial, necessitating expenditure of but a few pounds. The hapless householder would then be presented with an estimate for £150 or so. If he demurred, he (or more usually she) would be told that the company had already done £100 worth of work in stripping down the boiler, and only on payment of such sum would the parts be returned. The company's office was stacked high with boxes of assorted boiler parts, whose unfortunate owners could not afford to redeem. The workman recalled an occasion when he was called to an old lady's house to rectify inadequate water pressure. He noticed at once that the stopcock was half closed, but explained to his customer that the cause of the trouble was a blockage in a section of pipe behind the bath. The lady, having to go out for the day, left the plumber to carry out the repair. He himself left as soon as she had gone (having given the stopcock a couple of twists); and returned in the evening shortly before she did, to present her with a bill for £400

– which she gratefully paid, exclaiming that she had never had water pressure so good.

'A nation of fiddlers' was how a 'Man Alive' television programme once described us, and it seems that one way or another most of us do it. The verb *to cheat* is one of those strange irregular verbs which we instinctively learn to conjugate: I doodle, you diddle, he fiddles, they swindle. Neither does it seem to make any difference to our grasp of this particular verb whether we went to the posh school, or the state school round the corner. For every pound fiddled by the tricky barman, his better educated brother on the local Council, with his fingers in many lucrative pies, salts away a thousand.

What obviously do vary from trade to trade are the *opportunities* for fiddling. Thus when I buy the Sunday Times the newsagent cannot overcharge me, because the price is clearly printed on each copy; neither can he palm me off with the Sunday Express, because I can tell the difference. But I can't tell the difference between a vintage burgundy and a perfectly respectable *vin ordinaire*. (In fact, according to an expert witness giving evidence during a prosecution of a group of French wine growers, until wine is four years old *no-one* can.) Therefore as like as not the wine-shipper will take advantage of my ignorance to misdescribe his wares, and inflate his prices accordingly. He is neither more nor less intrinsically dishonest than his news-vending cousin. The only reason my newsagent never cheats me is because he can't.

Given unlimited opportunities, *x*% of the operators will take unlimited advantage. Not always is it the customer who is the initial dupe. In some trades (notably building and catering) it is the management which is more likely to be swindled by its own workpeople — but as the management then passes its loss on to the customer, it comes to the same thing. And in many trades it is virtually impossible to prevent swindling. . .

Nevertheless, the amount of trickery which can be perpetrated in an open market is limited by three factors.

First, tradesmen do not operate monopolies. So on being told that his clutch needs renewing, the car owner can always get a second or third opinion. So our property owner, faced with an amazing report from a specialist firm that the damp-proof courses in eight adjoining shops had all broken down, and all needed renewing at the cost of several thousand pounds, can always ring up half a dozen *other* firms; and it is unlikely that those half dozen firms would all be dishonest, or if they were, that they would all be dishonest *in the same way*. The noise and crush of a crowded pub give the tricky barman a seemingly insuperable advantage over his customer, who cannot carry the price of a couple of dozen different drinks in his head, and in any case will be more concerned to rejoin his friends than count his pennies. Yet the barman must know how far he can go, and that if he goes there too often it is at the risk of ignominious exposure. The fruit and veg merchant can 'pull' a few 'strokes'. But if he pulls too many, he gets recognised and shunned. According to the Bad Food Guide,* some sort of swindle is probably being perpetrated by over two-thirds of those engaged in the catering trade. Yet if I get an obviously bad or overpriced meal, I'm unlikely to pay the restaurant a second visit.

Secondly, those who make our laws have decided that swindling is *illegal*. Therefore however safe a particular swindle may seem, a criminal prosecution is always a possibility to be uneasily borne in mind. So it came to pass that a British Rail five man dining car crew was once sentenced at the Old Bailey to a total of 12 years 8 months imprisonment. Their fiddle had been simple. Out of the portions allocated for a single breakfast they made two breakfasts, got cash for both, one lot going into the till, the other remaining in their pockets. Apparently the portions dispensed became ever more niggardly as the dining car crew got greedier, until eventually they resorted to the bizarre expedient of supplementing their pigmy breakfasts with *powdered soup*. Yet this racket had gone on for several years before the transport police were finally alerted, and converged in large numbers and plain clothes on the dining car in question, to witness the phenomenon first hand. The fiddlers five had correctly assessed a fundamental British characteristic: the willingness to suffer almost any outrage rather than complain. But they failed to take account of an even more basic law — that however ingenious the trick and naive the dupe, you can't expect to get away with it *indefinitely*. The tricky barman knows that sooner or later he's going to hear an angry voice proclaim: 'But look here, you made exactly the same mistake when I was in here

* *The Bad Food Guide* by Derek Cooper, published by Routledge & Kegan Paul.

before.' The corrupt civic councillor, however apparently secure, knows that bags containing cats occasionally come untied. Ineffective as legal sanctions obviously are, at least they go a long way to prevent the illicit riches actually being *enjoyed*. Not to the Poulsons or T. Dan Smiths of this realm is the philosophers' stone vouchsafed.

Even those enterprising gentlemen whose grasp of company law enables them to leave a trail of disgruntled creditors battering at the locked doors of their wound up limited companies, while they drive round in the latest model of Mercedes (all perfectly legal), may unexpectedly find themselves at the end of the intrepid Roger Cook's telephone line, or perhaps a fist wielded by a more than usually robust creditor.

The third factor which limits trickery is the customer's ultimate freedom to dispense with the commodity or services altogether. If the menu becomes too pretentious, I can always stay at home. If the wine shipper's chicanery gets too outrageous, I can drink beer instead. If the brewers inject all their beers with carbon dioxide and chemicals to make life easier for *them, I* can drink water. If the cross-channel ferry operators simultaneously decide to double their tariff, I can take my holidays in Bognor. If I'm dissatisfied with British Leyland's after-sales service, next time I can buy a foreign car, or get a bicycle, or walk.

So the world revolves on its axis, and by and large an uneasy balance seems to be maintained. On one end of the see-saw sits ordinary man's love of money, unfettered by moral scruple as to how he gets it. On the other end sit the practicalities of competition, the customer's freedom of choice, and the fear of sanctions if the rules are broken too inexpertly or too persistently.

But if competition, the customer's freedom of choice, and the fear of sanctions balance (or go some way to balancing) ordinary man's love of money, and his unscrupulousness in its pursuit, what of extraordinary man — that is, *professional* man — who is *not* subject to competition, whose services can *not* be dispensed with, and who does not find the rules particularly irksome since it was he who drew them up in the first place? What therefore keeps professional man in check, if he is as greedy and unscrupulous as the rest of mankind?

The answer, happily, is a simple one. He isn't. Professional people have a high degree of detachment and integrity and, above all, they have a strong sense of responsibility and an exceptional commitment to the interests of their clients which transcends all other commitments. This is what I read in the leader columns of The Times (January 5 1980), so it must be true.

We find similar sentiments in the 1970 report of the Monopolies Commission: 'A transaction for the supply of professional services can never be settled as a simple bargain between purchaser and seller, each acting to further his own interest. A seller of *professional* services is expected to subordinate his self-interest to the client's interest' (para 286).

And again, in a pamphlet published by the General Dental Council: 'One of the most important distinguishing characteristics of a profession is that its members acknowledge an overriding responsibility to maintain certain standards of conduct. . .From the time he is engaged to serve his client he [the professional] is expected to identify himself with his client's interests even, if need be, at the expense of his own.'

And again, this time from the Lord Chancellor, Lord Hailsham: 'Lawyers and other members of the professions serve the public by. . .practice involving a considerable degree of self-denial, and a habit of disinterested professional judgment.' (Address to the Law Society's Conference, 1982).

And, more succinctly, from the Monopolies and Mergers Commission Report 1976: a professional man 'always puts his clients' interests before his own.'

In other words, the butcher, the baker, the candlestick maker, are all busy furthering their own interests: and human nature being what it is, as we have seen, some of them go further than others. But the hallmark of a professional man is that he subordinates *his* self interest to the interests of his clients.

So it is that Parliament, realizing that ordinary man is divided into the scrupulous and the unscrupulous, has issued a spate of legislation to protect us against the latter category. But at the same time Parliament realizes that professional men, by and large, can be safely left to regulate themselves without interference from outside. There was a debate in the House of Commons on this very point.

Most of this 'consumer' legislation, by its nature, does not apply to the professions, who do not, for example, advertise their goods or services, and so are unaffected by the provisions of the Trade Descriptions Act; who do not proffer contracts containing exclusion clauses, so are unaffected by the Unfair Contract Terms Act; who do not manufacture or supply goods, so are not caught by the Restrictive Trade Practices Act, and so on. But there *was* a piece of legislation which could indeed have had far reaching effects for the professional.

Under the Fair Trading Act 1973 the Secretary of State may 'designate' any particular body which provides a service; and once designated, any restrictive practice operated by that body shall be invalid *unless it can satisfy the Court that the restrictive practice is in the public interest*. Now whereas the professions do not advertise, nor hide behind exclusion clauses, nor peddle mortgages etc. they *do* operate restrictive practices. The question was, should the restrictive practices operated by the professions be treated in the same way as the restrictive practices operated by anyone else, or should they be exempt? The Act, as originally drafted, did contain such an exemption (a provision that professional services, as listed in the 4th Schedule, shall never be designated). But some Members of Parliament rebelled, and called a debate in which they argued that there was no justification for treating a professional restrictive practice any differently to a non-professional one, and that both should be subject to scrutiny by the Court. But they were outvoted. The majority of the House endorsed the opinion of the Under Secretary of State:—

> 'The professions are distinguished by a high degree of skill and learning acquired after long and specialized courses of intellectual study and practical training. They maintain standards of ethical conduct beyond those required of the ordinary citizen by the law, and accept personal responsibility to those whom they serve.' (Notice, incidentally, the assumption that a 'high degree of skill and learning' leads to superior 'standards of ethical conduct');

and of Sir Geoffrey Howe Q.C.:

> 'The professions, and the institutions by which they are governed, have held an honourable and long established place in the pattern of our society. One should pay respect to the institutions whereby the professions have governed

> themselves for many years. . . They have codes by which they regulate and conduct themselves. That is the argument behind the difference.' (Hansard, April 12 1973).

In other words, the Court has no need to examine whether a restrictive practice operated by a *profession* is against the public interest because professional man, by virtue of his superior ethical standards, would never operate a restrictive practice *unless* it was in the public interest. Accordingly the Fair Trading Act was passed, with the clause excluding the professions from its potentially stringent provisions intact.

Just as a professional man (unlike an ordinary man) would never operate a restrictive practice unless it was in the public interest, so he would never take advantage of his client's ignorance – unlike, e.g., a landlord, moneylender or finance company. So legislation lays down that if a landlord gives his tenant notice to quit or notice to repair, the notice must also give details (in letters no smaller than the rest of the notice) of the tenant's legal rights to counter such notice. Likewise the Hire Purchase Acts and the Moneylenders Acts stipulate certain information which must be given by the finance company or moneylender to the purchaser or borrower, with dramatic penalties if such provisions are overlooked. Parliament realizes that it is no use giving a weaker party legal rights against a stronger party, unless there is an obligation on the part of the stronger to notify the weaker of those rights. But in the rare case of a client being given a statutory right against his *solicitor* – the right to require the solicitor to get a certificate from the Law Society that his bill is reasonable – no-one thought to include an obligation by the solicitor to *notify* the client of that right. Moreover once the client has paid the bill that right is lost, even if he only paid as a result of being threatened with legal proceedings. The relevant provision is the Solicitors' Remuneration Order 1972, which was not considered important enough to merit a separate debate. But if there had been a debate, we may surmise that the 'argument behind the difference' would similarly have been: professional men maintain standards of ethical conduct superior to finance companies, moneylenders and landlords, and therefore you don't need to tell professional men what information they must give to their clients; still less do you dictate the size of the letters they must use to impart it.

In May 1981, the Acheson report on London doctors indicated that in some respects the service they gave was below standard, e.g. some doctors did not retire when they should, some waiting rooms were sordid, and so on. The Minister of Health, Gerard Vaughan, was interviewed on this report on television.* Did the Minister think that the report's recommendations should be implemented by legislation? 'No I don't think so,' he replied. 'These are professional people and should be left to run their own business. G.P.'s have a professional wish of their own to improve their service.' In other words, you don't need to control *professional* people by legislation; you merely point out the areas where there is room for improvement and they themselves will attend to them, by reason of their *professional* desire to improve their service.

Because an overtired lorry driver is a danger to the public, Parliament regulates the number of hours he may drive at a stretch; not only that but makes it compulsory for every lorry to be fitted with a tachograph (spy in the cab), so that the lorry drivers' hours and distances can be monitored. Equally dangerous is an overtired hospital doctor. What action, the Minister of Health (Kenneth Clarke) was asked in Parliament, was the government taking to reduce the excessive hours worked by junior hospital doctors (i.e. those below the rank of consultant)? Replied the Minister: 'Broadly speaking there was general agreement that the hours of work of some junior doctors are unacceptable. The participants agreed that action to reduce hours had to be taken locally in consultation with all concerned. I have asked officials to hold discussions with representatives of the profession to *agree* a framework within which local reviews of hours can take place.' (Hansard, March 22 1982.) Doctors, unlike lorry drivers, are professional people. Therefore if some hospital doctors are working 'unacceptable' hours, the profession itself will take the necessary steps to reduce them after 'consultation with all concerned'.

After one or two unfortunate mishaps, it became recognised that it was dangerous for a dentist to act simultaneously as both anaesthetist and operator. When a recurrent and potentially fatal practice can be pinpointed in a non-professional sphere, it is made the subject of an Act of Parliament (e.g. The Factories Act 1961 contains 180 pages of detailed provisions). But dentists

---

* I.T.V. The London Programme, May 22 1981.

being professionals, all that is required is for the Department of Health and Social Security to send a letter (June 26 1975) to all practitioners pointing out the danger, and urging 'any in the profession who may still be following the practice [of simultaneously acting as both anaesthetist and operator] to cease it.'

A provision in the Estate Agents Act obliges estate agents to pass on to the client any interest earned by his deposit. Solicitors also hold housebuyers' deposits, but no corresponding provision appears in the Solicitors' Act. Unlike estate agents, solicitors are profesional people, and will therefore deal fairly with their clients without any legislation *telling* them to.

Professional people 'have a high degree of detachment and integrity and, above all, they have a strong sense of responsibility and an exceptional commitment to the interests of their clients which transcends all other commitments.' This is what I read in the leader columns of The Times, so it must be true. Or rather, this is what I read in the leader columns of The Times, so a lot of important people must *believe* it to be true.

Having seen some instances of how our Cabinet Ministers and Members of Parliament – to whom we entrust the fiddly little job of making our laws – act on this belief, let's look at some other groups of equally important people: the Judges (who make the rest of our law), the Magistrates (who try 96% of all criminal cases), the Disciplinary Committees (which police the professions), the Consumers' Association (which publishes fearless independent reports), the Royal Commission on Legal Services (which has given us a four-volume report on the legal profession), the Newspaper Editors (who tell us what to think), the B.B.C. (which has a monopoly of national broadcasting) – and see how, like our Times leader writer, they also seem to jettison their critical faculties when dealing with professional men.

2 How the judges and commentators abandon their critical faculties when dealing with professional man

(1) Judges and Magistrates

We all know that in the eyes of the law all men are equal. It is the rock on which the whole edifice of British Justice is built. But as anyone who has had a lawsuit with a professional man will also know, some men are more equal than others. Your average judge seems to have an unconscious (and sometimes not so unconscious) affinity with a fellow professional. This does not mean, of course, that he always finds in his favour. But it means that in a legal tussle between ordinary man and professional man, ordinary man will be at a disadvantage — equivalent perhaps to playing a tennis match with his opponent starting each game with a three point lead.

Such legal tussle will usually be an action for negligence. Negligence, in this context, means failure to take reasonable care or exercise reasonable skill, which results in someone else suffering injury or financial loss. And the law makes the ordinary man — tradesman, taxi-driver, craftsman, or whoever — who is proved to have been negligent, pay compensation to the injured party.*

However, in the middle of the last century the Courts devised the term 'crassa neglentia' to describe 'crass' or 'gross' negligence, as distinct from ordinary negligence, and held that a *professional* man was not liable for ordinary negligence, only for gross negligence. As Lord Denning writes (*Discipline of Law* p.237):

'At one time the Courts held that a professional man was not

* This is a branch of the *Civil* law, which lays down what rights one individual has against another. It has nothing to do with the *Criminal* law.

liable for ordinary negligence but only for gross negligence or 'crassa neglentia', as it was called. There is a tendency today to draw the distinction again. It is done so as to protect a professional man from having his reputation unjustly be-smirched.'

Lord Denning implies that the Courts are *coming back* to the idea that professional man is liable only for gross negligence, not for ordinary negligence. In fact they probably never departed from it.

For instance, giving judgment in 1979 in a negligence action against two firms of solicitors (Stewart Wrightson v. Crocker), Lord Denning states: 'The case was embarrassing for two of the most eminent firms of solicitors in the City of London. They should not be found guilty of negligence *unless it was most clearly established*. The ruling that an error of judgment was not negligence was as important for solicitors as for doctors. They should not be harassed by claims for negligence years after the event.' (All negligence actions come to Court years after the event.)

Although he is thought of as an innovator, in expressing these views Lord Denning is merely echoing the philosophy of his predecessors over the years. Thus in 1927, a judge giving judgment stated: 'It was a most unfortunate litigation against a solicitor for negligence . . . the allegation of negligence was serious and *should be approached with the greatest care*' (Ellis v. Sampson). In 1899 a judge stated: 'Where a client sued his solicitor for negligence he must prove it distinctly because the charge was a *serious* one to make against a solicitor' (Farmer v. Turner). In 1845 the judge, in somewhat more forthright terms, ruled that for an action against a solicitor to succeed, there has to be 'negligence of a *crass description*, there must be *gross ignorance*' (Purves v. Landell).

The reasoning behind these decisions seems to be that as an action for negligence against a professional is more serious for him than for an ordinary man, a higher degree of proof by the plaintiff, and a greater degree of negligence on the part of the defendant, are required for the action to succeed. But there is another strand implied in the passage I quoted from Lord Denning's book. The tendency to distinguish between ordinary and gross negligence, and to hold the professional liable only for the latter, 'is done so as to protect a professional man from having his reputation unjustly besmirched.' Now a finding of negligence against a professional man may well be unfortunate for him, but it can only be *unjust* if he has not been negligent at all. The implication is that professional men *are not negligent*; and only if it is conclusively proved that this professional man has been *outrageously* negligent will I, the judge, be prepared to hold that he is an exception and find against him. Let's see this reasoning operating in two more negligence cases against solicitors.

A client, who was buying and selling a house, claimed that his solicitor's negligence had made him bankrupt. His solicitor had exchanged contracts on his purchase before his own buyer was ready to exchange. His buyer then withdrew, the market turned, and he found he could not sell his house at all, but nevertheless had to complete the purchase of the other house with a high interest bank loan. The solicitor claimed that the client had *instructed* him to exchange on the purchase and risk the sale falling through, although he could produce no written evidence — not even a copy letter he had written to the client confirming such instructions. The client argued that he had never so instructed the solicitor but had always emphasized that his purchase was dependent on his sale: and at the trial four separate documents (notes of telephone conversations, internal memoranda) were produced, all supporting the client's contention. The judge found for the solicitor. 'I don't think solicitors of the standing of Messrs *XY* would have made such a fundamental mistake of committing their client to a purchase without having secured his sale *unless they had clear instructions to do so*.' (Daily Mail, May 11 1977).

In the second case, a house purchaser found himself involved in a bitter boundary dispute, having entered into a contract containing a clause giving the seller the right, after completion, to take back up to one tenth of the land conveyed. The purchaser sued his solicitor, claiming that when he went through the contract with his solicitor he had specifically instructed him *not* to accept that clause; and the solicitor had said that he would get it deleted, but nevertheless invited him to sign the contract to save time. The solicitor, on the other hand, claimed that he *never* went through the contract with his client, but as there was some urgency in the matter he approved it on his behalf, and subsequently exchanged it. Said the judge in giving judgment for the solicitor: 'I have to choose between these two accounts . . . So far as Mr. Z is concerned, he seemed to be an ordinary thoroughly reliable solicitor. So far as Mr. Piotrowski is concerned, I gave very careful attention to his evidence but I am afraid I cannot accept that he is accurate about this . . . and I reject his assertion that he gave his solicitor instructions that this clause should be deleted. *It really seems to me quite inconceivable that if he had given such instructions that the solicitor should have taken no action upon them.*' Such a finding, of course, invites the further question: why did this thoroughly reliable solicitor not warn his client of the clause in point? But after stating that there is indeed an obligation on the part of a solicitor to warn his client of any *unusual* clause in a purchase contract, the judge blandly observes: 'I am certainly not prepared to regard this as an unusual clause.'*

See how the judges in these two cases start with the assumption that a professional man is not negligent, and then bend the facts to fit that assumption. Because Messrs *XY*, solicitors, are professional men they are not negligent. Therefore they would not exchange contracts on a client's house purchase without exchanging on his sale, unless they had their client's instructions to do so. As on this occasion they *did* exchange the purchase contract without exchanging on the sale, *therefore* they must have had their client's instructions to do so. This inexorable logic overrides any mere evidence there may be to the contrary. Because Mr. Z, solicitor, is a professional man, he is thoroughly reliable. Therefore he would warn his client of any unusual clause in a purchase contract. As he *didn't* warn his client of this particular clause (which gives the seller the right to take back up to one tenth of the land conveyed), *therefore it cannot be an unusual clause.*†

Because it is impossible to sue teachers for professional (as opposed to administrative) negligence, and because barristers enjoy a special immunity, the majority of professional negligence actions are against solicitors and medical men. Having looked at some cases involving solicitors, let's turn to medical men.

---

* High Court of Justice, October 24 1979, Action no. 2623.

† N.B. When solicitors *are* successfully sued for negligence it is usually in respect of the solicitor's failure to take some formal step in time (e.g. issue a writ, serve a notice or counter-notice under the Landlord and Tenant Act), as a result of which the client's rights are irretrievably lost. These cases are usually settled out of Court as there will be no defence.

First a case in which a lady sued the Health Authority in respect of a routine operation, which had left her permanently paralysed. The surgeon who did the operation was himself a very sick man, suffering from diabetes and terminal cancer (in fact he died eight weeks later); and the basis of her action was that the surgeon should not have carried out the operation, knowing that he was a very sick man. She lost her case and appealed to the Court of Appeal, which gave the following judgment:

'Lord Justice Denning said that Mrs. Nickolls had gone into hospital for what should have been quite a simple operation, but it had been followed by tragic consequences and her life had been ruined . . . His Lordship could not help feeling that *owing to Mr. Joll's [the surgeon's] state of health for some reason or other something went wrong in the operation and damage was done to both these nerves*. But that could not be said to be negligence unless one was to say that every time a surgeon was taken ill in an operating theatre that would be negligence . . . Surgeons ought not to operate unless they were fit to do it. But the trial judge made no error when he came to the very firm conclusion that Mr. Joll was quite fit to perform this particular operation . . . *One could not say that he was unfit to operate.*'*

Again the conclusion — that this professional man was not negligent —comes first, and the logic is twisted to support it. And the more eminent the professional man, the less it seems to matter how blatantly it is twisted. Notice, for instance, the contradiction in the two statements in italics. If the operation went wrong owing to the surgeon's chronic ill health, then clearly he was unfit to operate. Notice also the bizarre non-sequitur — that if one held that *this* surgeon was negligent in that he performed an operation knowing that he was critically ill, then one would have to hold that *every* surgeon who was taken ill during an operation was negligent.

Now to another judgment of Lord Denning — Whitehouse v. Jordan (1980) — a case in which the Court of Appeal reversed a finding of negligence against an obstetrician. The alleged negligence was that in trying to deliver a baby by forceps, the obstetrician pulled too hard and too long, thereby causing him brain damage. Denning, Master of the Rolls, opens his judgment by observing that birth is a dangerous time for a baby, and continues thus:

---

* Nickolls v. Minister of Health, The Times, February 4 1955.

'The specialist maternity unit [which delivered the baby] is held in the highest regard by the medical profession. The doctor in charge of the unit was Professor McLaren of international reputation. The delivery was expected to be troublesome. A very good team was gathered for it. The child was delivered by a very able and promising senior registrar, Mr. Jordan. Soon afterwards he attained the status of a consultant. He was assisted by a good younger man, Dr. Skinner, and two midwives. Also there was the anaesthetist. At hand were the paediatricians to take over the baby. With that assembly of skill you would not think that anything would go wrong on the medical side.'

In that passage there are seven separate references to the eminence and general skill of the medical team involved. If it was a *non*-professional man being sued for negligence, none of this would be relevant. A car mechanic is alleged to have negligently failed to rectify a steering defect, and thus caused a serious accident. That motor workshop is held in the highest regard in the motor industry; the company chairman is of international reputation; the repair was carried out by a very able and promising senior mechanic, who has since attained the status of manager. *Irrelevant*. We're not interested in the reputation of the workshop or the company chairman, nor whether the mechanic was considered able and promising by his colleagues, nor whether he has since been promoted. We, the judges, are interested only in whether he did or didn't rectify the steering defect. Why then are we, the judges, interested in the status and reputation of those involved in a *medical* negligence case? Presumably because of the underlying assumption that people at the top, or on their way to the top, of their profession are unlikely to be negligent; and moreover, that their evidence is more reliable than the evidence of ordinary people.

In fact, for Lord Denning it is such a small step from *stating* their evidence to *accepting* their evidence, that in the passage immediately following the one I quoted, it is only by careful analysis that one realizes that such a step has indeed been taken:

'Nor did it [go wrong on the medical side] by their accounts. None of them noticed anything untoward at all. Their evidence was that Mr. Jordan skilfully carried out a trial of labour to see if the baby could be safely delivered by forceps.

> As a result of the trial, it appeared that it would not be safe for the baby. So Mr. Jordan decided to switch over to a Caesarian Section: and that was performed most skilfully. Yet despite all that skill and care, the baby was born with severe brain damage.'

The first three sentences are clearly the medical team's version: *their* accounts; none of *them* noticed anything untoward; *their* evidence was that Mr. Jordan skilfully carried out a trial by forceps. But is the statement in the next sentence but one — that the Caesarian 'was performed most skilfully' — still *their* evidence, or Denning's own finding? It could be either. However, in the last sentence it seems that we have left what is merely an account of 'their evidence', and imperceptibly arrived at the *judge's own conclusion*, viz. that despite all that skill and care (in carrying out a trial by forceps and then delivery by Caesarian), the baby was born with severe brain damage. This must be so because Denning then says (after describing the child's present dismal condition) that the *saddest* part of it is that the mother blames it all on the hospital and the obstetrician.

Accordingly, Lord Denning reverses the trial judge's finding that the obstetrician pulled too hard and too long. But Denning goes further:

> 'We must say, and say firmly, that *in a professional man* an error of judgment is not negligent. To test it I would suggest that you ask the average competent and careful practitioner: Is this the sort of mistake that you yourself *might* have made? If he says: Yes, even doing the best I could it might have happened to me, then it is not negligent. In saying this I am only [following previous cases]. Applying this test I am clearly of opinion that, even accepting the judge's view that Mr. Jordan pulled too hard and too long, it was not negligent. It was at worst an error of judgment.'*

In other words, ordinary men make mistakes for which — if such mistakes result in damage — they are liable. But professional men make *errors of judgment* for which they should not be liable,

---

* The House of Lords, to which Mrs. Whitehouse appealed, unanimously upheld Denning's decision. However three of the five Law Lords did say that Denning's statement 'in a professional man an error of judgment is not negligent' needed some qualification. But none of the Law Lords questioned his suggested test for determining what, in a professional man, *does* amount to negligence.

unless the error is so gross that an average competent practitioner would say: I could *never* have made such an error.

Lawton L.J., sitting with Lord Denning and delivering a concurring judgment, seems to come to the same conclusion, albeit by a different route:

'The more serious the allegation, the higher the degree of probability [i.e. proof] that is required. In my opinion allegations of negligence against medical practitioners should be considered as serious. First, the defendant's *professional* reputation is under attack. A finding of negligence against him may jeopardize his career and cause him substantial financial loss over many years.' The judge goes on to observe that the mother was not in a position to 'give any worthwhile evidence on the question whether the obstetrician pulled too hard and too long.'

Therefore if, in a medical negligence case, a high degree of proof is required, and as first-hand evidence can normally only come from the doctor who is being accused of negligence or his colleagues present at the time, it follows that only in cases of extreme (gross) negligence is the plaintiff likely to succeed.

I mentioned that barristers enjoy a special immunity; they may not be sued either for breach of contract with their client, however reckless; or for their performance in Court, however negligent. This has been generally accepted over the last 150 years, but the judges of the High Court, Court of Appeal, and House of Lords unanimously affirmed it — and particularly the latter proposition — in a judicial decision, Rondel v. Worsley. The actual reasons the judges gave for giving barristers this immunity from negligence actions are so tenuous that even the Times leader writer raised an eyebrow (October 22 1966). For instance, the main reason given was that it was in the interests of *public policy*, because a barrister has a duty to the Court to disclose all documents and facts in his possession, even if detrimental to his client's case. It is equally in the public interest that a journalist writes the truth, even if prima facie libellous. Yet he is not given a blanket immunity from libel actions on that account, but simply a defence if he can show that what he wrote was true. Another reason their lordships gave was that if barristers could be sued for negligence it would make them even more prolix (heaven forfend!) One could as well argue that a taxi driver should enjoy a similar immunity; otherwise he would drive at a snail's pace.

But the real reasons for protecting barristers in this way can be discerned from one or two passages in their Lordships' judgments:

It is 'to prevent him being harassed by vexatious actions such as this present one now before us.' (Denning L.J.)

'Mr. Worsley [the defendant barrister] has been treated abominably by the bringing of this action and the conduct of the plaintiff, and those who have sought to embarrass the Bar for their own selfish and opinionated ends.' (Danckwerts L.J.)

'It is a fearsome thing for a barrister to have an action brought against him. To have his reputation besmirched by a charge of negligence. . .to be put to all the anxiety and all the cost of defending himself, even though in the end he should win.' (Denning, again.)

'It is of great public importance that they should all perform their respective duties free from the fear that any disgruntled and possibly impecunious litigant or other person may subsequently involve them in costly litigation. This Court in which we sit is a Temple of Justice, and the advocate at the Bar as well as the judge are equally Ministers in that Temple . . . Our system of justice has gained the admiration of the whole civilised world. . . There is no country in which justice is administered more impartially, efficiently or speedily.' (Salmon L.J.)

So here we may see the same philosophy at work, which gives professional man his favoured treatment. But whereas accusations of negligence against professional man, in general, 'should be approached with the greatest care', barristers are the most exalted of all professional men — being Ministers in a Temple of Justice, no less. And for a disgruntled (and no doubt impecunious) litigant to accuse a Minister in a Temple of Justice of common or garden negligence borders on sacrilege.

So far we have looked at some negligence cases involving professional men. Negligence forms part of the *civil* law, i.e. that branch of the law which determines rights between individuals. If we turn to the *criminal* law, we see that the magistrates and judges show the same tendency to discriminate in favour of the professional.

Let's see how a Mr. John Watson, unqualified conveyancer, got on with the Bradford-on-Avon Magistrates in his battle with the Law Society over the Solicitors' Act.

The relevant section lays down that anyone who is not a solicitor, who for a fee or other reward prepares a conveyance or transfer (i.e. the actual document which transfers a house from seller to buyer), is guilty of a criminal offence. Mr. Watson, himself the object of unfavourable attention from the Law Society, retaliated by bringing a private prosecution against an unqualified conveyancing clerk *employed* by a firm of solicitors, who had prepared a transfer. Now it is common knowledge (at any rate within the profession) that unqualified clerks do conveyancing from start to finish without any supervision — as the Law Society itself acknowledges, by publishing in its Gazette solicitors' advertisements for unqualified conveyancing clerks who 'must be able to work without supervision'. Moreover the Solicitors' Act is unambiguous on this point: simply that anyone who is not a solicitor who prepares a transfer is guilty of a criminal offence. There are three exceptions — barrister, notary, and typist who is employed to type out the document — but a solicitor's *clerk* is not one of them. Thus it would seem that Mr. Watson was about to expose the interesting fact that practically every firm of solicitors in the country was profiting from the crimes of its employees. In view of the importance of the case, the Law Society engaged a Queen's Counsel for the defence.

And how did our judiciary, so renowned for its impartiality, discharge its uncomfortable duty on this occasion? Although the case lasted two days, the Magistrates took less than five minutes to reach their verdict. They dismissed the case — and ordered Mr. Watson to pay all the legal costs of the defence and the Law Society — on the grounds that although the defendant was unqualified and *had* prepared the transfer, he had been acting *on behalf of* the solicitors employing him, and therefore was not guilty of infringing the Solicitors' Act. An illogical decision, of course. By the same reasoning a surgeon could employ a navvy to perform an operation as his agent. But given the axiom that professional men do *not* connive at and profit by the crimes of their employees, it was the only decision possible.

I once had occasion to serve a solicitor with a writ for negligence, when I was acting for one of his former clients. I called at his office and told his receptionist that I had a document to give him personally (as the rules then required). She relayed the message, but he refused to see me except I make an appointment (although he was alone at the time and all he had to do was to take the document). Whereupon I went into his room and gave him the writ; whereupon he assaulted me, causing actual bodily harm. I brought a private prosecution in the Magistrates Court. The solicitor, who engaged one of the most eminent Queen's Counsel to defend him, pleaded not guilty — claiming that although he was absolutely furious at being served with the writ, and that I had got my injuries on his premises, *he* had not caused them but that I had somehow caused them myself. After a full day's hearing the Magistrate gave judgment. 'I am in some difficulty', she said, 'because I find this case proved.' But because she based her findings on recklessness rather than intent, and because there had been extreme provocation, she gave the defendant an absolute discharge. Several times she stressed that she was giving the solicitor an absolute discharge, that he would not have a criminal record; and as she and everyone else in the Court room fought to choke back their sobs, she concluded that it had been a sad day for everyone. When Bill Bloggs, electrical components wholesaler, on being served with a writ assaults the process-server and does him a damage (a not unusual reaction I believe), does the magistrate say: '*I am in some difficulty because I find this case proved*'? And does the magistrate then give Mr. Bloggs an absolute discharge on account of the *extreme provocation* he suffered, in that the process-server entered his office uninvited?.

Lord Justice Cantley, summing up in a more celebrated case, has no compunction in calling the prosecution witness, Norman Scott (unemployed male model), 'a liar'. But when in the same summing up his Lordship deals with the explanations given by the defendant, one Jeremy Thorpe (former leader of the Liberal Party, ex-president of the Oxford Union, Barrister-at-law), as to some missing party funds, he says: 'he has given explanations not all of which can be true.'

Another example of this reluctance of judges to call a professional man a liar is the case of Mr. Glanville Davies, a solicitor (and member of the Council of the Law Society), who, after acting in a commercial case, submitted a bill of costs for £198,000. The client appealed against this bill to a taxing master, who concluded that the bill was based largely on fictitious attendance notes (containing false times, false dates and often duplicating or triplicating the same event), and bogus claims for time spent in perusing documents; and he reduced the bill from

£198,000 to £68,000. The solicitor's explanation for his fictitious attendance notes was that the originals had been damaged by *rain penetrating his office*, and he had consequently destroyed them; and for reasons unexplained *he had also destroyed all his diaries* (which would of course have shown his actual attendances). It fell to two High Court judges, on two separate occasions, to consider the solicitor's conduct. Neither of them could bring themselves to state that he had been fraudulent; only that he had been guilty of *misconduct*.

If a tradesman tries to overcharge his customer by £130,000, by submitting a bill based on palpably false records (having destroyed the originals), it is fraud. If a solicitor does it, it is misconduct. Norman Scott tells lies. Jeremy Thorpe gives explanations not all of which can be true. Ordinary men make mistakes. Professional men make errors of judgment.

In October 1981 a dentist, contrary to innumerable professional guidelines, not only administered a general anaesthetic and operated on a patient without any assistant being present, but left the patient alone for ten minutes. During that period the patient died. By a unanimous verdict the jury convicted the dentist of manslaughter, finding that during the period the patient had been left (not having recovered from the anaesthetic) she vomited and choked to death. At the trial, Home Office pathologist, Dr. B.T. Davis, testified that he carried out a post mortem (in the presence of the coroner), and found the windpipe was blocked with vomit — of which he took a specimen on a slide. The Court of Appeal quashed the dentist's conviction on the grounds that *new evidence* had come to light casting doubt on Dr. Davis's findings. Yet there was no new evidence; only the *opinions* of three other experts, who had not testified at the trial (and one of whom was not a pathologist), to the effect that Dr. Davis's conclusion that the patient had choked to death was unsafe, and that she could have died from heart failure. Although Dr. Davis was present during the appeal, he was not called upon to confirm his evidence or defend his findings. If a jury convicts a reckless lorry driver of manslaughter, it is manslaughter. If a jury convicts a reckless dentist of manslaughter (which has happened only once), it is a miscarriage of justice, and the conviction must be overturned.

As professional men invariably come from the middle class,

the professional issue to a certain extent is a class issue.

Just as judges are themselves professional men, so are they drawn exclusively from the middle class, and three-quarters of them have been to Oxford or Cambridge. And just as judges evidently feel some affinity with their fellow professionals, it would be surprising if some of them did not feel similar affinity with members of their own class; and it would be surprising if such feelings did not occasionally seep into their judgements. Look through a couple of random newspapers and you'll probably come across an example – how an M.P.'s son, who robbed a tourist at knifepoint, was given an absolute discharge 'after the Court heard how he suffered from having a famous family'; how a magistrate, a vicar's wife, who drove the wrong way down a dual carriageway thereby causing a serious accident, was acquitted of careless driving, and so on. The goddess of Justice may be blindfold but she hears the defendant's voice, and thereby learns his class, with her *ears*.

In February 1980 the wife of a Co-op director was kidnapped and hit over the head several times with a car jack, suffering a fractured skull, a broken jaw, and several broken teeth. Her assailant telephoned her husband and threatened to mutilate his wife still further, unless he brought a ransom of £50,000 to the international departure lounge of Manchester airport. Nasty. The assailant, fearing a trap, did not keep the rendezvous, and was subsequently arrested. He pleaded guilty. But he was an Oxford man, and a director of a large weaving company to boot. Moreover he was defended by an eminent Queen's Counsel (the same gentleman, incidentally, who defended Jeremy Thorpe). The medical officer at the remand centre, where the defendant had been detained pending trial, gave evidence that the defendant 'was a man of *high intellect*, but had been very ill at the time of the offence. His remorse is totally genuine.' (The Times, July 24 1980).

Ill he may have been, and remorseful at what he had done. Nevertheless he had evidently planned the crime in some detail, having called at his victim's house armed with chloroform padding, rope, adhesive tape, and had a reversible coat with which to effect a disguise. He had only used the jack when the lady showed unexpected spirit in resisting the chloroform. Said the judge in sending him to a mental hospital for treatment: 'If I were not satisfied that you were suffering from a serious mental disorder, you would have gone to prison for a very long time.' Chaps of high intellect *don't* hit ladies over the head with a car jack and kidnap them, *unless* they are suffering from a serious mental disorder.

Chaps lower down the intellectual ladder tend to get rather different treatment. I remember the firm where I was articled, defending a lorry driver (R. v. Wadham 1960). Having had a meal at a café with some mates in boisterous mood, he had called out to the proprietress, across the other diners' tables: 'We're from the protection gang, babe, so you better have some money ready when we call back tonight.' She telephoned the police. At his trial at the Old Bailey, where he was charged with demanding money with menaces, he claimed that his words had been said as a joke; that if he had really been a member of a protection gang he would scarcely have advertised the fact to everyone else in the café. For the tastelessness of his jest he paid dearly: two years imprisonment (six months more, incidentally, than a dentist who defrauded the National Health Service of £300,000*). And Bentley, still further down the intellectual ladder, being mentally subnormal, paid even more dearly for his alleged utterance of five ambiguous words† – he was hanged.

I am not saying that all judges and magistrates are influenced by the status or calling of the defendant. Obviously some will hold an even balance. But let's briefly return to negligence actions, and give the last word to Lord Denning. In a foreword to a textbook, *Professional Negligence* by J.P. Eddy, Lord Denning writes:

> 'Another difference [between negligence actions against professional men and negligence actions against anyone else] is in the standard of care which is exacted. The Courts have no hesitation in holding that mistakes made by car drivers or employers are visited by damages: but they make allowances for the mistakes of professional men. They realise that a finding of negligence against a professional man is a serious matter for him. It is not so much the money because he is often insured against it. It is the injury to his reputation which a finding of negligence involves. One hundred years ago the Courts said that a solicitor was not liable except for gross

---

* The Times, November 24 1982.

† 'Let him have it, Chris.'

> negligence. This phrase has been discarded but the cases are treated much the same now as then. The Courts hesitate long before holding that a solicitor is negligent. Likewise with doctors and hospitals.'

Lord Denning has a certain reputation for eccentricity, but in this respect his eccentricity probably lies only in his frankness. Most judges would, I think, be chary of expressing themselves in such terms, albeit subscribing — consciously or unconsciously – to the same philosophy. Anyway, this is how Lord Denning describes the judiciary's favoured treatment of professional men. And having over his long and distinguished career decided more cases than anyone else, alive or dead, he ought to know.

How the judges and commentators abandon their critical faculties when dealing with professional man (2) Disciplinary tribunals

As we have seen, the law which the judges administer is divided into two broad categories: the *civil* law, which lays down what *rights* one individual has over another (e.g. the right of someone to sue someone else whose negligence has caused him injury); and the *criminal* law, which *punishes* those who infringe it. But the law, covering as it does the whole spectrum of human activities, is too blunt an instrument to regulate the special relationship between a professional and his client. For this reason the professions impose upon their members their own particular codes of conduct and standards. Indeed it is this ability to discipline itself, and impose on its members *higher* standards than are required by law, which distinguishes a profession from a trade or business.

'There is general agreement that one of the most important distinguishing characteristics of a profession is the fact that its members acknowledge an overriding responsibility to maintain certain standards of conduct as a corollary of the special relationship of trust in which a professional man stands to his client. The professional man is called upon to give advice which the client is for the most part not qualified to criticise.' (Pamphlet published by the General Dental Council.)

'A profession involves a particular kind of relationship with clients or patients, arising from the complexity of the subject matter which deprives the client of the ability to make informed judgments for himself, and so renders him to a large extent dependent upon the professional man. A self-imposed code of professional ethics is intended to correct the imbalance in the relationship between the professional man and his client.' (Report of Ormrod Committee 1971.)

'A profession. . .may be described as a body of men and women. . .recognised as having a special skill and learning in some field of activity in which the public needs protection against incompetence, the standards of skill and learning being prescribed by the profession itself. . .[and] voluntarily submitting themselves to standards of ethical conduct beyond those required of the ordinary citizen by law.' (Statement by the Law Society to Monopolies Commission.)

'In order to protect its clients and provide a service of the necessary standard, a profession must impose on its members high standards of conduct and performance above those required by the general law.' (Bennion, *Professional Ethics*.)

Although these quotations come from diverse sources, they carry the same message: because of the public's disadvantage in its dealings with the professional, the professions ensure that their members observe 'standards of conduct', 'a code of professional ethics', 'standards of ethical conduct', 'standards of conduct and performance', *higher* than the law requires of the non-professional.

Moreover, as the Law Society states, a profession is a body of people 'having a special skill in some field of activity in which the public needs protection against incompetence'. Therefore it must follow that the various professional bodies, as well as being concerned with their members' ethics, are equally concerned to ensure their members' *competence*. Which, of course, they are:

'There has grown up an additional relationship between each recognised profession and the society in which it exists, in the form of an undertaking by the profession that it will, through its members, provide the best advice and service attainable within the scope of contemporary knowledge. . .A framework for the exercise of this special responsibility, and *sanctions for its enforcement*, are provided by a Council [whose] purpose is to ensure that the individual member of the profession honours both his relationship of trust to his clients, and the implicit contract between the profession and society.' (Pamphlet published by the General Dental Council.)

'The general duty of the Council is to protect the public

[which it does] by taking action against registered doctors if it appears that they have become unfit to practise.' (Pamphlet published by General Medical Council.)

'The Law Society representing and *ensuring the highest standards of service by solicitors to the public...*' (Full page advertisement on rear cover of a magazine published by the Law Society.)

'One of our most important objectives, referred to more than once in the Royal Commission report, is the maintenance of high standards not only of honesty and integrity but of *competence*.' (President of the Law Society's Annual Report 1980/81.)

'Incompetence ought to be controlled whether or not barristers are liable at law for negligence.' (Statement by Bar Council to Royal Commission.)

'In the case of a lawyer, the Law Society is a pretty hard taskmaster, as is the Bar Council. I do not know of any other group or association outside this profession which carries out such detailed and searching enquiries as the Law Society and the Bar Council, when allegations are made against solicitors and barristers.' (Stanley Davis M.P., Fair Trading Bill debate, Hansard April 12 1973).

The machinery by which the professions achieve this self-discipline is in most cases the same. Each profession has a Disciplinary Committee, and a Disciplinary Tribunal. The Disciplinary *Committee* acts as a clearing house for every complaint received about a member of that profession (whether from the public or from within the profession itself), and makes a preliminary investigation. If it then appears that the complaint requires further action, the Committee refers it to a separate Disciplinary *Tribunal*, which formally investigates the complaint, and in appropriate cases suspends the member or strikes him off.

At least that is the theory. However, if we look at how the gentlemen who sit on these disciplinary Committees and Tribunals actually deal with complaints about members of their profession, we see that their philosophy is somewhat at variance with the high-flown sentiments of their professions' script-writers.

Let's begin with the Law Society, whose claims that it ensures that its members conform to the highest standards of conduct are more strident than those of the other professions – possibly because it feels more threatened by unqualified competition.

The Law Society

(1) I presented fairly conclusive evidence, some of it written, to the Law Society that a certain eminent solicitor had successfully bribed a witness I intended calling in proceedings before the Industrial Tribunal. Replied the Law Society:

'Your letter alleges the commission of a criminal offence. I think it would be quite improper and certainly contrary to the usual practice of the Law Society for the Society to comment on your allegations or to take any action in the matter. . .The proper authority to whom to refer the commission of a criminal offence is the Police. This is a matter entirely for you. You may think in all the circumstances that you will be well advised to take separate legal advice.'

(2) Another solicitor exchanged contracts on his client's house sale without having exchanged on the dependent purchase, which subsequently fell through. When the client sued him for negligence the solicitor forged a note of a fictitious telephone conversation, in which he claimed that he had warned the client of the danger of exchanging the sale contract when the purchase contract might fall through, but that the client instructed him to exchange on the sale and take the risk. That the note of the telephone conversation was a fraudulent invention to cover up his mistake, was evident from a letter he had previously written to the client: 'We have now exchanged contracts on your sale *and your purchase*.' Thus at the time of the alleged telephone conversation he erroneously believed that he *had* successfully exchanged the purchase contract (when he had merely sent his client's part of the contract to the other side). A complaint about the solicitor, together with the supporting evidence, was sent to the Law Society, who acknowledged it but took no further action, and simply ignored all subsequent letters from the complainant.

(3) A solicitor, who acted for a client on the sale of her house, refused to hand over the proceeds of sale after completion, despite repeated requests. Eventually the client complained to the Law Society, which replied:

'At this stage I would not wish to make any further comments on the matter until I hear further from [the solicitor] to whom you will recall I wrote again, but generally speaking you should be advised by your new solicitor.'

A month after that letter (it being six months since the sale was completed, and the client having heard nothing meanwhile), I telephoned the Law Society official in question, and told him I was investigating the client's complaint in my capacity as a journalist. He promptly put the phone down but, surprise surprise, *the day after my telephone call* the lady received a cheque for her money (with interest) from her erstwhile solicitor, with a letter explaining that he had retained it 'in accordance with our understanding of what you instructed us to do.' As she had been continually demanding her money – and even went so far as to report him to the Law Society when he refused to hand it over – this was a blatant lie. Yet the Law Society in its final letter to her stated: 'I do not find your complaint has been substantiated.'

(4) Normally the Law Society's letter to the complainant, dismissing the complaint, is the end of the matter. But it so happened that on one occasion it *wasn't* the end of the matter. Mr. Leslie Parsons, a businessman, complained to the Law Society that his solicitor tried to overcharge him by £130,000. The solicitor had submitted a bill for £198,000 which the taxing master had reduced to £68,000, finding that the bill had been based largely on fictitious attendance notes (containing false times, false dates, and often duplicating or triplicating the same event), and bogus claims for time spent in perusing documents. The Law Society dismissed Mr. Parsons's complaint, and stated that no further correspondence would be entered into. *Consequently Mr. Parsons himself took High Court proceedings and had the solicitor struck off, which the solicitor did not even oppose.*

So much for the 'standards of ethical conduct beyond those required of the ordinary citizen by law' to which the profession voluntarily submits. Had it been 'the law' investigating the above four cases, and had they involved ordinary citizens rather than solicitors, one may assume the outcome would have been rather different for some of the practitioners involved.

But as the President of the Law Society stated in the 1980/81 Annual Report: 'One of our most important objectives. . .is the maintenance of high standards not only of honesty and integrity but of *competence*.' However, anyone who complains about their solicitor's incompetence will receive some such letter as (to quote from actual examples in my possession):

'The Society is only concerned with the professional conduct of solicitors. The Society has no power to tell a solicitor how to do his work.'

'You really must understand that the Law Society cannot be concerned in any way with the details of your case or with any disagreement with your solicitors, unless it is quite clear that there is some substantial element of professional misconduct on their part. Professional misconduct is not in any way concerned with the nature of the advice given to you, or the competence of the solicitors involved.'

'I must make it absolutely clear to you that the Law Society cannot entertain from a member of the public a complaint that a solicitor has been professionally negligent. The Law Society's jurisdiction is limited strictly to dealing complaints (sic) alleging actual professional conduct (sic). Alleged professional negligence does not raise an issue of conduct. The remedy for professional negligence is damages. . .For this purpose you need legal advice and this advice can be provided only by a solicitor either in private practise (sic) or at a Law Centre.'*

In one letter, the Law Society even indicates that it is in the aggrieved client's interest that it does *not* discipline a negligent solicitor: 'If the negligent solicitor is suspended or struck off, the client's position may become worse because prospects of recovery from the solicitor are reduced.'

According to a letter from the President of the Law Society (April 19 1984), the Law Society currently receives 9,000 complaints a year about solicitors. It deals with about 99% of these complaints (which come from clients) by sending the solicitor in question a copy of the client's letter of complaint, and sending the client a copy of the solicitor's reply. The remaining 1%, which are referred to the Disciplinary Tribunal, and which *do* result in disciplinary action being taken against the solicitor, almost invariably involve a breach of the Solicitors' Accounts Rules. Never once has a solicitor been disciplined for incompetence.

---

* I once wrote to the Law Society asking *how* it ensured 'the highest standards of service by solicitors to the public.' An official replied that it did so by 'insisting on high standards of education'!

The Bar Council

The Bar Council, which is the barristers' governing body, receives yearly between one hundred and two hundred complaints about its members – far fewer than the Law Society. This is because there are far fewer barristers than solicitors, and also because they are once removed from their clients. But although fewer, such complaints are likely to be more bitter: the barristers' most aggrieved clients will probably be in gaol.

The most common complaint by members of the public is that they saw their barrister for the first time only a few minutes before the trial (and consequently there was insufficient time to go over vital points), and that the barrister had an inadequate grasp of the case. According to a survey by Michael Zander (Legal Advice and Criminal Appeals, 1972), 'this complaint comes up again and again.' And according to another survey by Bottoms and McClean (Defendants in the Criminal Process, 1976), 79% of those defendants in the higher Criminal Courts who wished to plead innocent, saw their barrister for the first time on the morning of the trial. Another survey (*Negotiated Justice* by Baldwin and McConville) revealed numerous cases of barristers seeing their clients for the first time a few minutes before the trial, and persuading them against their will – and their interests – to plead guilty. Here again the allegation that the barrister had an inadequate grasp of the case 'was raised spontaneously by so many defendants' (p.58).

As part of this pattern, a significant proportion of complaints about barristers come from solicitors, and *their* most common complaint is that, having agreed to take a case and having been briefed, the barrister – through his clerk – tells the solicitor at the last minute that he cannot take the case after all. The solicitor then has to accept whatever substitute barrister the clerk offers. Sometimes this is not the fault of the original barrister, whose previous case overruns its expected time. But frequently it is because the barrister (through his clerk) cannot bring himself to refuse work, and consequently accepts more engagements than he could possibly handle – in the expectation that some will be settled prematurely and he will be able somehow to juggle around with the others. If he cannot, he will have to farm some of them out to other (possibly more junior and inexperienced) barristers in his chambers.

As a barrister himself has written (*The Bar on Trial*, Robert

Hazell): 'The clerks overload their principals with engagements in the hope that where two cases conflict one will settle or go short, so that the barrister will still be able to do both cases and collect two fees instead of one. If this hope does not materialize, one brief will have to be returned. . .For the Bar returns are an everyday occurrence, indeed they are the staple diet of the beginner' (p.120).

Even the Law Society has described this as 'a common and serious source of complaint.' (1964 Memorandum.)

As is usual, the Bar Council's machinery for dealing with complaints about its members consists of a Committee and a Disciplinary Tribunal. The Committee acts as a clearing house, and either dismisses the complaint, deals with it informally by giving the barrister some paternal and private advice, or else refers it to the Tribunal for possible disciplinary action. In fact only a very few complaints get beyond the Committee.

Between 1974 (the year in which these disciplinary bodies were constituted in their present form, and from when I was given records) and 1981, the Bar Council received between one hundred and two hundred complaints a year. Of these complaints, only an average of ten a year were referred by the Committee to the Tribunal; and of these, only an average of three a year resulted in the barrister being disciplined (by which I mean disbarred or suspended, not merely reprimanded).

No details of the complaints received are published, except the tiny minority which result in the barrister being disbarred or suspended (or, *at the Tribunal's discretion*, reprimanded). Nevertheless I think we can assume that if the most frequently heard complaint is that the barrister had an inadequate grasp of the case, either because he was incompetent or because he was a last minute substitute – as to which even the Law Society has expressed its disquiet – then this will also be the most common complaint made to the barristers' governing body.

The following complaint to the Bar Council by an acquaintance of mine is, I imagine, a typical example:

'Although Mr. X was instructed in this matter on September 18th 1981 and told of the Notice of Motion to be heard on September 21st 1981, he was unavailable for the hearing. It is disgraceful that he should take on work if he knew he could not attend, especially as this was a case concerning the liberty of the subject. Because of his failure to attend [he sent a substitute] I was fined £1,700 and given a suspended prison sentence. I know he had another case on, *but then so did the clerk on 18th September when he accepted the brief.*'

Equally typical is the reply: 'After careful consideration of all the documents the Committee agreed that there was no evidence of any professional misconduct by Mr. X.' The Committee gives no reasons for its decisions; neither does it send the complainant a copy of the barrister's reply to the complaint.

Looking down the list I was given, I see that between 1974 and 1981 only one complaint of overbooking was referred by the Committee to the Tribunal, which dealt with it as follows: *'Failure of duty to clients by accepting Briefs for two heavy cases which were bound to clash.' Allegation proved. Barrister reprimanded. Tribunal ordered no publication. (case D74/2).*

So it seems that if a barrister accepts briefs for two *heavy* cases which are *inevitably* going to clash, he runs an infinitesimal risk of being privately reprimanded by the Disciplinary Tribunal; but the fact that in eight years, this is the only complaint of overbooking to have got past the clearing Committee suggests that if he accepts two *ordinary* cases which are going to clash, he does not risk even that.

Similarly, between 1974 and 1981 only *two* complaints of *incompetence* were referred by the Committee to the Disciplinary Tribunal, both of which were dismissed. As the deputy Secretary of the Bar Council told me: 'You can't give a man competence by disciplining him.'

So in what circumstances *does* the Disciplinary Tribunal take action? Between 1974 and 1981 a total of 25 barristers practising in Britain were disciplined. Of these, 11 were disciplined for variations of dealing directly with the client without the intervention of a solicitor; 9 were for criminal convictions unconnected with their practice; 1 for touting; 1 for submitting false legal aid claims; and 3 miscellaneous.

The claim, that the professional has to observe *higher* standards than the law imposes on the ordinary citizen, has an even more hollow ring in the case of barristers. Not only does their disciplinary body fail to discipline them for incompetence (however gross), or for breach of agreement caused by overbooking (however reckless) – and however disastrous the result may be for their clients. As we have seen (p. 21), they enjoy a special immunity from ordinary *legal* proceedings in respect of such matters.

The General Dental Council

The Dental Council is less coy than the Bar Council (and the Law Society) as to how it exercises its disciplinary jurisdiction – having published a pamphlet in which it gives figures, under six headings, of all cases referred to its Disciplinary Tribunal since 1922, the year it was constituted. (Actually before 1957 it was the Dental *Board*, but for convenience I refer to it throughout as the Dental Council.)

In the 61 years from 1922 to 1982 the Dental Council has disciplined – by striking off, which is the only disciplinary action available to it – a total of 180 dentists. Again note the average of three a year. Of these cases, 97 were in respect of convictions by the Courts for criminal offences; 18 for advertising; 11 for employing an unqualified assistant to do dentistry; 5 for indecent behaviour to the patient; and 10 miscellaneous. This leaves 39 for 'false certification', that is, fraudulently claiming for treatments not carried out. This is an interesting category.

Just as overbooking is the most obvious temptation for a barrister, so is 'false certification' for a dentist. And on the assumption that all (professional) men are created equal, the one is probably as prevalent as the other. As the General Dental Council says in its pamphlet:

'In 1932 the Dental [Council] decided that the practice of making false statements on dental benefit forms under the National Health Insurance Acts had become *too common to ignore*.' In the ten years up to 1932 the Council had disciplined only *one* dentist for this, but in the next ten years (1932 to 1941) the Council investigated 46 such cases and disciplined – struck off– 28 dentists for this offence.

The pamphlet continues: 'In 1948 dental benefit cases gave way to National Health Service cases, but the nature of the misconduct involved has remained much the same – claiming fees for treatment not provided, claiming fees from patients in excess of the statutory charges, false certification, and similar forms of malpractice.'

But if the nature of the misconduct has remained much the same, the Council's reaction to it seems to have mellowed over the years. Having in the 10 years from 1932 to 1941 investigated 46 cases and struck off 28 dentists for making false claims, over the next 21 years (1942 to 1962) the Council investigated 40 cases and struck off 9 dentists; and during the last 20 years (1963 to

1982) it investigated 8 cases and struck off *one* dentist. In other words, having decided that the practice of dentists making fraudulent claims under the NHS 'had become too common to ignore', the dentists' governing body currently disciplines dentists for this malpractice at the rate of one every twenty years.

Here we might mention the concurrent jurisdiction of the Family Practitioner Committee to investigate overcharging by a dentist (and doctor), practising under the National Health Service. Unlike proceedings before the Disciplinary Tribunal of the Dental Council, this is not disciplinary jurisdiction – the FPC has no power to strike off – but more resembles an action for breach of contract (the contract being between the practitioner and the Health Authority), and before an incredibly benign judge. The overcharging usually comes to light as a result of random checks by NHS inspectors on patients; and where the FPC finds that the dentist has overcharged, the usual order it makes is that the amount of overpayment will be stopped out of the dentist's future NHS payments. Persistent or extreme offenders, *whose names are never disclosed*, will be fined.

A solicitor acquaintance told me how he once served as the lay member on such a Committee, which heard the case of a dentist who admitted having made fraudulent claims over a number of years. He was fined £50. A more ambitious dentist claimed NHS fees for one year (1981) totalling £288,779. This rather excessive claim coincided with complaints by some of his patients of *unnecessary treatments.* Accordingly the FPC investigated and in March 1982, deciding that the dentist was in breach of his terms of service in respect of both overcharging and unnecessary treatment, it fined him £50,000 – which was deducted from his NHS claims. Thus his remuneration for the year in question was reduced to £238,779. (The Times, September 29 1982.) The case was referred to the Disciplinary Tribunal, which decided that *'no sufficient evidence has been adduced'*, and dismissed the case. Incidentally, the dentist's fees for the *previous* year (so I was told by the relevant FPC) were slightly less than half his 1981 claim –i.e. about £140,000 – which had been paid without query, since no complaint had been received.

Notice how the claim that the professional man has to observe more exacting standards than the law imposes on the ordinary man, again seems to fall down. If perchance it came to light that a

NHS *clerk* had been fraudulently making out cheques in his favour to the tune of a quarter of a million pounds, one assumes he would receive more than a private request to return £50,000.

The Dental Council in its pamphlet states that it provides sanctions for the enforcement of the 'undertaking by the profession that it will, through its members, provide the best advice and service attainable within the scope of contemporary knowledge'. Yet in the 61 years from 1922 to 1982 it has never once disciplined a dentist for incompetence – even when that incompetence was so gross that it caused the patient's death.

This, when it happens, is usually the result of a dentist acting simultaneously as *both anaesthetist and dentist*, and therefore being unable to monitor the effects of the anaesthetic while carrying out the dental treatment. The danger is well recognised, and since 1967 dentists have been given numerous official warnings against such practice. According to the Medical Defence Union's 1982 report: 'there have been perhaps 100 dental anaesthetic deaths in the UK over the last 20 years associated with this dual role', which figure presumably represents only those cases which have come to the MDU's notice.

Yet of those hundred deaths, only two have been investigated by the Dental Council up to the end of 1982. In the first case (May 1979), the Disciplinary Tribunal found that the dentist had 'ignored the many warnings which have been issued to the profession', and administered a general anaesthetic without a second qualified person being present, with fatal results. But because the dentist promised not to do it again, and because of the 'terrible experience' which *he* had undergone, the Tribunal took no disciplinary action. Likewise in the second case (November 1982), where the facts were similar, the Tribunal took no action against the dentist because 'the knowledge of the tragic consequences of the negligence, which you have admitted, will always remain with you'.

However, on another occasion a dentist not only administered a general anaesthetic without *any* assistant being present, but left the unconscious patient unattended, during which time she died. This was in January 1981. Eight years previously he had similarly acted as both anaesthetist and operator on another patient, who had also died. On October

26th 1981 the dentist was convicted of manslaughter, but the conviction was quashed by the Court of Appeal (see p. 25), although it was not disputed that he had acted as both anaesthetist and operator without assistance, and had left the patient while unconscious. In November 1983 – nearly three years after the *second* death – the Disciplinary Tribunal finally struck the dentist off. The moral seems to be that to kill one patient, by ignoring the professional guidelines, may be regarded as a misfortune; but to kill two – at any rate if the second incident attracts unfavourable publicity in the shape of criminal proceedings – looks very much like carelessness.

The General Medical Council

As with the dentists' disciplinary body, so with the doctors'. A Harley Street doctor, prior to carrying out a routine and minor operation to remove a wart, injected his patient with more than ten times the correct dose of a general anaesthetic (methohexitone); not only that, but he also had no assistant with him, contrary to proper medical practice (for the reasons explained); not only that, but he falsely told the hospital, to which the unconscious patient was taken, that he had injected valium not methohexitone. The patient died; doctor cleared of manslaughter;* no disciplinary action taken by the Medical Council.

The activities of another doctor (Dr. Terence Lawlor), a consultant psychiatrist at a mental hospital, were the subject of a massive Government Inquiry – which concluded that he ran an abusive and tyrannical regime, that he was a liar who did not scruple to mislead the inquiry, that he was primarily responsible for the appalling conditions of the 200 patients in the hospital, and that he was in serious breach of his duty for most of his time at the hospital. (The Times, November 22 1978.) No disciplinary action taken by the Medical Council.

On the other hand, a doctor who 'had formed and maintained an improper relationship with a lady who was his patient', and had tried to persuade her to abandon her complaint, was struck off. (General Medical Council's annual report, 1981.) If instead – or even as well – he had killed her by his gross incompetence, presumably he would have been in the clear.

---

* The Times, July 7/15 1981.

Teachers

Built in to every contract of employment with ordinary man is an implied condition that if he is incompetent he can be dismissed. Not so with professional man, who is almost never sacked. This is most notable in the case of teachers, who are invariably *employed* – unlike the majority of other professionals. Teachers *can* be dismissed but the procedures are complicated, and it seems they are never invoked for incompetence, however extreme. Ask any headteacher or head of department, and you will hear the same story: a teacher can be incompetent, lazy, need never set or mark any homework, but there is nothing the Head can do. In extreme cases, e.g. if parents start complaining, and the Head in turn complains to the Education Authority (the teacher's *employer*), he will probably be met with one of the stock platitudes kept for such occasions: 'you've got to give and take', 'we'll keep an eye on the situation', 'let me know if it happens again' etc. Only if a teacher commits a criminal offence (and a fairly serious one at that) will he be sacked. Otherwise the worst that can happen to him is that he is transferred to another school.

At a conference, the General Secretary of the National Association of Headteachers mentioned the case of an incompetent teacher who had been shunted from school to school by the local Education Authority until he was now in his *fourteenth* school, although still in his 30's. Another headteacher recounted how he had agreed to exchange one of his incompetent teachers for another in a colleague's school, thinking that the replacement could not be as bad as the one he got rid of. He was wrong. She brought with her a psychiatrist's statement that she was *sane* (the result of an earlier attempt by the Education Authority to get rid of her), could neither teach nor control a class, refused to accept simple instructions, sang arias loudly from 9 a.m. to 4 p.m., and walked in the middle of the road to instil into the children a sense of road safety. (The Times, May 29, 1981.)

But whereas in extreme cases incompetent teachers can be transferred, an incompetent *head* teacher, it seems, can neither be sacked nor transferred.

Once upon a time there was appointed to William Tyndale primary Junior School a headmaster who considered that conventional education ill fitted children to modern life, particularly those from a working class background. And he sought to provide an alternative, in which authority was less assertive, and the children could choose their own activities. Unfortunately his theories, when put into practice, were not a success. As the headmaster himself was to acknowledge: 'many children from formal classrooms were unused to fluidity.'* The headmistress of the separate infants' school, housed in the same building, described the resulting chaos more bluntly:

> 'Large numbers of the Junior School children were completely uncontrolled, roaming the schools' building at will, including the infants' school classrooms, taking little notice of any reprimands from her or her staff. . . Throwing stones and spitting through the windows of the infants' school during class, knocking infants' work to the floor, shouting and rushing about the building during class periods, bullying the infants, laughing and swearing at the teachers.' (Auld Report, paragraphs 583/254).

Within two terms of the headmaster taking over the Junior School, conventional teaching had largely been abandoned, discipline had broken down, and the school roll had dropped by nearly a third.

The Education Authorities (both at local and County Hall level) were alerted from several quarters – dissenting teachers, parents and particularly the school managers – to what was happening; but instead of taking any action they took refuge in the standard platitudes. The dissenting teachers 'should try to co-operate with the headmaster'; 'pressure on the school from County Hall would be inopportune and premature'; 'Mr Hinds† will of course monitor all the developments closely', and so on. Relations between managers and staff deteriorated until finally the managers leaked something of the situation to the press – the first article appearing in The Times on July 2 1975. Whereupon the Education Authorities decided that they had better do something; and eight days later (July 10 1975) they ordered an inspection of the school, to be followed by a public inquiry.

When the day came for the inspection to start, the headmaster (and six out of the eight teachers, who supported him) went on

---

* *William Tyndale, The Teachers' Story* p.21.

† Harvey Hinds, Chairman of I.L.E.A. Schools Sub-Committee, second only to Sir Ashley Bramall in the I.L.E.A. hierarchy.

strike and closed the school in an attempt to thwart it. The Authority in turn enlisted temporary teachers, reopened the school, and the inspection went ahead – resulting in a fairly damning (although obviously incomplete) report. The headmaster and his colleagues then returned to the school, and after some indecision announced their intention to resume their previous posts.

In an attempt to avoid further disruption of the children's education, the managers had a meeting with the Education Authorities (with Sir Ashley Bramall, leader of the I.L.E.A. in the chair) to try to persuade them to suspend the headmaster and his colleagues, at any rate until after the public inquiry. The authorities demurred. During this meeting the following revealing exchange took place:

> Manager: 'Police officers subject to an inquiry are suspended while the inquiry is in hand, are they not?'
> Bramall:'We are not dealing with policemen but *teachers* . . . And I think that suspension, even with full pay, is regarded in a sense as derogatory. There are powers in sufficiently serious cases for the Education Officer to suspend, but this is not a normal sort of case where suspension is used. It is only used in cases of *criminal* offences.' (Meeting at County Hall, October 17 1975.)

In other words, despite the fact that within two terms of a headmaster taking over an apparently normal and healthy school it had almost literally gone to pieces, and the headmaster had gone on 'strike' and closed the school in an attempt to prevent an inspection which they had ordered, the Education Authorities refused even to suspend him on full pay – because that would be considered *derogatory*. As Harvey Hinds said (in a previous meeting, July 8 1975): 'It is almost impossible to sack the head: it is easier to close the school.'*

But it is not only teachers or headteachers who are never sacked for incompetence. No senior professional is. Consider our consultant psychiatrist whom a Government Inquiry (costing

---

* In fact nearly two years later, after two inspections, a public enquiry, and a hearing before the I.L.E.A. Disciplinary Tribunal, the headmaster (and five of his colleagues) *were* sacked – though not for incompetence, but for indiscipline in unlawfully closing the school. But for that 'error of judgment' he would merely have been downgraded for 'inefficiency'.

about £½ million) reported as running 'an abusive and tyrannical regime'; that he was 'a liar who did not scruple to mislead the inquiry'; that he was 'primarily responsible for the appalling conditions of the 200 patients' and the fact that 'every aspect of the hospital was deplorable'; that he was 'in serious breach of duty for most of his time at the hospital'. After this report he was sacked, but his dismissal was reversed. So having been suspended on full pay (approximately £15,000 p.a.) since 1976, in 1980 he was allowed to retire prematurely on *medical* grounds, with a pension of £6,500 and a substantial gratuity. (Evening Standard, January 24 1980.)

Another example is the Home Office forensic scientist, Dr Alan Clift, whose unfortunate tendency to give inaccurate evidence on behalf of the prosecution resulted in numerous innocent people being convicted and imprisoned. At the last count, seven have been released, including two who had served 16 years and 8 years respectively of a life sentence for murder, three who had each served 3 years of a 6 year sentence for robbery, and one who had been detained in a mental hospital for 6 years for assault. In fact since 1977 the good doctor had been suspended on full pay (£12,500 p.a.) because of 'possible irregularities' – since when the Home Office had been pressing him to retire, but without success. Accordingly in August 1981 the Home Office, having referred the matter to the Departmental Retirement Board, accepted its recommendation that the doctor be given six months' notice, not of dismissal – you can't sack a *doctor* even if he has caused *x* number of innocent people to be put away for *y* number of years – but of compulsory retirement on grounds of 'limited efficiency', retirement gratuity and pension intact.

How the judges and commentators abandon their critical faculties when dealing with professional man (3) Consumers' Association

Because what you read in the newspapers tends to be coloured by the politics and prejudices of the newspaper proprietors, or the requirements of their advertisers on whom they rely for their revenue, the Consumers' Association was founded. This Association, in its monthly magazine *Which?*, publishes reports on a wide range of products and services. And because it is non-profitmaking and carries no advertising, it is totally independent. 'This total independence means that we can be completely objective and outspoken in reporting our test results to you. Our responsibility is to you, the consumer.' (Circular from Consumers' Association.) In other words, unlike the newspapers whose responsibility is to their owners and advertisers, *Which?*'s responsibility is solely to its readers.

When *Which?* sees a spade, it calls it a spade. When its investigations show that a certain product or service is useless, it *says* that it is useless (e.g. hair restorers and baldness treatments, August 1973). When it considers that an advertising campaign makes 'disgracefully false and misleading claims', it says so (off-peak electricity, December 1978).

On car servicing it has this to say: 'Over the last ten years we have revealed an appalling picture of incompetence, wastefulness and even dishonesty. . . Out of 50 garages tested [for this current report] only 2 came anywhere near to carrying out a full service in line with the maker's specifications. Of the rest, 10 were rated poor, 34 very poor, 3 appalling, and 1 'words fail us.' ' (January 1981.) And on travel agents: 'We were appalled by the results of our tests. On too many occasions we were given outrageously bad advice or absolutely wrong information.' (September 1980.)

But *Which?* does not only report on tradesmen's products and services; it also reports on professional services, e.g. doctors, dentists and solicitors. And here, mercifully, it has found that the public is well served by its professionals – unlike its car repairers, travel agents and hair restorers.

'Most people are very happy with their family doctor: they think he's interested in them and that he helps them when they're ill. That's the main message from the surveys we've done.' (January 1974.)

'In our survey members were in general satisfied with the work done by solicitors.' 'Almost all members found their solicitor friendly. About half were very satisfied and a further quarter were fairly satisfied. . .One in ten of our members said that, overall, they were dissatisfied.' (May 1977.)

'Our members were generally very satisfied with the dental treatment they had had.' (March 1973.)

Now the value of *Which?* lies in its vast resources, which enable it to carry out ruthless tests on products and services which the man in the street has little chance of assessing for himself. For instance, unless you are yourself an able mechanic (in which case you would do your own car servicing anyway), you don't know whether the garage, which has serviced your car and has charged you £100, has done a good or a bad job – or whether it has done anything at all. Accordingly, for the previously mentioned report on car servicing *Which?* booked a car, with deliberately induced faults, into 50 garages for a major service; and afterwards checked which of the faults (if any) had been rectified, and what items of a normal service had been carried out.

This is a brutal way to check someone's competence, but in fact it is the only way. *Which?* does not base its report on the *customer's opinion* of the garage, because it realizes that the customer is in no position to give an informed opinion. As the report says: 'The sort of checks we do to find out how well a car has been serviced are obviously not really on for the average motorist . . . and many need test equipment even an avid home mechanic won't have.'

But if the man in the street is ill equipped to assess the service he gets from his car repairer and his travel agent, he is infinitely less well equipped to assess the service he gets from his doctor, dentist and solicitor. To test car repairers' competence, *Which?* takes a car with deliberately induced faults to 50 unsuspecting garages. Subjecting doctors to an equivalent test would be much easier. Simply take, say, a diabetic child to 50 random doctors and posing as his parent explain that he has suddenly begun persistently to wet the bed (the symptom of the untreated disease); and note how many doctors at once dropped a 'clinitest' tablet into a specimen of urine and diagnosed diabetes within a couple of minutes; how many told the 'parent' to take a specimen of urine to the laboratory of the local hospital (which might take a week, whereas early diagnosis is vital); how many told the 'parent' that it is probably her fussing which is disturbing the child. Alternatively a *Which?* inspector, simulating the symptoms of depression, could visit 50 random doctors, and note how many did or said anything useful, how many simply wrote out a prescription for valium.

But for its report on doctors *Which?* does neither of these things. Instead, 'to look more closely at what happens when people go to the doctor with a problem . . . *we asked people in detail* about the last visit they had made to the doctor. We excluded those people who hadn't been in the last year – leaving us with over 2,600 people' (January 1974).

To find out what kind of service travel agents give, *Which?* sent anonymous inspectors to 115 random travel agents all over England. Posing as would-be holiday makers, the inspectors asked advice about two fairly standard holiday locations abroad, and *Which?* then compared the advice the travel agents gave with the facts as it knew them to be – with the result previously stated. Again, it would be just as feasible to subject solicitors to an equivalent test. Plant a simulated road accident victim on 115 random solicitors, and monitor how their claims for compensation progressed over the next three years.*

For its report on solicitors, however, *Which?* adopted a rather different method: 'Solicitors can be expensive. Are they worth it? Can you manage without? For this report *some 2,800 members told us what they thought about the legal profession*.' (May 1977.)

My wife, who was a dental nurse, tells me that some naughty dentists she worked for sometimes did unnecessary fillings; and

---

* In addition to the planted 'client' it would need one co-operative solicitor to act for the fictitious 'other driver' and his insurance company, a 'doctor' to write some medical reports, and perhaps a couple of 'witnesses'.

in the case of other fillings, unnecessarily extended them so that a greater number of the tooth's surfaces would be disturbed, thus increasing the dentist's remuneration. For its report on dentists does *Which?* therefore plant a patient with a carefully vetted mouth, and see how widespread these practices are? And the answer, as you will have guessed, is it does not. 'We've drawn on the experiences of nearly 2,000 of our members with their dentists' (March 1973) – which presumably means we've *asked* nearly 2,000 of our members what they thought about their dentists.

Now *Which?*'s responsibility, as it says, is to *you*, the consumer. And you, the consumer, are just as interested in the competence and honesty of your doctor, dentist and solicitor as you are in the competence and honesty of your car repairer, travel agent and hair restorer. Why, then, does *Which?* not subject the former group of people to the same stringent tests as it applies to the latter? The answer must be that it does not consider that it needs to. The former group are *professional* people, whose competence and honesty can, therefore, by and large be taken for granted.

Thus *Which?* notes that the Motor Agents' Code of Practice is not concerned with standards of workmanship, and finds this a 'glaring omission', 'a paradox', and concludes: 'We remain convinced that what is needed is a watchdog with teeth.'(January 1981.) But as to the *professional* governing bodies' equal disinterest in allegations of incompetence on the part of their members, *Which?* merely observes: 'It would help if the professional bodies clarified their guidelines and took a more severe view of simple inefficiency.' (July 1983.) To suggest that *professional* men need watchdogs with teeth is just not on.

One of the services the Automobile Association provides (for a fee) is to check the condition of a second-hand car you are contemplating buying. Now suppose the A.A. did not actually inspect the vehicle in question, but did its checking by sending the seller a list of questions: 'Is the clutch showing any signs of wear?' 'How often in the last two years has the vehicle broken down?' 'When was it last serviced?' etc. If *Which?* did a report on this service, one imagines that it would have some pretty objective and outspoken comments to make.

Now there are no less than nine *Which?* reports on solicitors' conveyancing, including a full length book on the subject published by the Consumers' Association. Yet in none of these publications will you find a single line questioning the purchaser's *solicitor's* traditional practice of checking the house being bought, by sending a printed form of questions to the seller's solicitor. Indeed this solicitors' question and answer routine is described with apparent approval: 'There are many questions which the buyer's solicitor has to ask the seller's solicitor. This is done mainly on a printed form called 'enquiries before contract'. This form asks questions about the boundaries of the property, about the way in which the main services are laid on, about rights of way, about planning consents . . . and other things.' (The Legal Side of Buying a House, p.4.) 'The buyer's solicitor sends a standard form asking, for example, where the boundaries are, whether the owner has any special obligations, and to confirm that the buyer will get vacant possession. There are standard – in the main rather non-committal – answers to the questions on this form.' (*Which?* report on Conveyancing, June 1979.)

It so happened that the lady who organised this latter report – whose avowed object was to 'suggest ways in which the system could be improved' – asked me for my views on the subject beforehand. These I duly submitted, and when she sent me a draft of the final report I expressed interest as to why my views had not been incorporated. Did she not agree, I asked, that sending the seller a list of questions about the thing he is selling is a fatuous way for an 'expert' to check it? If she didn't, I would explain more fully; if she did, why did she not say so in the report? The representative of this objective and outspoken organisation was silent for a few moments. Then she said: 'Well, we do suggest that the purchaser should be allowed to *see* his building society surveyor's report.'

In other words, I had as little chance of convincing her that our conveyancing system is absurd as I would have in convincing the Pope that God does not exist. Baldness treatments and vitamin pills might be useless, travel agents and car repairers might give appalling service, but professional men *don't* devise and operate absurd systems for their own gain.

How the judges and commentators abandon their critical faculties when dealing with professional man (4) Royal Commission on Legal Services

When Harold Wilson set up a Royal Commission in 1976 to investigate legal services, the legal profession, not surprisingly, viewed the prospect of an independent investigation with some alarm. After some blustering by the then Lord Chancellor and other legal dignitaries, the profession put as brave a face on the inevitable as it could muster. The Law Society and the Bar Council issued a joint statement welcoming the prospect of a 'comprehensive examination'; and the President of the Law Society made a statement that he welcomed the appointment of the Royal Commission which 'I am confident will vindicate the lawyers in the country'. Just *how* confident he was may be judged from the fact that the Law Society decided to retain 40% of the £680,000, which it had raised in 1978 to pay for a national advertising campaign, to pay for a *further* advertising campaign to coincide with the publication of the Commission's report, and to counter its expected criticisms.

In the event (as it should have known) the Law Society had nothing to worry about: the Royal Commissioners came out of the same stable as the judges and the writers of the *Which?* reports. Indeed the first three names on the list are the Chairman, Sir Henry Benson O.B.E. (now Lord Benson), former President of the Institute of Chartered Accountants; Sir Sydney Templeman M.B.E., a High Court judge; and Peter Goldman C.B.E., director of the Consumers' Association.

The key section in the Report comes in the introductory chapter (entitled The Legal Profession), under the subheading *Characteristics of a Profession:*

> 'We summarise below what appear to us to be the main features of a profession, with particular reference to the legal profession: . . .A profession is given a measure of self-regulation so that it may require its members to observe higher standards than could be successfully imposed from without. In order to protect its clients and provide a service of the necessary standard, a profession must impose on its members *high standards of conduct and performance* above those required by the general law, and it must see that these standards are observed.' (Paragraph 3.18.)

The Commissioners go on to quote, with approval, the Law Society's definition of a profession:

> 'In order to maintain their own repute and understanding and to retain public confidence in their abilities, these groups imposed upon themselves a discipline and adopted ethical rules and restrictions, sometimes to their own personal disadvantage but always designed to establish their *probity and competence* in the eyes of the public . . .' (3.19.)

From stating the characteristics which, ideally, a profession *ought* to have, it seems to be a natural step for the Commissioners to assume that these are the characteristics which the professions *do* in fact have:

> 'We think that the characteristics outlined above collectively provide the profession with a sense of corporate identity and independence which is of value not only to its members but to the public at large. It is founded on the ability of its members to speak with knowledge and authority in a particular field of learning. . .; the power to regulate their affairs so as to enhance the prestige and standing of their calling; the sense that its members are directly serving the public to whom they are answerable for their actions; the importance of high standards beyond those required by the law, voluntarily set and maintained.' (3.25.)

These, then, are the characteristics of a profession, according to our Royal Commissioners. And of the legal profession in particular: 'We have been conscious throughout our work of the long history and achievements of both branches of the legal profession. They occupy an important place in our history. . . Our contacts abroad have left us in no doubt that the standing of our legal profession is high in the eyes of the rest of the world.' (3.14.)

Then almost by way of apology for presuming to investigate the legal profession at all: 'It is common experience that any institution or organisation *however venerable* will at times benefit from. . .a study of the potential value of changes in its structure and practices.' (3.15.) I look up 'venerable' and see that it means 'worthy of deep respect on account of noble qualities or associations'.

After this introductory chapter on the characteristics of a profession, it would be reasonable to expect some evidence as to whether or not the actual performance of the legal profession measures up to these ideals. But it seems that the Commissioners are better at delivering windy generalizations about the superior standards of a profession than they are at producing any evidence to support them.

So in the chapter entitled 'Quality of Service', the Commissioners state: 'The evidence before us shows that year by year most legal work is transacted well and efficiently.' (22.16.)

But a couple of pages further on we read: 'The analysis of the time taken in the Queen's Bench Division [i.e. those cases where someone injured in an accident claims compensation] in 1977 shows that the average lapse of time between cause of action and trial was four years'. And 'on average 17 months elapse before a writ is issued.' (22.25.)

Now a reasonably efficient solicitor should be able to get a complicated personal injury case to trial within two years – one year to get the evidence and complete the pre-trial procedures; another year after that, while the case is waiting its turn to come to Court. So the Commissioners' findings (based on evidence supplied by the Lord Chancellor's office) that the average case takes *double* that period to come to Court, and that it takes the plaintiff's solicitor nearly a year and a half to issue a writ – which is the *first* step in a legal action – would seem to be pretty conclusive evidence that most legal work, at any rate Court work, is done badly and inefficiently.

Following the Commissioners' conclusion that most legal work is transacted well and efficiently, comes another conclusion: 'Most clients are satisfied with the service they receive.' (22.16.)

Yet on the previous page we read: 'In response to our requests to the public to submit evidence, we received nearly 1,500 letters making complaints, and relatively few expressing approval.' (22.10.)

If you're a Royal Commissioner investigating the legal profession, your conclusions come first – that the professions in general, and the legal profession in particular, impose on their members high standards of conduct and performance; that most legal work is done well and efficiently; that most clients are satisfied with their legal services, and so on. Evidence comes second. And not to worry if the evidence contradicts the conclusions, because the only people who will look at the report will be lawyers and journalists who won't be interested in reading the evidence anyway.

As we have seen, the professions claim that they impose on their members higher standards of conduct and competence than the law requires of the ordinary man (which according to the Commissioners is one of the most important characteristics of a profession). And as we have also seen, in actuality they do no such thing. In particular, anyone who complains to the Law Society about his solicitor's incompetence will merely receive a stereotyped letter saying that the Society cannot investigate the complaint, and that the complainant's only course is to instruct another solicitor to sue the first one for negligence (see p. 34). As the Commissioners themselves state: 'Complaints of bad professional work are not further examined by the Law Society.'* (25.17.)

A couple of pages further on, however, the Commissioners quote the Law Society as stating: 'It follows that the Society accepts, and has accepted for a great number of years, responsibility not only for the maintainance of professional standards of behaviour *but also for the maintainance of professional standards of competence and efficiency*.' (25.22.)

And how do the Commissioners react to this barefaced lie on the part of the Law Society? 'We are not satisfied that the above principle is always observed; in consequence, many complaints

---

* Actually the Commissioners add the proviso: 'unless they are of so grave a character as to amount to professional misconduct'. But as six Law Society officials who were quizzed by the Commissioners on this point could not recall a single case where bad professional work *had* been considered to amount to professional misconduct, I think this proviso may be ignored.

alleging bad professional work are not investigated.' (25.23.)

Norman Scott is a liar. Jeremy Thorpe gives explanations not all of which can be true. A tradesman tells lies about his services. A professional body enunciates a principle which is not always observed.

When it comes to Barristers – the most exalted of all professions – the Commissioners cannot bring themselves to utter even that mild admonishment. After observing that 'it is incumbent upon the profession to lay down and enforce strict standards both of professional conduct and of competence in the services it provides' (26.1), the Commissioners come to the conclusion: 'We are satisfied that the existing system whereby the Bar lays down rules of conduct for its members is sound and operates in the public interest' (26.4); and 'We are satisfied that the Bar has been punctilious in examining complaints' (26.14).

Yet the barristers' governing body has never once disciplined a barrister either for incompetence, or for overbooking. What, therefore, is the basis for the Commissioners' conclusion that the barristers' disciplinary system is sound and operates in the public interest, and that the Bar has been punctilious in examining complaints? Apparently it is nothing more than *a statement by the barristers' governing body itself*:

'The Senate. . .said in its evidence to us that incompetence ought to be controlled whether or not barristers are liable at law for negligence.' (26.5.)* The Commissioners go on to say: '*This has already been reflected in practice for some years in serious cases.*' (26.6.)

Note the difference in the Commissioners' treatment of the two branches of the legal profession on this prickly point – that is, to what extent (if at all) the professional governing bodies *do* enforce standards of competence. The Commissioners quote the Law Society's palpably false claim, merely adding the gentlest of caveats. But the barristers' profession, from which come our Judges, Master of the Rolls and Lord Chancellor, must not be tainted by *any* suggestion that it fails in its duty to the public. Accordingly our Royal Commissioners obligingly make the false claim on its behalf.

---

* Incidentally, two other important conclusions – that solicitors do not overcharge for conveyancing, and that most conveyancing is done by the actual solicitor not his clerk – are based on nothing more than what solicitors *told* the Commissioners in answer to a questionnaire designed in consultation with the Law Society! (A. 6.1.1.)

Let's go back to the Commissioners' central conclusion: 'The evidence before us shows that year by year most legal work is transacted well and efficiently.' (22.16.) What evidence? Well, the Commissioners carried out two surveys. One was done by placing advertisements in the national press asking for the public's comments on legal services. As mentioned, this produced 'nearly 1,500 letters making complaints and relatively few expressing approval.' This survey the Commissioners dismiss with the words: 'This was to be expected. There would have been the same result if comments had been invited on any service available to the public. Those with a grievance come forward, the satisfied do not' (22. 10). (Why, then, advertise for comments in the first place?) As to the other survey: 'We conducted a survey amongst a random sample of 16,000 people of whom over 2,000 had recently made use of legal services . . . *to provide balanced information upon which an assessment of the quality of service could be based.*' (22.7.)

The fact that 'two-thirds of clients said they were completely satisfied and more than four out of five said they were either completely or fairly satisfied' apparently constitutes the *evidence* which shows that 'most legal work is transacted well and efficiently.'

But of course this fact shows nothing of the kind, since the average client is incapable of assessing the quality of a professional's work. Mrs. Moo's regular solicitor or doctor might be an incompetent ass; but because he has a kindly manner and pats her on the shoulder she might think he's wonderful. On the other hand, she may have no time for his far more competent (albeit more brusque) partner. This the Commissioners themselves acknowledge, for in another part of the report we read: 'In most cases their [the clients who filled in the questionnaire] judgment of the quality of the services given them is probably not professional or expert. That they are dissatisfied does not mean that they necessarily have good reason for dissatisfaction. *Nor, conversely, does the fact that they are satisfied mean that the services given them are necessarily of a high standard.*' (8.213.)

In other words, the Commissioners purport to base their central conclusion – that most legal work is done well and efficiently – on evidence which they know does not support it.

How then *should* our Royal Commissioners have gone about their task of finding out how well or badly lawyers do their job –

assuming that they wanted to know?

In the introduction to the chapter entitled 'Quality of Service', the Commissioners state: 'There are no simple tests of the quality of legal services. The requirements cannot be specified in the same way as those relating to products and some other types of service . . . *The standard of any piece of legal work is largely a matter of opinion.*' (22.3.) Convenient as such a get-out might be, this statement is as absurd as a body, set up (at the cost of £1.25 million) to investigate the motor repair trade, saying: 'the standard of any car repair or service is largely a matter of opinion.'

You can test the quality of legal services in the same way as you can test the quality of any other service – in the same way as *Which?* tests car repairers and travel agents. Mock up a personal injury case, get the 'injured party' to instruct a hundred random solicitors to claim compensation on his behalf, call in all the files after two years, and compare how the hundred solicitors got on with how they *should* have got on. (As the Commissioners include a High Court judge, a Queen's Counsel and two solicitors, they will presumably know how they should have got on.) Alternatively, instruct a hundred random solicitors to do the conveyancing on behalf of a 'purchaser' of a house with a known legal defect (e.g. no right of way to the garage), and see how many solicitors found out and warned him of the defect. Alternatively, ask a hundred random solicitors and barristers to advise on a certain set of facts, and compare the advice given with the advice which *should* have been given.

Such methods are the only way to test *any* kind of service. But just as the Consumers' Association, publishers of *Which?*, considers that while they are appropriate for car repairers and travel agents, it would be unseemly to use them on professional men, so evidently do the Royal Commissioners. Indeed for Sir Henry Benson and Co. to plant a fictitious accident victim on a hundred unsuspecting members of the legal profession, with its 'long history and achievements' and its 'important place in our history' and its 'high standing in the eyes of the rest of the world', would be as unthinkable as for the floor manager of Fortnum and Masons to ask the Queen to open her handbag to check she hadn't been shop-lifting.

When the Commissioners state: 'There are no simple tests of the quality of legal services. The requirements cannot be specified in the same way as those relating to . . . other types of service', what they presumably mean is: there *are* simple tests to assess the quality of legal services (just as there are to assess the quality of any other type of service), but you don't subject professional men – particularly legal professional men – to such tests. And the reason that you don't is because if '*the professions in this country on the whole compare very favourably with those in any other part of the world, and in many respects they are the acknowledged leaders. . .because by their written constitutions and by tradition they seek year after year to improve the quality of service which they give to the public,*'* there isn't any need to.

---

* Lord Benson's letter to The Times, December 14 1983.

How the judges and commentators abandon their critical faculties when dealing with professional man (5) The Press

Having looked at the way in which the judges – judges, that is, in the broadest sense of the word, not just the wigged variety – abandon their critical faculties when dealing with professional man, we continue our catalogue of professionals' lackeys with the Press. At first sight this might seem misguided. Are we not continually reading in our newspapers about this solicitor's chicanery, that doctor's misdiagnosis, that headmaster's unspeakable practices? Well, yes and no. From time to time we do indeed read about such unfortunate incidents. On the other hand we virtually never read anything which questions the professional's underlying *system.*

For example, we read about the solicitor who tried to overcharge his client by £130,000 by submitting a largely fictitious bill. And we read how, when the Law Society dismissed the client's complaint, the client himself took High Court proceedings and had the solicitor struck off. But you may be sure we would never read anything touching on the *implications* of the story – that is, that solicitors (and other professions) escape outside interference by virtue of their claim that through their disciplinary body they ensure higher standards of conduct on the part of their members than are required by law; but in actuality they do no such thing. In other words, the press may from time to time print material hostile or embarrassing to the professions; but never in such a way as to expose the real issues and so cause the professions any real damage.

Conveyancing is a case in point. This being a 'consumer' issue which impinges on a million householders each year, as well as being a professional issue, there have been acres of newsprint on the subject; and some of it has indeed been critical of the cost and delay (which is no doubt why solicitors are forever complaining about their hostile press). Yet in all those acres of newsprint you will not find a single line suggesting that the conveyancing *system* – whereby the purchaser's solicitor checks that the house his client is buying is 'all right' by sending printed forms of questions to the seller's solicitor and to the local Council – is *absurd.* Occasionally even a full page article will appear purporting to 'expose' solicitors' excessive conveyancing costs. But the far more pertinent accusation, that the actual work which accounts for those costs in palpably *useless*, is never made.

In any case, the critical articles are the exception. When the serious press comments on conveyancing, it is usually content to parrot the Law Society's own propaganda. Solicitors may complain about their hostile press but, ironically, without the support of the serious press (and other organs of the media), it is doubtful whether they could have maintained such a ludicrous system over the years. I quote:

When selling a house 'you should reckon that between 6% and 10% of the price will go to others, including the solicitor *who is usually well worth his fee*.' (The Times, November 25 1978.) I doubt whether even the Law Society would dare tell such a whopper – that someone who charges between £350 and £700 for a couple of hours routine clerical work, usually delegated to a clerk or secretary, is 'usually well worth his fee'.

A reader wrote in to the *Guardian*'s money advice column asking where he could get information on D.I.Y. conveyancing. He was advised that although there were books on the subject, 'I do urge you to be very careful. This is really a matter which should be left to the experts . . . and you would be wise to utilize the services of a solicitor from the outset.' (*Guardian*, May 28 1983.)

On the advantages of using a solicitor for your house purchase: 'All solicitors are covered by the Law Society's rules . . . as well as having insurance against the risk that you sue them successfully for negligence.' (*Guardian*, August 2 1980.) Just as this is the standard Law Society justification, so it is the standard middlebrow media comment. The journalists who make it have no interest in pointing out that there are numerous avoidable quasi-legal pitfalls in buying a house, against which employing a solicitor affords not the slightest protection; and neither will falling into one give rise to any action for negligence against the solicitor.

The editor of the *Guardian*'s Family Finance page, who was the 'expert consultant' on a Radio 4 series on house buying and selling, was asked at the end of a programme whether he would do his own conveyancing. Replied he: 'No. Firstly, because I'm lazy; secondly, because I would want someone to blame if things went wrong.' ('Your Move or Mine', February 11 1982.) Again the standard 'professional' argument. Again neither he, nor any other newspaper man,* shows the slightest interest in the fact that things are far *less* likely to go wrong if you do your own conveyancing intelligently than if you go to a solicitor – as the most cursory examination of the solicitors' conveyancing procedures would at once reveal.

Incidentally, apropos the argument that you can always sue your solicitor if he makes a mistake, I have recounted how I once served a writ for negligence on a solicitor, who assaulted me causing actual bodily harm. He was found guilty after a full day's hearing in the Magistrates Court, during which the press bench was full to capacity. But, surprise surprise, only *The Sun* – an organ not primarily noted for its interest in matters legal – gave the case any mention (under the headline *Law Men's Tussle ends in Blood*).

After conveyancing, the lawyers' activity which impinges most on the public is litigation – the process whereby someone who is injured in an accident (whether on the roads, at work or wherever) seeks to obtain compensation for his injuries through the Courts.

Here the press is equally docile. On December 7 1979 every national newspaper reported the case of Whitehouse v. Jordan (which I have previously mentioned).In this case the Court of Appeal reversed a finding of negligence against an obstetrician; and quashed the award of £100,000 compensation, which had been made against him, in favour of a ten year old child, in respect of brain damage which the child had received at birth. So in the event the child got nothing. Now the *Times* also reported that the obstetrician's barrister (when applying for an order in

---

* With the exception of David Lewis, editor of the Money Mail section in the Daily Mail.

respect of his client's costs) stated that the total legal costs of the case were likely to exceed £150,000. The *Daily Telegraph* also mentioned the sum of 'about £150,000' in legal costs. So did the *Mirror*. All those hawk-eyed journalists. Yet none of them can manage the comment that a legal system which costs over £150,000 to decide an issue involving £100,000 is *absurd*.

Not only did every newspaper report the case. Several devoted leaders to it. The *Guardian*'s leader writer welcomed the Court of Appeal's decision: 'The problem for medical men is that the consequences of their mistakes are so much more dire than for most other professional people.' The *Guardian* omits to mention that this might also be a problem for some of their patients. The *Daily Telegraph* not only welcomed the Court of Appeal's decision, but found it a cause for rejoicing. After sternly warning us that our natural reaction of indignation at the mother's plight is '*morally misguided*', it continues: 'Others as well as Mrs. Whitehouse have suffered anguish – notably the obstetrician whom the Court of Appeal now finds to have been guilty merely of an error of judgment, in which negligence played no part. If that decision is correct we should all rejoice at it as warmly as we sympathize with Mrs. Whitehouse's *misfortune*.'

Consider, if you will, another aspect of that case. Look again at the facts. The Court of Appeal decided that a ten year old child should not get compensation for the brain damage he received at birth, because the obstetrician who delivered him had not been negligent. In other words, it took the legal system *ten years* to decide the question. All those hawk-eyed journalists. All those pontificating leader writers telling us what we should and shouldn't feel about the case. Yet none of them can manage the comment that a legal system which takes ten years to decide whether or not an obstetrician was negligent in delivering a baby, is *absurd*. Next time you see a newspaper report of a personal injury case, note the date of the accident; then note the date of the newspaper reporting the Court's judgment in respect of it, and you will see that the normal period between the two is four years, and that five or six years is not uncommon. Yet never will you see in the newspaper carrying that report any comment that a legal system which takes four to six years to decide a negligence case – which often turns on just one or two not too complicated facts* –

---

* In Whitehouse v. Jordan it was just one question which had to be decided: in trying to deliver the baby by forceps did the obstetrician pull too hard and for too long before abandoning the attempt, and proceeding to Caesarian section?

is *absurd.* Professional men *don't* devise and operate absurd systems.

Litigation, not being a 'consumer' issue, is of less interest to the press than conveyancing; and for the most part attracts a discreet silence. Of course if a case does have a particularly dramatic element, or an exceptionally high sum is involved, or when Ken Loach *famous film director* has a car crash with tragic consequences, but finds that under our legal system he can get no compensation, there will be some press coverage. But there is little interest in the predicament of the grey mass of litigants who aren't film directors, whose cases have no dramatic element, who year in year out shuffle through our Courts. Only one journalist seems to take any consistent interest in their plight – Phillip Knightley who, as well as writing two pieces on Ken Loach's case, was responsible for a short editorial in the *Sunday Times* (February 8 1981) on the defects in our litigation system; and who wrote an article in the same paper (February 15 1981) on four people who were seriously injured, but unable to obtain compensation. Mr. Knightley's explanation for his lone stand (when I asked him) is that he is the only journalist to have done his homework thoroughly enough to be able to argue successfully with the paper's libel lawyers.

This may have something to do with it – not so much that the newspapers' lawyers are concerned to protect their profession, as fearful (as are the journalists) that anything attacking the *legal* profession will provoke an avalanche of writs. But it cannot be the whole explanation, because when dealing with the other professions the press (particularly the 'serious' press) is equally bland.

In May 1981 David Woodhouse went into hospital for a routine appendix operation, and thence into an irreversible coma, because something had gone amiss with the anaesthetic. The Area Health Authority wanted to hold an independent inquiry to find out what had happened, and prevent it hapening again. But the inquiry could not take place because the doctors refused to co-operate, as advised by the Medical Defence Union, in case it unearthed evidence which could be used by the relatives in subsequent negligence proceedings. A few eyebrows raised; a few comments in the serious press that such a situation is not exactly satisfactory. But certainly no cry of anger. All those pontificating leader writers who are forever telling the politicians and management and unions what they should and shouldn't do. Yet none of them suggest that *every* serious hospital mishap should automatically be followed by an independent inquiry; and that if it was, there might be less of them. All those hawk-eyed journalists. Yet none of them comment on the fact that the doctor responsible – who, according to a subsequent report, failed to understand the anaesthetic equipment he was using, failed to make the right connexions to the breathing apparatus, failed to act when Mr. Woodhouse went blue, failed to get help until it was too late – should immediately take up another appointment in an Essex hospital as an obstetrician. And only one journalist (Oliver Gillie, Sunday Times, March 7 1982) comments on the fact that an identical accident had occurred three years previously, when an independent inquiry set up by the Health Authority was similarly thwarted by the doctors.

In January 1981 a dentist administered a general anaesthetic, and operated, without a qualified assistant being present – contrary to the professional guidelines – and the patient died. The dentist was charged with manslaughter, and initially found guilty on October 27 1981. One or two papers reporting the incident laconically let fall the fact that the same dentist had done the same thing, with the same result, eight years previously. Compare the discreet few column inches of newsprint which appeared on this item, with the furore if a criminal released on parole commits a murder. Compare the discreet few column inches when a child dies as the result of a doctor's negligence, with the screams of rage, accompanied by strident demands for a public enquiry, when a child dies as a result of a *social worker's* negligence.

On September 29 1982 another discreet item appeared in the papers about an unnamed dentist who gave patients unnecessary treatments, and whose N.H.S. fees for the 1981 financial year came to £288,779. He was fined £50,000 by the Herts Family Practitioner Committee for breach of his terms of service. Thus his net fees for the year in question came to £238,779. Again, no cry of protest, no indignant editorials, no interest in what the dentist's fees had been for the *previous* year (approximately £140,000, paid without query). No comment on the fact that if a dentist makes fraudulent claims in the region of a quarter of a million pounds a year, it seems that the Dental Estimates Board might be alerted, but apparently not if he lirnits them to, say £100,000 a year.* And again, no journalist can manage the question touching on the real issue – by how many millions each year is the N.H.S. being milked in this way, and how many hospitals would not have to be closed down if it wasn't?

Of course, here and there one comes across a journalist writing on professional matters, who *does* try to do a bit more than merely paraphrase the press handouts.† But one or two journalists on their own (whose efforts in any case are dependent on the whim of their editors) are pretty powerless, and cannot do more than inflict the occasional flesh wound.

'Journalists plainly have special responsibilities and . . . must necessarily be in the front line of any resistance.' So says the Deputy General Secretary of the National Union of Journalists in a pamphlet, *Taking Liberties*. If half the gentlemen of the press – that is, journalists, editors and proprietors – went half way to meeting those responsibilities, the solicitors just could not get away with a conveyancing system which finds out virtually nothing of any use about the house being bought; the barristers just could not get away with rules which permit them to ditch their client at the last minute if it suits them; the Dental Estimates Board just could not get away with a system which permits a dentist to defraud the N.H.S. by £100,000 a year; the doctors just could not get away with refusing to co-operate with an independent inquiry to determine the cause of a medical mishap; the professional governing bodies just could not get away with pontificating about how they ensure that their members observe the highest standards – and then take no action against, e.g., a hundred dentists who gassed a hundred patients, and so on.

The free press is our only watchdog against tyranny, corruption and hypocrisy. But it's as if there is an invisible charter which delimits what it does and what it does not watch.

---

* 'The general dental service operates on the principle of good faith . . . it is quite impossible for us to check every claim.' – Chairman of the Dental Estimates Board (The Times, November 25 1982).

† E.g. Phillip Knightley on legal matters; Oliver Gillie on medical matters.

How the judges and commentators abandon their critical faculties when dealing with professional man (6) B.B.C.

Once upon a time, many years ago, I heard a radio programme which, by means of a fictional narrative, showed how an injured person obtains compensation through the Courts. A window cleaner had fallen from an outside ledge, and had permanently injured his back. His attitude to this cruel turn of fate was stoical –'If I couldn't take a joke I shouldn't have gone in for the job.' But his wife, not sharing her husband's fatalism, insists he takes the matter further and sees a solicitor. 'So with some trepidation' Mr. and Mrs. Ex-window cleaner penetrate the rather imposing offices of a solicitor in the nearby town. It proves less of an ordeal than they imagined, and the solicitor advises the ex-window cleaner that he may well have a claim against his erstwhile employers for failing to provide a safe system of work. The solicitor duly submits an application for legal aid (a scheme whereby people of limited means can bring a case to Court and have their legal fees paid for by the State). Cut to Legal Aid Committee in session. Pompous voice: 'Damn fool. Stood on a ledge which was obviously too narrow. No claim here.' Testy voice: 'We can't all read as quickly as you, Smithers . . . hmm . . . [in more reflective tone] Blank & Co. don't seem to be too careful about the system of work they provide for their employees.'

The Committee agrees to allow the applicant's solicitor to take a barrister's opinion, which proves favourable, and so legal aid is granted. . .Final scene, the Court room, in which the judge is giving judgment for the window cleaner: '. . .and I therefore award Mr. Johnson £6,500 [or whatever it was] general damages, and to this I add the further sum of £5. Mr. Johnson has said that the evening following his accident he was due to play the trumpet in his local band. Now it may be that the local citizenry did not suffer unduly in missing Mr. Johnson's performance; but he has said that he was looking forward to it, and so in addition to the general damages he shall have an extra £5 for that disappointment.' Final comment by the presenter: 'With the compensation Mr. and Mrs. Johnson bought a small newsagents business, and Mr. Johnson himself now gives the odd bit of legal advice to his customers. Well, in the circumstances you can hardly blame him.'

Many years after that programme, I wrote to the BBC, querying why a certain 'consumer' radio programme – on the delays involved in injured people obtaining compensation through the Courts – was not more critical of the legal system, but accepted it at its face value. The editor replied: 'Our function is to give *useful information* to our listeners, and *controversy* is normally left to those programmes which exist to show trends in current thought.' In answer to a further letter, the producer wrote: 'It is not the purpose of this programme to discuss *political* proposals and suggested changes in the law; our job is to discuss the law as it is now.'

Once I got through to a 'Tuesday Call' phone-in programme on housebuying, when the discussion had strayed on to the thorny question of gazumping. I put the point that gazumping is caused by the delay in exchanging contracts, which in turn is caused by the solicitors' useless conveyancing ritual – which ensures that it takes one or two months, whereas under an efficient system it need take only one or two hours. I was unceremoniously cut off, because (as the BBC explained in a letter to a listener who complained that my point had not been adequately dealt with) the programme 'was merely trying to give practical advice and not engage in *politics*.'

From my observations, reinforced by these revealing snippets, it seems that the BBC puts documentary material, whether on legal matters or any other, into one of three categories: (1) Useful Information; (2) Controversial; (3) Political.

Into the first category falls that material which conforms to the established accepted thinking, as the BBC understands it. Into the second falls: (a) those subjects on which there is no established accepted thinking, but which tend to attract widely differing opinions; and (b) unconventional and potentially disturbing views. As to the third category, 'political' (meaning factious or partisan, rather than pertaining to government) is simply a convenient pejorative label for 'unacceptable.'

The third category, therefore, has no place in the BBC. The first and second do. The difference between them is that 'useful information' needs no balancing, whereas 'controversial' must always be balanced.

Those programmes which are *specifically* designed to accommodate controversial material (e.g. 'Any Questions', 'You the Jury') have a debating hall or Court room format, so that the arguments on both sides of the question (e.g. blood sports, euthanasia, private medicine, whether it is better to have your baby at home, etc.) can be put. In the case of a controversial *interview* (which can occur on any of the news and comment programmes), the opposing point of view must always be put. For instance, if someone is asserting that a large number of social workers are incompetent because students aspiring to that calling are never failed, then the Secretary of the Social Workers' Association will be given equal time in the same item to refute the allegation.

So 'controversial' has to be balanced; 'useful information' doesn't. Another rule is that when that 'useful information' concerns professional matters, it will be purveyed by a professional. This is because only a professional is presumed to be capable of speaking authoritatively on professional matters. As the editor of 'You and Yours' – the longest running and most regular of BBC consumer programmes – wrote to me: 'We don't use solicitors to put the point of view of their professional body, *but as people who understand the law to explain it to the lay public.*'

The BBC's categorizing documentary material in this manner, and the rules it applies to each category, may seem unexceptionable. The fact that for information on professional matters it will go to a professional, may seem equally unexceptionable. But these apparently unexceptionable rules, taken together, have a most profound result. Which is that the professionals, and their lackeys, are given freedom of the air to put their point of view ('useful information') unopposed; whereas anything which *questions* their point of view ('controversial') is permitted only if balanced by a simultaneous counter-argument. Moreover, anything which questions the professional's point of view in such a way as to admit *no* balancing counter-argument is labelled 'political', and therefore is not allowed at all.

Thus the window cleaner's half hour saga (obviously written by a lawyer), which purports to explain to the lay public how someone who is injured gets compensation through the Courts, falls in the 'useful information' category. It would never have occured to the producer that the information which that programme did purvey – that the legal system is run by competent humane people, and will uphold the rights of the little man – is just as controversial as any party political broadcast. Incidentally, that little touch at the end, where the judge awards him an extra £5 to compensate him for missing his trumpet performance, is legally incorrect (because such 'damage' would not be foreseeable), but was presumably deliberately inserted to show the humour and humanity of our judges.

Into the 'useful information' category also fall such statements as: 'Our two-tier system [i.e. the division of lawyers into solicitors and barristers] is the admiration of overseas organizations' (Lord Benson, The World Tonight, October 3 1979); and 'The legal system in Britain is rightly esteemed as a pillar of our democracy,incorruptible and remarkably independent. Most of us breathe more easily because it is there' (presenter of Newsweek, May 24 1979). Because this is the established accepted view – that the British legal system is the admiration of foreigners, and the embodiment of excellence – such statements likewise need no balancing.

As we saw in the previous section on the Press, conveyancing, being a popular 'consumer' issue as well as a professional issue, provides a neat illustration of how these unwritten rules operate.

Now just as there are strongly held and opposing views on capital punishment, blood sports, etc., so there are on conveyancing. One is that when you buy and sell your house you should employ a *solicitor* to do the conveyancing. The other is that solicitors' conveyancing services are useless or worse, and that you are better off doing the job yourself. The first, being the established or *professional* view, falls in the 'useful information' category. Thus those who purvey it are allowed to do so unopposed. For example:

'You and Yours' (Radio 4, February 20 1981). Solicitor talked for ten minutes about what 'we professionals' do on behalf of someone buying a flat, at the end of which the presenter gave details of a Law Society booklet and where it could be obtained, which urges the potential purchaser to consult a solicitor.

That same morning, also on Radio 4: 'Buying a Dream'. A 45 minute documentary programme (repeated) on how a couple, Bob and Deirdre, set about buying their house. We hear them being shown round the house in question, and then we are told by the presenter: 'Bob and Deirdre already had a solicitor lined up, and they went to see him that afternoon.' In other words, that is the way to buy a house.

'Tuesday Call' (Radio 4, July 5 1983). Chartered surveyor answering questions on housebuying: 'I do have a very high regard for the work solicitors do in conveyancing . . . If you've got all the time you *can* do your own conveyancing, but this is a very big transaction you're involved in and *you can't sue yourself for negligence*.' 'I'm sorry to have to bring in solicitors all the while, but it does emphasize the role they play in house purchase and selling.'

'Woman's Hour' (Radio 4, January 9 1984). Architect and author of a book on housebuying is being interviewed, and mentions the various fees involved in a move: 'And of course you'll have to pay legal fees to your solicitor. In general they give jolly good value. Of course you *can* do it yourself but I wouldn't advise it. I've known too many cases of D.I.Y. purchasers coming unstuck because they found they didn't own the land they wanted to build that garage on, or grandma turned out to be a sitting tenant.'

In three out of those four examples it is a professional giving the professional's point of view (although in the last two, significantly, it is not a member of the profession in question but a related profession). And as there is no-one to challenge such views, they assume the status of objective truths.

What happens to someone with equal credentials, who is concerned to put the *opposite* point of view – that the housebuyer is safer doing his own conveyancing and *not* going to a solicitor? At first sight this view would seem to fall into the 'controversial' category; that is, it may be aired provided there is someone from the professional camp to answer it. Nothing so grand as 'You the

Jury' for such an *eccentric* opinion, but perhaps a six minute discussion in a consumer or current affairs programme. And having written a book (Conveyancing Fraud) in which I do argue that point of view, I am indeed invited to take part in one or two broadcast discussions. I am allowed to expound my views for two or three minutes, someone from the legal establishment is given the equivalent time to explain that what I have said is nonsense, and give or take an interruption or two, that's that. A 'controversial' point of view has been put, honour has been honoured, balance has been balanced, and *what* a stimulating discussion that was and thank you both *so* much for coming along. (It comes as something of a shock to realize that the BBC female programme presenters don't all *look* the same.)

But over the years following the publication of my book, I gave several more recorded interviews for various current affairs programmes, without anyone from the legal establishment being present to oppose me – none of which were broadcast. In particular, I recorded an interview for 'The World at One' on my refusal to pay my contribution to the Law Society's advertising fund (levied on each solicitor), because I considered that its previous advertising campaign had made false claims. The presenter told me that the BBC lawyers had vetted and approved the item, and that it would be transmitted in an hour. But when I returned to listen to it I was told that 'it had been decided' not to use it after all. On another occasion I had a recorded discussion with a Law Society spokesman, which was broadcast at 6.40 a.m. ('Up to the Hour'). Although there would have been only a few lorry drivers and insomniacs around at that time, I subsequently heard from the presenter that he had been rebuked by his superior, who told him that as the Law Society spokesman had appeared so ineffectual *he should have either re-recorded the item or suppressed it altogether.*

In other words, an anti-professional – 'controversial' – argument is permitted only if it is balanced by the professional counter-argument. If there is no professional present to balance it, it is rejected because it breaks the rules. If there is a professional present, but his counter-arguments are so feeble that they do not effectively balance it, then it is (or should be) equally rejected, because it then falls into the 'political' category. Thus the point I made on Tuesday Call – that gazumping was caused by the solicitors' absurd conveyancing ritual – would have been 'controversial' had the professional taking the calls been able to answer it. But as he wasn't, it was 'political' and I was at once cut off – on the grounds that the programme '*was merely trying to give practical advice and not engage in politics*.'

So far my examples have been taken from the current affairs, consumer, and phone-in programmes broadcast during the day. But the real plums are the evening phone-in programmes, such as 'It's Your Line' and 'Person to Person'. Here people who have risen to the top of their profession answer questions from the public, and in so doing they can explain to their several million listeners the value of their profession's work. This, of course, falls in the 'useful information' category. Occasionally a hostile questioner is allowed to put his point, but he will normally be at a disadvantage, and in any case if he looks like seriously embarrassing the 'guest' he will simply be cut off. For example, when Sir Peter Rawlinson, Chairman of the Bar Council, was Robin Day's guest on 'It's Your Line', someone rang in to query why barristers charged such generous fees for a day's work arguing a case in Court. Sir Peter replied that what they did in Court was often only the tip of an iceberg, having regard to all the preparation they did beforehand. Does Mr. Questioner want to come back to Sir Peter on that one? asks Robin Day, but no he doesn't, thank you, and thank *you* Mr. Questioner. But ten minutes later comes Michael Zander on the line: if Sir Peter is claiming that what barristers do in Court is only the tip of an iceberg, then why did a survey in Leicester show that 80% of barristers surveyed saw their clients *for the first time on the morning of the trial?* To which Sir Peter can only bluster: 'I know you, Mr. Zander, and I know your views, and I won't alter your views just as you won't alter mine, so I don't quite know why you've bothered to come through to me.' 'Well, we must leave it there, Mr. Zander,' says Robin Day, 'you *are* a legal correspondent and so have other channels in which to air your views' – which of course he would have known before Zander put his point.

Sir Desmond Heap, President of the Law Society, was Robin Day's guest on another 'It's Your Line.' A lady rang in to say that she had done her own conveyancing, and queried whether the business was as complicated as solicitors make out. The President, with all the authority one would expect from someone in his position, warned her what a dangerous area she had been moving in (in view of all the 'cross covenants, rights of underground support, and overhead rights of aeroplanes'); and implied that because she had not used a solicitor she might find that her house was unsaleable. Robin Day then asked what *could* have gone wrong with the lady's purchase – an innocent enough question, but it evidently threw the President, who could only reply that he knew of a case where a *solicitor* acting for a purchaser had failed to find out about a neighbour's drain running under the garden, which prevented the purchaser building a garage. Robin Day refrains from making the obvious rejoinder – which would have knocked Sir Desmond and his claims for six – and tactfully hurries on to the next questioner.*

Following a Consumer Council's report on official gobbledy-gook, a Law Society spokesman was asked whether *lawyers* were not guilty of using deliberately obscure language ('Today', May 22 1980). Replied he: 'I don't know where that view comes from. The lawyer's job is to interpret and explain official red tape to his client.' Interviewer does not confront him with the verbal rubbish in, say, a typical clause in a typical lease.

In a fairly bland item on the case of the solicitor who tried to overcharge his client by £130,000 (see p. 33), and the Law Society's role in that case ('The World at One', October 17 1983), the Secretary General of the Law Society was asked whether there is any reason why the complaints procedure should not be taken out of the Law Society's hands and put in the hands of some independent body. He replied: 'Yes. Because I believe that a true profession must have self regulation.' To which the interviewer's reply is 'John Bowron, thank you very much' – not 'John Bowron, that's all very well, but what if the profession manifestly *fails* to regulate itself?' which rejoinder, or its equivalent, I imagine he would have had no difficulty in making had he been interviewing a trade union leader.

Lord Denning, Master of the Rolls, is the guest on 'Person to

---

* It is interesting to compare Robin Day's treatment of his professional guests with his astringent treatment of his *political* guests. For instance when Barbara Castle was his guest on 'It's Your Line', a questioner accused her of having attended a private nursing home (i.e. of being a hypocrite). She replied that she hadn't, and that if he didn't withdraw she would take libel proceedings. Robin Day: 'Well, Mr. Thing, are you going to withdraw? When a Minister has given her word it's usual to accept it. On the other hand you don't have to withdraw if you don't want to.' (In the event he did withdraw.)

Person'. (June 18 1980). He explains that the Pearson Commission made no radical suggestion to alter the existing litigation system. No-one points out to his lordship that the Pearson Commission recommended that *road accident victims should be taken out of the litigation system altogether*, and given automatic compensation from a fund financed by a levy on petrol – as radical a suggestion as anyone could wish for. And so on, and so on.

The professional is given freedom of the air to put his point of view. Nothing is permitted which effectively *refutes* that point of view.

So far my examples have been taken from the legal profession. But we may observe the same rules operating in respect of the medical and teaching professions.

The medical equivalent of the window cleaner's saga would be, say, 'A tale of two survivors' (Radio 4, May 5 1982, repeated), in which two accident victims recount their remarkable recoveries 'with the help of hospital experts who treated them'; and in which one patient says: 'there's a tremendous amount of skill. It's tremendous. It's our miracle.'

Just as 'Our two-tier system [dividing the legal profession into solicitors and barristers] is the admiration of overseas organisations', so 'Our doctors get better training than anywhere else in the world' ('Tuesday Call', November 15 1983). Just as 'The legal system in Britain is rightly esteemed as a pillar of our democracy, incorruptible and remarkably independent', so do 'we owe most doctors an enormous debt of gratitude for all their skill and care' ('That's Life', March 18 1984). Just as Lord Denning, Master of the Rolls, is not challenged when he says that the Pearson Commission made no radical suggestion to alter our legal system, neither is Dame Josephine Barnes, former President of the British Medical Association, when she says: 'When patients are injured by a doctor's negligence *they are compensated without question* . . . There is no argument about that.' ('Man Alive', May 15 1982.)

A lady, whose family has had successful treatment for cancer, says on 'Tuesday Call' (November 15 1983): 'We owe everything to our G.P.'s. They were absolutely wonderful.' Now I'm not suggesting that the lady's doctors were not wonderful. What I am saying is that had she wished to put the *opposite* point of view – that her doctors were absolutely awful and ruined her life – she probably would not have been allowed to. Thus on another 'Tuesday Call' a doctor on the answering panel, who was asked about the G.P.'s right to remove a patient from his list, explains that such a right is necessary 'because just occasionally a patient is so selfish and unreasonable that the doctor–patient relationship breaks down.' This being the professional's point of view, it falls in the 'useful information' category, which means it is purveyed as an absolute truth. The opposing point of view – that the selfishness and unreason are just as likely to be on the doctor's part as on the patient's, and to give the doctor the unquestioned right to remove a patient from his list is to give him a dangerous amount of power – would not be allowed to be voiced.

Turning briefly to schools and education, a lady made the point ('Tuesday Call' again) that whilst the education authorities paid lip service to the value of parents' involvement with their child's education, they nevertheless did nothing to make such involvement possible if the headteacher was against it; and what contact – if any – there was between parent and teacher is completely at the discretion of the individual head. Had her point concerned her difficulty in varying the sandwich fillings in the lunches she packed for her little laddie, or similar, it would have come under *useful information*, and she would probably have been invited to a prolonged cosy discussion. But because it implied a criticism of the system, after a few frosty words of reply she was cut off – no doubt on the grounds that the programme was merely trying to give practical advice, and not engage in *politics*. On another 'Tuesday Call' (July 7 1982), a caller is worried that the only available comprehensive school has a bad reputation. Advice from one member of the panel: 'Put pressure on the school to improve it'; and from the other (the education correspondent of The Guardian): 'If the school knows you expect jolly good teaching then there's no reason why your daughter shouldn't get good results.'

The notion that there might be lousy schools and lousy teachers about, and there's nothing you can do about it, has no place within the carpeted studios of Broadcasting House. Within those soundproofed walls so stout, keeping disturbing questions out, everyone is well-bred and decent – as typified by Mrs. Dale, the doctor's wife, of the serial of so many years ago. And well-bred decent people do not, for the most part, consider that there is anything fundamentally amiss with the system.

To this rule – that BBC radio programmes do not question the system – there is an exception. Roger Cook of Checkpoint, microphone in hand, will put all sorts of disturbing questions to all kinds of people. His usual subject is business fraud, but he has investigated corruption in local government, the remand system where innocent people are locked up in worse conditions than the guilty, people who are wrongly incarcerated in prisons or criminal mental institutions, building societies' callous treatment of borrowers who fall behind in their mortgage repayments, and similar. But although in the eleven years since the programme started there have been a few items on the professionals, Cook (or more probably his producer) seems chary of them.

Now when I wrote an article in the Daily Mail (Money Mail section) critical of how lawyers had handled a personal injury case, there was appended a little note stating that I was writing a book on the legal system, and would welcome readers' experiences. As a result I got a sackful of readers' disastrous experiences, some of them clearly involving fraud, not only with lawyers but doctors, dentists and schoolteachers as well – enough material for a whole year's Checkpoint programmes. Checkpoint is a weekly programme, broadcast at peak listening time in the evening and repeated the following morning. At the end of each programme, listeners are invited to write in if they come across anything they think needs investigating. If a few lines added to a single newspaper article can get such a result for me, imagine what Checkpoint's continuous appeals must throw up. Checkpoint does a good job week after week, year after year, exposing fraud and injustice – especially fraud. But the occasions when it has exposed fraud perpetrated by a professional (qua professional) can be counted on the fingers of Django's right hand.

I asked the producer for a list of subjects which Checkpoint had investigated, but he seemed curiously coy in response to such a request.* Eventually I got a list from BBC Data Services for the period January 1979 to June 1981, when the microfiche system was discontinued. The first four items on the first sheet

---

* I was told there was no such list, or if there was, it contained other sensitive material; or that someone would have to go through it with me and there was no one available. Incidentally, the list of subjects printed at the end of the BBC's book on Checkpoint is too general to be of use.

are: Fraud, travel agencies; Fraud, mail order; Fraud, building firms; Fraud, car dealers. Then looking through the sheets I see amongst the titles: Fraud, vanity publishing; Fraud, fringe bank; Fraud, charity collections; Fraud, book retail trade; Fraud, private detection; Fraud, holiday housing abroad; Fraud, Australian land deals; Fraud, immigration; Fraud, windows; Fraud, jewellery; Fraud, cereal crops; Fraud, music industry; Fraud, hotels; Fraud, magazines; Fraud, plumbing; and so on. Looking through this list, one gets the impression that there is not an area of human activity on which Checkpoint has not exposed a fraud. Except one. *There is not a single item on fraud perpetrated by a professional.*

Not every Checkpoint subject is fraudulent. The programmes cover a wide spectrum of morals and activities, from the wicked to the misguided, from freemasonry in a local Council to the Sun's misreporting of skinhead violence, from fringe religion to Home Office injustice. The list covers a period of two and a half years, during which over 200 subjects were investigated. But there is only *one programme* on professionals* – complaints against doctors (July 20 1979).

One Checkpoint programme (after the period covered by my list, November 26 1981) concerned a man whose house had been ruined by a builder who, in the course of building an extension, had dug underneath the existing foundations, which had promptly collapsed. The unfortunate householder started legal proceedings against the builder, but seven years later he still cannot get his case to Court because his solicitor is demanding £12,000 on account of costs. 'I don't have that sort of money; not many people do.' We hear Cook questioning the builder over the telephone, then the builder's insurance company – but not the *solicitor* who has made such an outrageous demand.

Moreover, in the rare instances that Checkpoint does turn its attention to the professionals, they tend to get different treatment from its usual subjects. For instance on September 2 1982 there was a six minute item on a solicitor who, because he had omitted a routine 'Land Registry search', had not realized that the house which his client was buying from a builder fell *outside* the

---

* By professional I mean a member of an established profession who is operating within its traditional ambit, i.e. *not* someone who claims to have psychical healing powers. I also mean professional *qua* professional, i.e. not a shady hotelier who also *happens* to be a barrister.

boundary of the land which the builder owned. Having bought the house, the purchaser was unable to sell it, and was in fact liable to be dispossessed at any time. 'Our solicitor doesn't seem to have done his job properly,' says the aggrieved purchaser. 'That's probably true,' says the reporter. Probably true? I later spoke to the reporter (not Roger Cook, as it happened), who agreed that it was *unquestionably* true. No such pussyfooting when Checkpoint is on the trail of a central heating contractor, or similar. 'We asked the solicitor what he had to say, but he refused an interview and instead insisted on reading from a prepared statement.' Recording of solicitor's voice: 'I try to be an honourable professional man . . .' When Checkpoint's usual subjects refuse an interview, Roger Cook gets his foot in their door and asks the questions whether they want to answer them or not. Why not when the subject is an 'honourable professional man'?

In another item (September 15 1983) Checkpoint investigated an entrepreneur whose chain of cosmetic surgery clinics results in wealth for him but 'surgical mutilation' for many of his clients. For 23 minutes out of the 25 minute programme, the non-professional entrepreneur is given the full Checkpoint treatment, down to the final confrontation (which he tries to avoid by locking himself in the lavatory, while Cook is set on by his staff). But the professional doctors (that is, qualified G.P.'s but evidently unskilled in surgery) who, in the last two minutes of the programme, we are given to understand actually did most of the mutilating, retain their anonymity; and escape with the most casual of references – merely that none of them had been struck off by the General Medical Council, who had said that 'striking off a doctor is a serious matter'.

Although BBC television is a more virile and independent medium, with some hard hitting exposés (e.g. drug companies, the asbestos industry) to its credit, when it comes to the professional it seems to follow in Auntie's cautious footsteps.

If a professional is interviewed he must not be challenged or embarrassed – unlike a trade union leader or politician, who may be grilled mercilessly. For instance, in all the interviews of Lord Denning it is accepted that he is the judge who stands up for the little man against the big institution. No-one reminds him of his advice to the mother of the brain-damaged child, with which he concluded his judgement quashing her award of £100,000 compensation: 'She should be grateful for all that has been done for her without laying blame on the doctors.' Christmas Humphreys, the Buddhist barrister who refused a judgeship because it would be against his religion to sentence someone to death, was interviewed both on radio and television. On neither occasion was he asked about his role as prosecuting Counsel in two of the most notorious cases where innocent men were hanged (Evans and Bentley). Dame Josephine Barnes, former President of the British Medical Association, says: 'When patients are injured by a doctor's negligence they are compensated without question' ('Man Alive', May 15 1982). No reminder of instances where the Medical Defence Union ordered the doctors involved not to co-operate in an independent inquiry to find out the cause of a medical mishap, lest it uncover evidence which could be used in subsequent negligence proceedings. (See p. 63).

'Out of Court' had an item about a man who was ruined because he bought a 'hotel' which turned out to be an annexe to an existing hotel, and so had no separate planning permission. We see the reporter tracking down the vendor, whom he describes as 'a 'crook'. But he makes no attempt to interview the purchaser's solicitor to ask him *why* he hadn't found out about the lack of planning permission.

And just as the 'useful information' put out by BBC radio is that you should use a solicitor for your conveyancing because 'you can't sue yourself for negligence', so it is on BBC television – where ten million viewers are told: 'That's why it's important always to use a solicitor. Not all solicitors are perfect, but if they're negligent you can at least sue them.' (The ubiquitous David Tench, giving advice on That's Life, May 29 1983.)

If the programme on the professional is fictional, almost invariably it will be written *by* the professional. If documentary, it will be written either by or in collaboration with the professional. Which is why if we see a barrister in a fictional programme, he will be conducting a skilful cross-examination; in a documentary he will be expounding the law – usually against a background of law books from floor to ceiling; in a series designed to show the operation of the legal system ('useful information') he will be competently advising his clients in conference. If we see a surgeon, he will be carrying out an intricate operation, or reassuring the patient beforehand or afterwards. If we see a psychiatrist, he will be sympathetic and understanding (although in a fictional series he himself may crack up through overwork). If we see a teacher, he or she will be dedicated and competent.

Whether the BBC programme is on radio or television, whether documentary or soap opera, whether consumer advice or phone-in, the message is the same: that professionals are caring and competent. We never see or hear about a useless psychiatrist, or an ignorant doctor.* We are never shown a barrister seeing his client for the first time a few minutes before the trial, and clearly knowing almost nothing about the case; or a solicitor farming out a serious personal injury case to an illiterate and incompetent clerk; or a lazy incompetent teacher being shunted from school to school because he can't be sacked.

There have, of course, been a few programmes which have criticised the professional. Over the last eleven years one or two Checkpoint programmes *have* been on doctors' mistakes, and *have* criticised the legal system. Esther Rantzen's survey of antenatal care – and one or two items on That's Life – have criticised doctors. And 'Out of Court' has directed a couple of well aimed darts into the Law Society's well-padded side. But to what avail is a handful of exceptions over the years to redress the bias of even *one evening's* BBC television fare?

I pick up the Radio Times for December 21 1982, and what do I see? 'Kingswood: A Comprehensive School', the last of a documentary series of ten programmes. Throughout the series all the teachers shown have been dedicated, sympathetic and competent. Followed by 'Your Life in their Hands', a documentary series on the medical profession. This episode shows a surgeon performing a nifty bit of brain surgery whereby, with the aid of a high-powered microscope, he successfully blocks off some faulty blood vessels deep inside the brain. His anaesthetist then explains what a job *he* had keeping the patient's blood pressure constant during the operation. Followed by a discussion on the Kingswood series, in which the speakers agree what a very caring school it is, and another speaker (a headmaster) exclaims irritably (but quite seriously) '*All schools are caring*'. Followed by the news, the chief item being the birth of Siamese twins in an Oxford hospital where, we are told, 'a team of highly trained medical

* 'The Nation's Health' by G.F. Newman, be it noted, was on Channel 4.

experts is waiting to carry out the operation to separate them.' Perhaps not a typical evening's viewing, but not so untypical either.

Moreover it is interesting to note the ambivalence of some of the apparently anti-professional exceptions.

I have in mind two quasi-documentary television plays, 'Wednesday's Child', and 'Minor Complications'. Both plays were on medical negligence, dealing with the legal as well as the medical profession. And both plays have happy endings in so far as the victim of the medical negligence gets a satisfactory settlement in the end. In 'Wednesday's Child' the case goes to Court, and the plaintiff's success derives from his barrister's grasp of complicated medical matters, and consequent brilliant cross-examination of the anaesthetist – and, of course, an unbiased and understanding judge: 'On this occasion I find that Dr. X fell below his usual high standards.'

In 'Minor Complications' (by Peter Ransley) the settlement is made out of Court. This play tells of a lady who goes into hospital for a routine sterilization operation, and is permanently incapacitated as a result. The Health Authority denies negligence, and she instructs a firm of solicitors to sue for compensation. Then come the 'minor complications'. At one point her solicitor tells her that the £250 she initially paid on account has been expended, and asks for a further £250 if he is to continue the proceedings – which sum she does not possess. In real life, hundreds of thousands of valid negligence claims founder because the plaintiff, while not qualifying for legal aid, nevertheless cannot afford the lawyers' fees. Is the BBC actually going to *show* this happening and thus expose this glaring defect in our legal system which is 'the admiration of overseas organizations'? But fortunately ex-hubby (who hadn't featured hitherto) suddenly pops up with the proceeds of a second mortgage, and we then see the lady happily instructing her solicitor to get the best Q.C. as 'expense is now no object'. Another problem is that an independent consultant is unwilling to state that the hospital surgeon was negligent, and his report is unhelpful. In real life, of course, this is another often insuperable obstacle facing a plaintiff suing a medical man. Is the BBC actually going to *show* us a consultant refusing to testify to a clear-cut case of medical negligence, and so expose another glaring defect in our legal system – which enables most of us to 'breathe more easily because it is there'? But happily the difficulty is resolved, and when pressed the consultant comes clean. 'Well of course it was negligence,' he says.

The different treatment of the three professions involved is revealing. The nurses get a drubbing, being depicted as sluttish and brutal. At one point one of them refers to the agonized patient as 'Lady Muck'. The medics are treated more cautiously. Yes, the original surgeon *did* obstinately refuse to diagnose obstruction after the operation (despite the obvious symptoms), which caused the bowel to become gangrenous. But then another surgeon who carried out a subsequent emergency operation '*did* save my life [this is mentioned twice] and afterwards he was always kind'.* The lawyers come over as neutral. Ineffective at first, this is hardly their fault in view of the consultant's negative report. At any rate they are instrumental in getting the lady her satisfactory settlement, as she herself acknowledges. 'I'm more grateful to you than I can ever say for supporting me,' she tells them – and the consultant – in the final scene in the barrister's chambers.

At one point in the play she complains that her case is getting nowhere after *ten months*; and a note appearing at the end states that the settlement was achieved after one year eight months. In real life most plaintiffs are not so fortunate . . .

In real life, hundreds of thousands of perfectly valid negligence claims get nowhere after *four or five years*. In real life, three-quarters of the stories of those who sue medical men for negligence do *not* have happy endings, but the injured patient gets no compensation – merely a massive bill for legal costs. In real life, thousands of plaintiffs' cases are dealt with not by the solicitor, but by his unqualified and incompetent clerk. In real life, there's a fair chance that the plaintiff's barrister will not turn up for the trial, but will send along a substitute who picked up the papers for the first time the previous evening.

* This difference in the treatment of 'fringe' professionals and 'real' professionals pops up in other contexts. For instance on the 'Today' programme (January 25 1984), someone was claiming that students aspiring to be social workers are never failed, so there are a lot of incompetent social workers about. If this is true of social workers it is equally true of *teachers*, but such a comment about teachers would never be made. Similarly it is permissible to say on a 'consumer' programme that estate agents are useless, but not that *solicitors* are useless.

In real life, conveyancing solicitors, assisted by the lies of the Law Society, swindle the public out of several hundred million pounds a year (as I prove in my book, of which not a single sentence has been faulted). In real life, the professions escape outside interference by virtue of their claim that they impose *higher* standards than are required by law. Yet if a solicitor bribes a witness or tries to overcharge his client by £130,000, or if a doctor or dentist kills his patient by his gross incompetence, the professional body in question takes no action. In real life, student teachers are almost never failed; and once they qualify they cannot be sacked, however incompetent, only shunted from school to school.

But if such facts exist, Mrs. Dale does not want to know about them. Mrs. Dale, the doctor's wife, who epitomizes the philosophy of the BBC, inhabits a comfortable well-ordered world – a world where, by and large, the system works well, and we all breathe more easily because our incorruptible and remarkably independent legal system is there to protect our rights; a world where judges are impartial and teachers are dedicated; where psychiatrists are wise and barristers are brilliant; where solicitors are competent and surgeons are superhuman. In Mrs. Dale's world, if a medical man should, unfortunately, have a lapse from his usual high standards (or if a window cleaner slips off an outside ledge) the injured patient (or window cleaner) need only instruct one of these competent solicitors, who will engage one of these brilliant barristers, and at the end of the play he or she will obtain generous compensation. In Mrs. Dale's world, if a parent is worried that the comprehensive school where he is obliged to send his child has a bad reputation, all he need do is to let the school know that he expects 'jolly good teaching' and his child will get good results (Mrs. Dale's children, one assumes, go to private schools or perhaps comprehensive schools in superior areas); if a doctor removes a patient from his list it will be because the patient is so unreasonable that the doctor–patient relationship broke down; if fraud is perpetrated it will be by the entrepreneur or businessman, never by the professional.

And so until we meet again on the next page, goodbye.

3 *Why the judges and commentators abandon their critical faculties when dealing with professional man*

In the last two chapters we saw how Parliament, the judges (in the broadest sense of the word), and the commentators – those watchdogs of our society who yap and snap at the heels of ordinary man whom they see straying from the narrow path of righteousness – fall silent as soon as they smell *professional* man (particularly legal professional man), their tails begin to wag, and they start fawning and pawing at the ground. Some years ago I noticed in the Sunday Times that a government inquiry was being set up to investigate complaints that some shops were making excessive profits on their bacon. Apparently housewives were being charged 20% more for sides of Danish bacon than they were two years previously, whereas the price to the retailer had risen by only 13%. Very reprehensible. When the said housewife and her husband get a building society mortgage, the building society insists that its printed form of mortgage is filled in by a *solicitor* – usually the same solicitor who is acting for them on their purchase – who charges anything from £50 to £150 *on top of his own fee* for so doing, which would pay for quite a bit of Danish bacon. Once the written instructions to argue a case in Court are delivered to a barrister, he gets his full fee – even if the case is settled before the trial and in the event he never has to untie the pink ribbon on his brief. No government enquiry on, nor mention by the Consumers' Association, or Royal Commission on Legal Services in its four-volume report, or the newspapers, of *these* little swindles. When dealing with professional man the lawmakers, judges and commentators abandon their critical faculties. The watchdog becomes a poodle.

Why?

There are some fairly straightforward reasons. As the majority of Members of Parliament are themselves professionals, it isn't too surprising that Parliament, while regulating the tradesman and businessman, believes that the professions can be safely left to regulate themselves. As judges are themselves professional men, it is natural that they will feel some sympathy with a fellow professional coming before them (as Lord Denning has so frankly acknowledged). As judges are the chief lawmakers, and as they are appointed exclusively from barristers, it isn't too surprising that the law favours barristers above any other body of men. As the professional governing bodies are required to perform two conflicting roles – further the interests of their members and protect the public *from* their members – and as they are mostly composed of practising members of the profession in question, it is natural that they should perform the former role more successfully than the latter. So on the rare occasions when a professional disciplinary body actually does any disciplining, it will almost invariably be for a misdemeanour which damages the profession rather than the client. So a barrister (Barry Payton) who is convicted of assault has brought his *profession* into disrepute and so must be suspended for six months; but a barrister who accepts 'briefs for two heavy cases which were bound to clash' (case no. D.74/2) has merely damaged his client, and so can be let off with a private reprimand. So a medical man who has an affair with his patient is struck off; but if instead he quietly kills her, that's O.K.

As both the press and the BBC employ libel lawyers to vet their material, who realize that professionals (particularly lawyers) are more adept at issuing libel writs than their non-professional brothers, it isn't too surprising that the press and the BBC are more chary of disparaging the professional than any other group.

Moreover, as regards the press, journalism is a pretty shallow affair. One week a journalist may be doing a feature on oil rigs, the next week on conveyancing, the next week on horse doping or whatever. He therefore has no time to investigate any one subject properly, but has to rely on a few hurried interviews with the most likely people who will speak to him, and then cobble together what he hopes is a reasonably plausible piece to meet the deadline. And as his piece is liable to be cut by up to a third to make way for advertisements (which always have priority), he has little incentive to do otherwise. Another reason for the general blandness of the press is that a journalist can usually get by with the information provided for him in the press handouts and bulletins, without actually having to make any investigations for himself (just as a conveyancing solicitor can get by by sending out forms of printed questions to the seller and local authority, without actually looking at the house and finding out anything about it). Most of us prefer an easier life to a more difficult one, and journalists are no exception. The romantic image of press men falling over each other in search of the scoop, bashing out their copy which will expose this injustice, take the lid off that scandal, rarely obtrudes into reality.

Nevertheless, there must be other underlying reasons for this ubiquitous deference to the professional on the part of the judges and commentators. For instance, after I gave an interview to 'The World at One' about why I was witholding part of my solicitors' practising certificate fee, being the contribution to the Law Society's advertising fund, the BBC's libel lawyers deleted only one word ('fraud'). It was some unseen and mysterious presence higher up the BBC hierarchy which deleted the whole interview.

What, then, are these other reasons? They can only be conjectured. I cannot climb into Sir Henry Benson's head. Neither do those who produce the *Which?* reports, or the BBC 'consumer' programmes, invite me to sit in on their editorial meetings. Neither does the President of the Dental Council confide in me the reasons why a dentist who gasses his patient (while in breach of clear professional guidelines) is not automatically struck off. Neither does the magistrate explain why she is in *some difficulty* because on the evidence presented to her (process-server serves solicitor with writ for negligence, solicitor becomes absolutely furious, process-server retires from solicitor's office with crushed and bleeding hand) she has to find that solicitor guilty of assault. I can only guess at why these people – society's watchdogs – act in the way they do; the guess guided by the occasional ray of light, the chance incident, the unguarded remark.

The Club

The point of a club is to secure privileges for its members, the value of which depends on the exclusiveness of the club in question. Some clubs give their members mechanical assistance at the roadside; others give the opportunity to see rare films. But the best club of all to belong to – and one to which every professional automatically *does* belong – is the middle class (i.e. *middle* middle and above), because membership secures the most valuable privilege of all: that should you have occasion to be judged, your judges will also be members; and recognising you as a fellow member, they will tend to give you sympathetic treatment.

'Out of the question to shoot an old Harrovian', says a Major in *Decline and Fall* (by Evelyn Waugh), who had been sent to preside over Captain Grimes's court-martial, and who turns out to have been at his old public school. In fact this is not such a parody as it seems. It *is* pretty well out of the question to imprison an old Oxford or Cambridge man. Thus Norman Scott (non-member) is a liar, but Jeremy Thorpe, Oxford man (member), has merely given explanations not all of which can be true. Vassall, junior admiralty clerk (non-member), who gave secrets to the Russians because he was blackmailed, gets 18 years imprisonment; Blunt, Cambridge man (member), who betrayed of his own free will, is let off with a caution and a knighthood. These are merely well known examples of what quietly goes on all the while. The unspoken philosophy of Lord Justice Cantley, who cannot bring himself to call Thorpe a liar, is the same as that of Lord Denning who (in his own words) makes 'allowances for the mistakes of professional men [because] a finding of negligence against a professional man is a serious matter for him'; is the same as that of the magistrate who finds herself 'in some difficulty' at having to find a solicitor guilty of assaulting a process-server; is the same as that of the Chairman of the Family Practitioner Committee who fines a fraudulent dentist £50.

But judges don't always wear wigs or preside over disciplinary Committees. They come in other guises, e.g. in the shape of newspaper editors and established journalists – in their way just as powerful as the wigged variety, and just as inevitably members of the club. And just as the wigged variety has no compunction in castigating a non-member but will tend to gloss over the transgressions of a member, so will the journalistic variety. Thus the dentist who kills a patient by giving a general anaesthetic and proceeding to operate, without a qualified assistant being present, and who is allowed to remain in practice and repeat his performance, gets a few discreet lines in the news section. If a *non-member* did the equivalent – e.g. if a prison authority released a violent criminal on parole who then committed a murder, and if it subsequently released him a *second* time with the same result – the editorial columns in every newpaper in the country would resound to outraged screams of protest.

Which? castigates the Electricity Board's advertising campaign for off-peak electricity, for making *'disgracefully false and misleading claims'* (December 1978). But in a report on conveyancing *Which?* actually reproduces the picture and caption in a Law Society's pamphlet – which makes the equally false and misleading claim that your solicitor will warn you of any future untoward developments in the neighbourhood of the house you are contemplating buying. In this case *Which?* merely observes: *'there is a limit to what your solicitor finds out about nearby developments although a Law Society pamphlet (see below) suggests he will find out about them.'*

By and by I will be chronicling the case of a child who lost an eye in a playground accident at school. One of his playmates had been larking about brandishing a broken car aerial, the jagged end of which went in his eye. Instead of at once driving the child to hospital or summoning an ambulance, the headmaster telephoned the child's *mother* – who worked on the other side of the town – to come to the school. When she arrived three-quarters of an hour later, the headmaster drove mother and injured child to hospital; so he reached hospital about an hour later than had he been driven there immediately. Within ten minutes of arrival the child was seen by an eye consultant, who injected antibiotics but to no avail. Infection had set in and the eye subsequently had to be removed. The mother sued the education authority for negligence, and the consultant was asked to write a report. He stated that infection was inevitable, and 'I would consider the treatment he received at school *was perfectly reasonable.*' This is another example of a judge judging a fellow member.

But not only will the judges (in whatever capacity) of professional men be members of the same class. They will usually be professional men themselves, and – especially in the case of lawyers – they will often be members of the *same* profession. So the club philosophy merges into the *Philby Philosophy*.

The Philby Philosophy

Philby, you may remember, was the 'third man' – a British born spy of impeccable pedigree (public school, Cambridge, Foreign Office) who spied for the Russians, until he finally defected to Russia in 1963. But what was remarkable in Philby's case was that in 1951, in view of the ominous evidence which had been accumulating against him over the years, he was given a mock trial by the Foreign Office. But he was cleared. And the reason he was cleared despite the evidence against him was, in the words of John le Carré:* *this club doesn't elect cheats and liars; therefore Philby cannot be a cheat and a liar.*

The judge who decides whether or not a lawyer has been negligent is himself a lawyer. The tribunal which determines a complaint against a doctor or dentist is itself composed of doctors or dentists. The Chairman of the Royal Commission on Legal Services is a former President of the Institute of Chartered Accountants. The Philby philosophy, in this context, becomes: this profession doesn't appoint incompetent or dishonest people to its ranks; therefore this lawyer, doctor, dentist, headteacher etc. cannot be incompetent or dishonest.

Fundamentally it is the inability to think disturbing thoughts. If this solicitor is incompetent or dishonest it means that some lawyers are incompetent or dishonest. But I, the judge, am a lawyer. Moreover I preside over a legal system which everyone knows is the best in the world; and a legal system which is the best in the world doesn't *have* incompetent or dishonest lawyers. Therefore I will blot out from my mind the evidence which shows that this solicitor is incompetent or dishonest. If this profession, which I, Sir Henry Benson, and my merry men are investigating, makes false claims and gives the public a lousy service, then this explodes the whole myth of professionalism. But I am myself a top professional man; and as we all know, the professions impose on their members 'high standards beyond those required by the law.' Therefore this profession, which I am investigating, does *not* make false claims or give the public a lousy service, and I will gloss over the evidence which shows that it does. If this eminent

* In his introduction to *Philby, the Spy who Betrayed a Generation* (by Bruce Page).

solicitor has bribed a witness it means that we, the Law Society, have elected a criminal into our exclusive club. But we don't *have* criminals in our club. Therefore this eminent solicitor cannot have bribed a witness, *and even if he has we don't want to know anything about it, and you'd better be careful before you go round making such allegations.*

If we, the education authorities, investigate what is happening at William Tyndale School, we will have to sack the headmaster for incompetence – because the evidence indicates that the school is physically disintegrating through lack of discipline. But our system *doesn't* appoint incompetent headteachers. Therefore we cannot sack him. Therefore we had better not investigate what is happening. If we, the Home Office, sack this forensic scientist who has an unfortunate penchant for giving inaccurate evidence and getting innocent people put away for long stretches, it means he must be incompetent or worse. But incompetent people *don't* hold responsible positions in our department. Therefore we cannot sack him. (On the other hand, if we continue to let him put away innocent people it could be embarrassing – so we'll try and get him to retire early on grounds of 'limited efficiency', with the offer of a fat pension and gratuity.) If we, the Dental Council, strike off this dentist who killed his patient by giving a general anaesthetic and proceeding to operate without a qualified assistant being present, it means he was unsafe to practise. But we *don't* have people who are unsafe to practise in our profession. Therefore we'll let him off with a caution, and hope that he will be a bit more careful next time.

Mixed up with the Philby philosophy is, I suspect, a measure of self protection. Those who sit on professional disciplinary tribunals and committees are, for the most part, themselves practising members of that profession. I have recounted how a Family Practitioner Committee imposed a £50 fine on a dentist, who admitted submitting fraudulent N.H.S. claims over a number of years. When my acquaintance – who was the lay member of the Committee in question, and who told me of the incident – remonstrated with the Chairman that not only should the dentist be struck off but prosecuted for fraud, the Chairman took him aside. 'I don't think we should be too hard on him, you know. *There but for the grace of God go any of us.*'

I have also recounted how I presented the Law Society with

written evidence that a certain eminent solicitor had bribed a witness, and how the Law Society took no action. I asked the senior official concerned why the Law Society had not investigated such a seemingly open and shut case. He replied that several things had to be considered in such cases, for instance the seriousness of the effect on the solicitor, and on the profession as a whole, if such matters came out into the open. 'I suppose', he concluded, 'that if someone told us that a solicitor had murdered his brother we'd *have* to take some sort of action.'*

Only professionals are qualified to comment on professional matters.

Just as professional men are the judges of professional men, so are they the exponents of professional matters in the media, particularly the BBC. This is because *only professionals are considered capable of understanding and explaining professional matters.* As the producer of 'You and Yours' wrote to me: 'We don't use solicitors to put the point of view of their professional body, but as people who understand the law to explain it to the lay public.' And just as a professional is considered the most appropriate person to talk about a profession, or answer questions on professional matters, so he is considered the most appropriate person to write a soap opera or fictional series about a profession – because he will *know* about it, and get the details right.

But a professional talking or writing about his profession cannot help but put over a partial point of view. And if that point of view is – in effect – the only one which is allowed to be transmitted, the public gets only one side of the argument. In the last chapter I gave some examples. Here are two more:

'That's Life' (November 21, 1982) had an item about a man who built a garage on what clearly seemed to be his own land, and within his own garden fence, but subsequently had to demolish part of the garage because it turned out that the garden fence had been in the wrong position, and the garage encroached on his neighbour's land. Advice from That's Life's legal eagle, solicitor David Tench: 'The plans you get from the solicitors aren't much use in the event of a boundary dispute. The best thing to do is to go round the place with your neighbour and try to agree the

---

* I wrote a column over a number of years in the Solicitors' Journal, and in one of the pieces (February 23 1973) I quoted this conversation. Sometimes a piece would elicit a reply from the Law Society, but this one did not.

boundary.' Quite so. But then why use a solicitor for your house purchase if his system is so useless as regards one of the most important legal aspects about a house, and when (so far as this point is concerned anyway) it seems that you can do the job better yourself? One might think that such a question would be relevant for a reputedly hard hitting 'consumer' programme. But as it would never occur to a *solicitor* to ask it, and as no-one *other* than a solicitor would be considered qualified to comment on boundaries and legal disputes, the question is never asked.

'You and Yours' had a talk by a solicitor on the delays suffered by accident victims in getting their claims settled. He explains that this is because the system requires that the injured person must prove that his injury was caused by someone else's fault. But *why* does the system so require? Again, such a question would never be asked, because a lawyer would not be interested in asking it; and someone who *wasn't* a lawyer would not be invited to talk about accident victims getting compensation under the legal system.

The professional point of view is, in fact, just as 'controversial' as the anti-professional point of view. And just as it would be unheard of for the BBC to allow anyone to put an anti-professional point of view without it being balanced, so (in the interests of impartiality) the same rule should apply to anyone putting over the *professional* point of view. And it should apply whether the professional point of view is put over in a talk or a 'Tuesday Call'; or – more subtly – in a soap opera or documentary.

So for every phone-in programme to a professional who has 'a very high regard for the work that solicitors do in conveyancing', there should be a phone-in to someone who believes that solicitors' conveyancing is not only useless but worse than useless. For every interview with Lord Benson and his ilk, who thinks that the division of lawyers into solicitors and barristers is the 'admiration of overseas organisations', an interview with someone who argues that such division makes for inefficiency and incompetence. For every programme on Bob and Deirdre, house buyers, who 'already had a solicitor lined up', a programme on Nigel and Susan, who did their own conveyancing. For every quasi-documentary showing an injured person getting a satisfactory settlement through the Courts, another showing a valid claim getting nowhere after five years.

For every Rumpole of the Bailey, Bumble of the Crown Court – an equally typical representative of his profession, who generally sees his client for the first time on the morning of the trial, having looked at the papers for the first time a couple of hours beforehand. For every Checkpoint programme exposing a fraudulent businessman, a Checkpoint exposing a fraudulent professional *qua* professional. For every documentary showing a brilliant surgeon in action, another on doctors overprescribing tranquillizers, or drugs for the elderly; or abusing their deputising services; or the ten thousand babies who are unnecessarily born dead or handicapped each year in Britain. For every ten-part documentary on a school staffed by competent dedicated teachers, a ten-part documentary on a school staffed by idle indifferent teachers.

The Best Things in Life go to those who do not query the system

Such proposals, however, are unlikely to appeal to the top men at the BBC, who will themselves be eminent members of the club, and currently enjoying the perquisites thereof – an Oxford or Cambridge degree, a glamorous job, a big house, a pretty wife. These are society's rewards meted out to those who prove best at observing its rules. Thus the people who are in a position to put their critical faculties to the greatest effect are the least likely to have any. Those who enjoy the best things in life have the least reason to query a particular aspect of a system which overall treats them so generously.

As with Auntie, so with Uncle – Auntie's half-brother, the serious press. A sharp and spiky journalist may join a paper determined to set the world to rights by exposing this injustice, taking the lid off that scandal. But by the time he has established his reputation – perhaps been given his own column – he will have mellowed considerably, and be less concerned with the world's injustices, more with enjoying the fruits of his own success. By the time he is promoted editor or assistant editor, he will have mellowed to such an extent that his outlook and income will probably be indistinguishable from that of a director of a bank or building society or any other pillar of the establishment. So while the news section might carry an item detrimental to the professional, the editorial section hardly ever does. The former is written by a journalist, the latter by someone higher up the journalistic hierarchy. I previously quoted from an article in The Times, which stated that the house seller's solicitor 'is usually well worth his fee'. I happened to speak to the writer of this article after he moved to another paper, and he let fall a derogatory remark about solicitors' excessive fees. I reminded him of his former contrary opinion. 'Oh, that would have been written in by the business editor as part of his policy', said he.

And they all lived happily ever after. Please buy my product

We know why film makers stick on happy endings: it makes their product more acceptable. They are in the business to make money, and you don't make money by sending people away disturbed. Similarly, the brewers and the food chain stores realize that in these days of mass marketing, the blander the product, the greater the sales. But just as a film and a pint of beer and a pound of cheese have to be sold to the public, so do a newspaper and a *Which?* report. And here, too, it seems that the blander the product, the greater the sales. Thus vast areas of potentially disturbing territory are virtually taboo. To give an industrial example, every year in Britain there are a hundred thousand car crashes causing death or serious injury. On March 17, 1981 a 'Man Alive' programme investigated how cars could easily and cheaply be designed to be significantly safer on collision, but weren't. The programme commented that whereas the *Which?* report on electric cookers gave points for safety, in all the *Which?* reports on cars, safety was nowhere mentioned. As the commentator drily observed: 'Whoever heard of anyone being killed by an electric cooker?'

Similarly, in all the *Which?* reports, and in all the newspaper coverage, on conveyancing, you will not find one line suggesting that the conveyancing system – whereby the buyer's solicitor purports to check the house is 'all right' by sending printed sheets of questions to the seller's solicitor and the local Council – is *absurd.* In our society cars are gleaming wonderful machines – perhaps a bit dangerous but then so are lots of things. The suggestion that they might be *needlessly* dangerous would be disturbing. So we all know that lawyers take an age to do anything and they charge like crazy; but we believe that at any rate the legal *system* is basically sound. Any suggestion that conveyancing, as carried out by solicitors, is nothing more than an elaborate confidence trick would be disturbing, because it would raise doubts about some of their other activities – and indeed it would call into question the whole concept of professionalism.

The judge sitting on high may not know what century he's living in, but when he finally gives judgment it will be the distillation of British Justice. And British Justice, as we all know, is the best in the world. The law may be an ass, but an ass with its heart in the right place. Any suggestion that the law is not so much an ass as a cruel and capricious monster would be *disturbing*. So while the Times, Guardian, and Telegraph devoted leaders to the case of Whitehouse v. Jordan, none of them – nor any other newspaper – could bring themselves to spell out the stark message of that case: that if you think your child has been permanently damaged by a doctor's negligence, trying to prove it could take ten years; and if you fail (as you probably will), not only will you get no compensation but you may have to pay £150,000 in legal fees. Such a message, when we believe that British Justice is the best in the world, would be *disturbing*.

This is not to say that nothing disturbing, or critical of the professions, will appear; but nothing which is *too* disturbing or *too* critical – that is to say, nothing which questions the professional's *system*.

We want something to be; therefore it is. We don't want something to be; therefore it isn't. We, the public, don't want to be disturbed. Therefore no-one who wants our money is going to disturb us. We have surrendered rather a lot of power to professional man. In fact, when you come to think about it, we have allowed him to devise and operate his own system without any outside controls or checks. But we needn't worry, because professional men 'have a high degree of detachment and integrity and. . .a strong sense of responsibility and an exceptional commitment to the interests of their clients which transcends all other commitments' – so they won't abuse their power. The function of newspapers is to increase their circulation. Telling the truth is an incidental luxury.

In the fairy tale, when the emperor struts about in his supposedly fine clothes, a little boy suddenly shouts out that he *hasn't* any clothes on, and the crowd takes up the theme. In reality the crowd would rather not know, and the little boy's message would be quietly suppressed by the assistant editor.

Let me end this section with a parochial example.

During the unusually hot summer of 1976, County Hall issued a verbal directive to all I.L.E.A. primary school head-teachers, giving them discretion to abandon afternoon school until further notice if conditions became too uncomfortable, provided they looked after those children whose parents were both out at work or otherwise could not conveniently have them at home. Accordingly the headmistress of a certain primary school decided to abandon afternoon school until further notice, giving the parents less than a day's notice of the fact – and initially not mentioning that children could still be kept at school if need be. A couple of days later a mother telephoned the headmistress, saying that her two children should stay at school that afternoon as she had a hospital appointment, which was agreed. However, after putting the phone down the headmistress promptly made the two children stand up in assembly, and asked for volunteers from the other children to take them home with them when the school 'closed' for the day at lunch time. In my capacity as parent manager I called a special Managers' meeting to protest about the incident, and the way in which the discretion to close the school was being exercised in general – and a fairly neutral account of the incident found its way onto the front page of our local paper.

Instantly a storm of protest broke over the head of the hapless editor, and he was inundated with enraged telephone calls and letters from teachers *and parents* of the 'oozi finki iz' variety – who did I think I was, telling *professional teachers* how they should do their job? The newspaper, realizing its blunder, in its next issue printed what purported to be an account of the special Managers' meeting (which hadn't even taken place), under the headline 'Managers Refute Criticism of School'; and subsequently carried a fulsome editorial praising the school and its headmistress, and bemoaning that such a fuss had arisen over such a trivial incident.

4 *The public also abandons its critical faculties when dealing with professional man*

When Orwell remarked on 'the considerable agreement that does unfortunately exist between the leaders and the led',* he was referring to the public's support of Chamberlain's foreign policy at Munich. His observation could equally apply to the public's faith in the professional. We have seen how the lawmakers, judges and commentators abandon their critical faculties when dealing with professional man. The public is even more uncritical.

This is not to say that the public never *criticizes* the professional. Many people have their favourite unflattering doctor, teacher or lawyer anecdote. But that's as far as the criticism goes. It is merely anecdotal or *superficial* criticism. Mr. and Mrs. Thing may well tell a pretty tale against the professional, but – like the newspapers – it will rarely, if ever, occur to them to question the *system* which gives rise to the anecdote.

So while the occasional disgruntled mum may wax indignant at the state of the school lavatories or that her Johnny is not allowed to take a packed lunch to school, she will not confront the headteacher with her complaint. Neither will she query why there is no parents' committee through which her complaint can be made. Still less would it occur to her to wonder what *use* are the subjects which her Johnny is being made to study at school for a dozen years. So while it is not uncommon to hear someone grumbling about his solicitor's conveyancing charges, probably less than one in a thousand people moving house wonder *why*

* England Your England (*Inside the Whale and other essays*), published by Penguin Books.

they should employ a solicitor. So while there are some quarter of a million people in Britain (mostly middle-aged housewives) who have been taking tranquillizers for over seven years, few of them will wonder what training their G.P.'s, who prescribed these drugs, had in pharmacology or treating depression, or where their knowledge of the drugs comes from. In other words, despite a bit of ineffectual carping here and there about, e.g., this headteacher's highhandedness, that solicitor's charges, that doctor's manner, the system under which the teachers, lawyers and doctors operate is almost never questioned.

Now the professions (that is, the big three) are more powerful than any trade union, more secure than any mafia. Yet in order to impose their systems, the professions never had to resort to the methods of those organisations. They never had to go on strike or threaten force – which indicates that the systems they have imposed have the public's approval. This approval is not, of course, express. It is tacit; or rather, it is *once removed*. The reason my son learns arithmetic at school is not because I want him to learn arithmetic at school; but because I have allowed someone else, the professional, to make the decision (under the hazy impression that he somehow has my son's interests at heart), and *he* wants my son to learn arithmetic at school. And having delegated the decision to the expert, I either have no strong feelings on the matter, or if I do, they are not *sufficiently* strong for me to do anything about them.

So we allow the professional to dictate the system.

If we want to go to university – and most professions are open only to those who do – we must get *x* number of *y* grade 'O' levels, and *y* number of *z* grade 'A' levels. And this we must do because teacher (that is, university teacher) *says* we must. And when our children go to school they will learn French for five or six years. But they won't be able to speak it or understand it when they leave, because the reason they learn French (or whatever) is to pass the *exam*, and the oral makes up only a small part of the exam – because teacher (that is, examining teacher) *says* it does. And when our children go to school, the education authorities will keep files on them. Mostly, of course, the information therein is innocuous, but occasionally it will be damaging, irrelevant, out of date or false. But we can't see the information which is being kept on our children (albeit it may be released to a variety of outside bodies), because the education authorities *say* we can't. And if our child is in the hands of a palpably incompetent teacher, we can't get that teacher sacked; because incompetent teachers *aren't* sacked.

And if we go into hospital, although there will be a consultant's name above our bed, we will actually be treated by a doctor who will probably have been on duty for 90 hours – and on call every single hour – during the preceding week. Because the senior doctors have decided that these are the hours their junior colleagues shall work. And if a routine operation leaves us permanently disabled, we will get compensation only if we can prove in a Court of law that a medical man was at fault. So we need to know what went wrong. But the hospital and the doctors needn't *tell* us, and neither need they give us the notes. So unless it's a very obvious case of negligence, we don't stand much chance. That's the system. And that's the system because the hospitals, doctors and lawyers have *decided* that it shall be the system. And if a routine operation goes seriously wrong, there won't be an independent inquiry to find out *why* it went wrong, to help prevent the same mishap recurring; because hospitals and doctors don't like independent inquiries.

And if we are seriously injured in an accident – on the roads, at work, or wherever – we will get compensation only if we can prove in Court that the accident was someone else's fault. And if when the case comes to Court in four to six years time, the judge decides that we haven't proved that the accident was this other person's fault, not only will we get no compensation but we will have to pay a five figure sum in legal costs (our own and those of the other party). That's the system. And that's the system because the judges have *decided* that it shall be the system. And to bring our case to Court we must instruct a solicitor, and our solicitor must instruct a barrister. We can't go direct to the barrister or ask a friend to represent us; and we can't because the lawyers *say* we can't. And if our barrister doesn't turn up for the hearing (because he's accepted a more lucrative engagement elsewhere), but instead sends along an untutored colleague – as a result of which we lose our case – we can't sue the original barrister, and it's no use complaining to his professional body. And we can't and it isn't, because the barristers and ex-barristers *say* that we can't and it isn't.

If Bill Bloggs owes us money we can sue him to recover it. Unless, that is, Bill Bloggs had the foresight to employ a lawyer or accountant to turn him into (and thereafter service) Bill Bloggs *Limited*, in which case we can whistle for our money. And when Bill Bloggs Ltd. is finally wound up, the learned gentlemen merely have to turn him into William Bloggs Ltd., whereupon he can run up another few thousand or hundred thousand pound bills which likewise he need never pay. All perfectly legal. That's the system. And that's the system because our members of Parliament (most of whom are either lawyers, accountants or company directors) have *decided* that it shall be the system.

And although the professions escape outside interference by virtue of their claim that they impose on their members *higher* standards than the law imposes on ordinary men, the professional bodies in question take no action against a doctor or dentist who kills his patient by his gross incompetence, or a solicitor who bribes a witness, or a barrister who accepts a case which he knows he won't be able to handle. And the professional bodies take no action because they choose not to take any action.

So we allow the teachers to decide our education system, the medical men to decide our medical system, the lawyers to decide our legal system, the professional bodies to decide whether or not to fulfil their claims. And having done so, we contentedly go about our daily business without giving the matter much further thought.

When Victor the Giraffe sat down and couldn't get up again, the interest of the whole nation was aroused. Hundreds of thousands of letters containing suggestions and offers of help poured into the zoo and the BBC; and there were daily news bulletins for about a week, during which time if you went into a shop you would hear total strangers discussing the unfortunate animal's predicament. If you stopped a man in the street and told him that if he or his child was permanently injured in an accident he would get no compensation unless he could prove in a Court of law that someone else was at fault, which process would take four to six years, and the legal costs – and emotional strain – of trying to do so might easily ruin him, he would stare at you. And if he replied at all, he would probably say 'so what?' or 'well, that's the system, isn't it?'

Having allowed the experts to decide the system, we seem to take remarkably little interest in how that decision has been exercised on our behalf.

* * * * * *

I suggested that the reason why the lawmakers, judges, and commentators jettison their critical faculties when dealing with professional man is that, broadly, for the most part they are professional men themselves; and those who are not it nevertheless suits to act as their lackeys. Why then are we, the public, so uncritical of professional man – or rather, the *system* he imposes on us? The answer, I think, is that we have been trained to be. That is to say, we have been trained not to question; in particular, not to question *authority*.

Authority is the Headteacher, the Teacher, the Consultant, the Doctor, the Judge, the Lawyer. But Authority is not necessarily a professional. Authority can also be the bank manager, the building society branch manager, the manager of a self-service cafeteria, even the waiter. In fact Authority is anyone who appears to have a pocket of direct power over us (even if only the power to make us look stupid). And we British respect authority, our respect bordering on fear – hence our notorious unwillingness to complain. That this national characteristic is usually remarked on in a culinary context is only because a café or restaurant is the most likely place for someone to be confronted with the choice between accepting what is offered, or complaining. We British choose the first alternative. We like good food as much as anyone else; yet compare the self-service cafeteria in Folkestone with the one twenty five miles away in Boulogne, or the English motorway restaurants with their German counterparts.

To borrow another example from the Bad Food Guide.* An official of the Good Food Association, having had lunch on a train, complained that the coffee tasted of *iron filings*. The waiter apologized and promptly replaced it with another cup of the same unappetizing liquid. When the official further remonstrated he was met by the invariable argument that no-one else had complained, which was obviously true. It so happened that the same dining car crew was in attendance for his return journey,

* *The Bad Food Guide* by Derek Cooper, published by Routledge & Kegan Paul.

and when he went for dinner the waiter told him that they had discovered the trouble with the lunchtime coffee. The coffee pot had been put on the stove in such a position as to allow condensation from an old and very rusty extractor hood to trickle into its spout. The resulting beverage was therefore a mixture of coffee and rust.

But the Englishman's unwillingness to complain, his stoical acceptance of whatever Authority dishes up, goes beyond mere eating matters. The Englishman accepts without question what he is offered in the self-service cafeteria and dining car, just as he accepts without question what he is offered by the doctors, by the hospitals, by the schools, by the law courts. And for the same reason. He has been *trained* to.

The training begins early; and the trainers – whether wittingly or unwittingly – do a good job. So that although we have long forgotten the date of the Armada, and how to conjugate a French irregular verb, and what the square on the hypotenuse equals, and who fought whom at the Battle of Naseby, few of us forget the *real* lesson of our schooldays: to learn what authority tells us to learn, and believe what authority tells us to believe.

So authority tells us to learn our lessons or we won't pass our exams, so we learn our lessons and we try to pass our exams. (There are rebels, of course, who don't try to learn their lessons and who don't pass their exams, but they don't usually get very far.) So authority tells us to eat our dinner up and think of all the starving children in Timbuctoo who would give their ears for such a dinner. So we eat our dinner up, and we think of all the starving children in Timbuctoo; and presumably we're still thinking of them when we file past the cash desk at the motorway cafeteria thirty years later. So authority tells us that Hitler is a good chap who will stand up to the Commies, and that's O.K. by us. Then authority decides that perhaps Hitler isn't such a good chap after all and we might even be going to war with him, so we stoically start digging trenches in Hyde Park. Then authority announces that it has made an *agreement* with Hitler and we won't be going to war after all, and we all cheer like mad. So authority tells us that it is going to war with Argentina to make the world a safer place for small nations against fascist dictatorships. And we're right behind the government on this one. And it never occurs to us to ask why, in that case, did it *sell* arms to Argentina in the first place. So authority tells us that the British legal system is the best in the world, and we believe that the British legal system is the best in the world. And it never occurs to us to ask why, if the British legal system is the best in the world, it takes ten years and costs £150,000 in legal fees to decide whether Mrs. Whitehouse should or should not receive compensation in respect of her brain-damaged child. People who have spent their childhood learning how to conjugate French irregular verbs, and who fought whom at the Battle of Naseby, don't ask why any more. People who have spent their childhood learning what the square on the hypotenuse equals and the formula for quadratic equations, because authority has *told* them to, tend not to question what authority tells them thereafter.

Those responsible for military training, incidentally, who require an *absolute* surrender of the soldier's critical faculties, go a step further, and instead of making him *learn* useless things they make him *do* useless things. A four weeks concentrated course of stamping about on the parade ground and polishing his belt brasses is all it takes to make the raw recruit into a good soldier, i.e. an automaton – which, of course, is the avowed aim of military training. Not that I am suggesting there is any similar *conscious* policy behind our education system. Rather it seems to be the product of that kind of mysterious instinct which guides swallows over oceans, and equally unerringly guides those in authority to devise systems which best serve their interests.

I look at a circular which my youngest child brought home, from the headteacher of his primary school (not, incidentally, the school previously mentioned). It gives parents a week's notice that school hours for juniors are to be cut by half an hour, and that thenceforth afternoon school will cease at 3.15 p.m. instead of 3.45 p.m.

'Dear Parents, It was brought to my attention last week that the children in our school were working quarter of an hour in excess of the hours laid down by the Department of Education and Science, *and so we had to shorten our day to keep within the law*'.

This school being in a 'mixed' area, many mothers would have a job, and would presumably find the change of hours a serious inconvenience. At least one had to give up her job. But out of the five hundred or so parents who received this circular, only about three complained, the majority view being summed up by one parent who told me: 'It seems a bit strange that the school was breaking the law all these years, but I suppose it must be true'. Of course it must be true. *Teacher* says so.

I sit at my desk in my first job as an assistant solicitor. In my room reposes the office safe – a great iron cavern without shelf or partition, filled from base to top with ill-assorted bundles and parcels. I watch as various members of the staff come into the room and proceed to unpack the contents, in an attempt to find a particular bundle. If it's near the top they find it in a few minutes. If it's near the bottom it takes half an hour. Yet it never occurs to anyone to suggest that a few partitions and an index would cut out this tedious procedure. That's the system laid down by authority; and you don't question the system laid down by authority.

I am meeting my mother at Victoria Station after she has spent a weekend in the West Country. To my surprise I see her on the platform surrounded by a little group of people apparently congratulating her. 'You were splendid. I don't know what we'd have done without you,' says a quite distinguished looking gentleman shaking her hand. 'She was absolutely splendid,' he says turning to me, 'but *she'll* tell you all about it.' What had my mum (83 years old and under five feet tall) been up to? Had the train been hijacked and had she alone disarmed the desperados? Had the engine driver had a stroke as the train hurtled towards the Penryn tunnel, and only by leaping to the controls had she averted what would otherwise have been the worst rail disaster for twenty years? It turned out that she had done neither of these things. The train had been full of old age pensioners taking advantage of an offer of unlimited travel for £1; and all the seats being taken, about a hundred of them were standing and sitting in the corridor. My mother, not fancying three hours of such discomfort, sat down in the practically empty dining car. And although she was told by the waiter that she couldn't remain there unless she was having a meal, she refused to budge. Nonplussed by this unprecedented rebellion, the waiter summoned a higher ranking official to deal with it – who decided that in the circumstances the rule could be relaxed; and announced over the tannoy that the seats in the virtually empty dining car could be used by passengers. And as the old folk gratefully clambered into the unexpectedly available seats, four out of the half dozen or so diners joyfully cancelled their orders.

I look at another document, the card issued by the British Diabetic Association which every diabetic on insulin is supposed to carry. It bears the message: 'I am a diabetic on insulin. If I am found ill, please give me two tablespoons of sugar or glucose preferably in water.' When a diabetic is on insulin injections his blood sugar may occasionally fall *too low*, in which case he becomes fuddled and confused and eventually goes into a coma. For this reason diabetics should always carry sugar lumps or sweets, so that if they feel such symptoms (which usually come on gradually) they merely eat the sugar lumps or sweets, which restore their blood sugar to normal, whereupon the symptoms disappear. The problem is that a diabetic experiencing the symptoms of too low blood sugar may have *forgotten* to carry sugar or sweets, or otherwise become so confused that he needs a stranger's help. Hence the card.

Now although drinking sugar (or glucose) dissolved in water is the quickest way to get sugar into the bloodstream, eating *any* concentrated carbohydrate (sweets, biscuits, chocolate etc) is almost as quick; but the card does not mention these alternatives. The diabetic in difficulties is most likely to need help from a stranger when he is in the street or other public place, where the stranger reading the card – being unlikely to have two tablespoons of sugar dissolved in a glass of water at the ready – would be unable to procure such ingredients quickly or at all. On the other hand, he would normally be able to get biscuits or chocolate within a couple of minutes, which the card fails to mention. Therefore the possibility of a diabetic unnecessarily going into a coma because of the incompetently worded card is not a remote one – *and this the diabetic himself must know*, since he carries out his own treatment and must necessarily know something about the subject. But because the card is issued by authority, authority moreover having some sort of professional connotation, it has evidently never been queried by any of the several million diabetics who have carried it over the years.

Authority does not have to be the professional: but when authority *is* the professional, it's authority plus. The professional has been to University. He's got *letters* after his name. Teacher has unbounded knowledge, as well as holding the golden key to our 'O' level results. Doctor carries a mysterious black bag and makes us well when we are ill. Lawyer knows off by heart whole legal tomes which we couldn't even begin to understand. Who are we, therefore, to question them? And having been conditioned not to question their expertise, it is but a small step not to question *anything* they tell us.

At a smart dental surgery where I go for a check-up, the dentist takes a couple of X-rays, which show no fillings are required, so he does a routine scaling. I sign for the treatment at the receptionist's counter on which reposes a framed printed notice: 'NHS Dental Charges. If you are 18 or over you normally pay £13.50 for each course of treatment.' I am asked to pay £13.50 which I do almost unthinkingly. I am, in fact, quite pleased with the outcome of my visit. But when I get home my wife, a former dental nurse, indignantly asks me how a scaling and a couple of X-rays can come to £13.50; to which question I have to confess that I have no idea, except that it must be right or they wouldn't have a *notice.* She ascertains from the Family Practitioner Committee that £13.50 is the *maximum* contribution, not the minimum as the notice implies, and that my treatment should have cost £6. Of course similar tricks are played all the while by tradesmen on their customers, but only a professional could exhibit such a deliberately misleading notice, secure in the knowledge that it will never be queried.*

Consider again the circular from the primary school head-teacher, giving notice that school hours for juniors (which were completely standard according to the Education Authority's guidelines) are to be cut by half an hour: 'Dear Parents, It was brought to my attention last week that the children in our school were working quarter of an hour in excess of the hours laid down by the Department of Education and Science, and so we had to shorten our day to keep within the law.' The hours laid down by the Department of Education and Science are not maximum but *minimum* hours. In any case they don't relate to the school day, but only to the period of actual instruction. Yet none of the parents who received this notice queried it. 'It seems a bit strange that the school was breaking the law all these years, but I suppose it must be true.' In this country, mercifully not ruled by the gun or rubber truncheon, only someone at the top of a *profession* could send out a circular containing such a barefaced lie to five hundred people, secure in the knowledge that none of them will question it.

---

* The local Fair Trading Officer to whom I complained, incidentally, said he had no jurisdiction over professionals.

The house buyer or seller is told that he needs to employ a solicitor to do the conveyancing because it is a very complicated and technical procedure. So every year a million people who move house employ a solicitor – at a cost of about £700 each – to do a few hours work, which is usually delegated to an unqualified clerk, and which is not only routine and unskilled but demonstrably useless. Only a profession could get away with such a confidence trick for close on two hundred years.

I give these examples (and they could be capped a thousand times) to illustrate our disinclination to question authority, particularly when in professional guise. But they illustrate another characteristic which we probably also owe to our education – perhaps reinforced by our long and happy hours in front of the box. We British are an apathetic lot. In fact only trivialities seem to rouse us. Both Victor the Giraffe (who sat down and couldn't get up again) and Mrs. Whitehouse (whose award of £100,000 compensation for negligence in respect of her brain-damaged child was quashed by the Court of Appeal) made television news. The predicament of the giraffe aroused national concern; the predicament of Mrs. Whitehouse – which if the scalpel slips or the wrong knobs are turned could be that of any parent – aroused almost none. More national interest was excited by who shot J.R. than by the major events of the first two years of the last war. Orwell observed in his War Diaries that during this period, when he went to the pub of an evening, he had to *ask* the barmaid to turn on the 9 o'clock news. On one occasion she demurred, on the grounds that the customers preferred listening to the piano.

* * * * * *

So given our disinclination to question authority, particularly when in professional guise, and given our apathy, it is not surprising that we have allowed the professionals to dictate the system: the teachers to dictate our education system, the doctors to dictate our medical system, the lawyers to dictate our legal system – and having done so, we go about our daily business without giving the matter much further thought.

Now as we have seen, one characteristic which every profession seems to share is an unbounded faith in its own moral superiority. Thus the Minister of Health, Dr. Gerard Vaughan, does not think that the recommendations of the Acheson report on doctors need be implemented by legislation, because doctors 'have a professional wish of their own to improve their service'. Geoffrey Howe Q.C. argues in the House of Commons – which of course agrees with him – that there is no need to subject the professions to the provisions of the Fair Trading Act, because 'they have codes by which they regulate and conduct themselves'. The President of the Law Society states that solicitors' standards, 'largely *self imposed*, are as high if not higher than those in other professions in this country'. (Eastbourne Conference 1980.) Lord Benson, former President of the Institute of Chartered Accountants, writes: 'The professions in this country. . .compare very favourably with those in any other part of the world, and in many respects they are the acknowledged leaders. This is because by their written constitutions and by tradition they seek year after year to improve the quality of service which they give to the public.' (Letter to The Times, December 14 1983.) Lord Justice Salmon believes that 'Our system of justice has gained the admiration of the whole civilised world. . .There is no country in which justice is administered more impartially, efficiently or speedily' – giving judgment in Rondel v. Worsley, a case which decided that barristers should be immune from negligence actions. And so on.

In other words the professional considers that whereas ordinary man needs checks from outside, he, the professional, does not. So having been allowed to dictate his own system, it follows that he will dictate a system which allows him to operate without any outside checks – indeed without any checks at all. And having allowed the professional to dictate his own system, and accepting the system he dictates without question, it follows that we in turn will neither require – nor even ask for – any checks in return.

The various Acts of Parliament designed to protect the public from the unscrupulous manufacturer, tradesman and businessman do not apply to the professional – either because the professional is specifically excluded from them (as in the Fair Trading Act 1973), or more usually because such Acts by their nature apply only to those activities carried on by the non-professional. The common law sanction of dismissal for incompetence, which is implied in every contract of employment with ordinary man, has no application to the professional. Neither need he fear any over-zealous investigation into his activities by his professional governing body; nor, it seems, by anyone else.

The teacher is unsackable, the headteacher is irremovable, the judge is unimpeachable, the barrister is unsuable, the dentist is unaccountable, the lawyer, doctor, and dentist are uncomplainable, the professional governing bodies are unanswerable, the hospital authorities are unquestionable, the education authorities are unassailable. And although the individual medical man and solicitor *can* be sued, the litigation procedures are so weighted in their favour that their erstwhile clients will find the contest resembles a tennis match with their opponent starting each game with a three point lead – and with bankruptcy the penalty for losing. In a word, we have surrendered power to the professional.

We British are an apathetic lot. Yet our forbears learned earlier than most other nations that kings were not to be trusted with unchecked power; and when a king once rashly claimed that he ruled by Divine Right, Parliament very sensibly cut his head off. Thereafter the British people realized that Parliament was not to be trusted with too much power either, and over the years they gradually evolved a system whereby the monarch, for all his splendour and adulation, has no power at all; and the government of the day can be sent packing every five years – often to the accompaniment of jeers and rotten tomatoes. If our forbears were possessed of this wisdom why, then, do we fail to understand that it is not only kings and governments who are not to be trusted with power, but that *no-one* is safe with the stuff?

And armed with such understanding, why do we not start imposing proper checks on professional man? Make the judges and the headteachers answerable for their decisions and actions in the same way that the Prime Minister is; set up robust independent tribunals to hear complaints about doctors, dentists, teachers, lawyers; sack incompetent teachers, consultants, and forensic scientists in the same way that we sack incompetent bus drivers; subject hospitals, doctors, dentists, teachers and lawyers to the same tests as *Which?* carries out on car repairers and travel agents, and publish the findings; set up as powerful a body to pursue individual claims for negligence against the professional as the professionals' insurers are in defending them; have the Restrictive Practices Court scrutinise the professions' restrictive practices in the same way as it scrutinises any other restrictive practice; examine what *use* are some of the commodities dispensed by the professional – the pills and 'A' levels and legal procedures – with the same critical eye with which we examine hair restorers? If our forbears were motivated to curtail the power of kings and governments, why are we not similarly concerned to curb the power of the professional?

For a number of reasons.

First of all, our forbears lived in an age before the stupefying effects of mass media and universal education.

Secondly, although we have conceded power to the professional, his power is unobtrusive, and its abuse concealed. Whereas the tyrants of yore locked their victims up in the Tower, the professional shakes *his* victim reassuringly by the hand, and then proceeds unnecessarily to drill his teeth, or advises him to accept the defendant's insurance company's derisory offer in settlement of his personal injury claim. The monarch who abused his power levied illicit taxes. The dentist who abuses his power silently helps himself to a hundred thousand pounds of *our* taxes, and no-one is any the wiser.

Thirdly, and perhaps most important, abuse of power by a monarch or government threatens us *collectively*, whereas abuse of power by a professional affects us only *individually*.

Thus the man in the street is not concerned that our legal system requires him to wait four to six years, and risk financial ruin, in order to get compensation for accident injuries however horrendous; or that he will be powerless in any altercation with his wife's doctor or his child's headteacher; or that if he is accused of a serious crime, his barrister need not turn up for the trial, but can with impunity send along an untutored substitute; or that if he is left paralysed after a routine operation, he probably will not be able to find out what went wrong; or that his child has a greater chance of being stillborn in Great Britain than in any other EEC and Scandinavian country* – because until they actually happen to him he does not feel threatened by such possibilities. And if and when they do happen to him, it will be to him as an individual. And just as he did not care very much before, he will

* W.H.O. Annual Statistical Report for 1977.

find that no-one else will care very much after.

A group of mothers, realizing that a hospital stay can be an unnecessarily frightening experience for a child, founded the National Association for the Welfare of Children in Hospital (NAWCH); and by extensive campaigning they achieved unrestricted visiting hours throughout the country. But as far as I know there has been no campaign to reverse the fact that being born in a British hospital is an unnecessarily *fatal* experience for 10,000 babies each year.* The NAWCH mothers evidently saw the traditional restricted hospital visiting hours as a *collective* threat, and sufficient numbers of them were therefore motivated to expend considerable energy in getting them altered. But the possibility of unnecessary medical mishap – being more remote – is *not* seen as a collective threat. Hence no campaign.

Therefore, because *collectively* we are not motivated to rebel against the professional, *individually* we are powerless against him. And sensing our powerlessness in any potential confrontation with the professional, we are more inclined to propitiate him than rebel against him – just as the ancient Greeks propitiated *their* gods by offering sacrifices, in the hope they would send them a fair wind and a calm sea rather than smite them with a thunderbolt.

So the anxious mum, concerned over the state of the school lavatories or that her Johnny isn't getting on very well with his teacher, will not confront the headteacher with her complaint, because she is fearful that her Johnny will not then be chosen for the school play, or get a good reference. So the old lady hobbles about in pain rather than tell her doctor that his pills are doing no good, and to get a second opinion, lest the doctor gets offended and strikes her off his list. So the house-buyer, trying to do his own conveyancing, will abandon the attempt as soon as he is told that if he doesn't get a solicitor he will lose the deal. So the accident victim will accept the other driver's insurance company's offer as soon as his own lawyer tells him that if he doesn't, he will lose his case, and end up getting nothing. Because the professional has power to affect our lives for good or ill, he must be propitiated. The more he is propitiated, the more power he has to affect our lives for good or ill.

We are therefore caught in a vicious circle. And not being motivated to break out of it, the only thing to do is to turn it into a

---

* Report by Parliamentary Select Committee on Social Services, 1980.

benign circle. We have allowed the professional to design his own system, and prescribe his own standards. In the case of ordinary man this would be a dangerous, even absurd, thing to do. But not to worry. If we invest professional man with superior morality he will put our interests above his own, and will prescribe *higher* standards for himself than the law requires of ordinary man. We have handed over rather a lot of power to the professional, without requiring any checks to monitor how that power is exercised. But not to worry. If we invest him with superior morality he won't abuse his power, doesn't *need* any checks. In fact we do not even have to invest him with superior morality. All we have to do is to accept that when professional man is forever telling us that he is morally superior, it is so.

* * * * * *

There is no satisfactory definition of 'profession' and 'professional'. If we consult our dictionaries we see that a profession is, amongst other things: 'an occupation requiring special training, advanced education, and intellectual skills' (Collins); 'a calling involving specialised knowledge and often long and intensive academic preparation' (Websters); 'a form of employment especially one that is respected in society as honourable and is possible only for an educated person, such as law, medicine and the Church' (Longmans); 'something usually or properly pursued from higher motives' (Oxford Illustrated). A *professional* is: 'one showing the skill, behaviour or standards appropriate in a member of a profession' (Chambers); 'one who belongs to one of the learned or skilled professions, who raises his trade to the dignity of a learned profession' (Shorter Oxford). Professional as an *adjective* means: 'of a very high standard' (Chambers Universal). *Professionalism* means: 'the competence or correct demeanour of those who are highly trained and disciplined' (Chambers).

In so far as these definitions imply that the difference between a professional and a non-professional occupation is that the former requires superior mental powers, they are on shaky ground. For instance, who decides that one occupation (e.g. lawyer, professional) requires more skill and learning than another (e.g. mechanic, non-professional), and what criteria does whoever it is who decides, use to *measure* the respective skill and learning required of each? Who has decided that the training, education and skills of a teacher (professional) are respectively more special, advanced and intellectual than those required of a trumpet player (non-professional), and why? In what way is the preparation needed to become an optician (professional) longer, more intensive, and more academic than that needed to become an airline pilot (non-professional)?

The dictionaries are nearer the mark when they hint that the difference between a professional and a non-professional is that the professional is morally superior – 'a form of employment *especially one that is respected in society as honourable*', an activity '*pursued from higher motives*', 'showing the skill, *behaviour or standards appropriate* in a member of a profession', 'who raises his trade to the *dignity* of a learned profession', 'the competence or *correct demeanour of those who are highly disciplined*'.

But as the dictionaries only hint at the true definition but cannot quite bring themselves to spell it out, let me do it for them: a profession is an occupation the nature of which (particularly in view of the absence of proper controls) makes it imperative that its practitioners are morally superior to those who do a job which is not a profession. And a professional is someone who engages in such an occupation, and *who therefore has the appropriate moral superiority*.

When the word 'professional' is used as an adjective, it means one of two things.* Firstly, morally superior by virtue of being engaged in a particular occupation, as in:

'Doctors are *professional* people, and have a *professional* wish of their own to improve their service.' (Dr. Gerard Vaughan, Minister of Health, explaining why legislation is not needed to implement the proposals in the Acheson report.)

'It is perhaps too much to expect *professional* standards from an unqualified man, but I would have thought that common honesty would have impelled him to bring the matter to the purchaser's attention.' (Judge in Petersfield County Court castigating an unqualified estate agent's sharp practice. Honesty evidently comes in two grades: your common honesty, and your superior professional honesty, and whilst an unqualified person cannot be expected to aspire to the latter, he should at any rate have the former.)

---

* Apart from the limited definition of someone who does something for a living as distinct from a hobby.

'Even *professional* men are prepared to behave in questionable ways if they feel their livelihood threatened.' (Michael Zander, *Lawyers and the Public Interest* p.178.)

'There is no doubt that forensic scientists are for the most part highly competent *and professional*.' (Panorama programme, reassuring us after mentioning one or two unfortunate exceptions.)

'I am disgusted that a man of such *professional* status as a solicitor should behave like this.' (Someone complaining on Checkpoint(!) that a solicitor's equivocal letter induced him to invest with a worthless insurance broker.)

'We have a lot of vested interests *even in the professions*.' (Kenneth Clarke, Minister of Health, L.B.C. October 2 1983.)

'As more occupations come to assume *professional* status it will be right to demand that the *qualities of professionalism* are in existence before its privileges are granted.' (The Times leader, January 5 1980.)

So that's the moral question settled. But it still leaves another problem.

We know that ordinary man is divided into two categories, competent and incompetent. For instance, I go into a small workshop with a fractured section of my tent frame and ask if it can be welded. Harry examines it cursorily: 'No, that's aluminium, it will only melt.' But Fred standing nearby suggests testing the metal, decides it is steel, puts on his goggles and gets to work. Harry knows nothing and cares less. Fred knows exactly what to do, and in a few moments has produced a perfect job. I go into a bookshop wanting a certain book. If I ask Harriet she will briefly raise her lacklustre eyes and say, with a vague wave of her hand, 'If we've got it, it will be over there.' If I ask Frieda she will know they haven't got it, will check with the publishers that it is still in print, and will offer to get it for me. This is obvious enough.

But what if this division between competent and incompetent applies to *professional* man as well? Suppose you are accused of a serious crime (of which you are innocent), and the judge assigned to your case happens to be his lordship Judge Harry? Suppose you've got a difficult pregnancy and your consultant gynaecologist happens to be Dr. Harry? Suppose you've got a case for personal injuries on which your future life depends, and your solicitor or barrister turns out to be Harry?

A disturbing thought. But fortunately there is another convenient solution on hand. Set the judge on high, put a wig on his head, address him as a god (my lord, your honour, your worship), and he will obligingly assume divine wisdom and impartiality. Give a man a university degree and put *letters* after his name, and not only do you thereby invest him with superior morality, but with superior competence to go with his superior morality.

So we need the second definition. And here the dictionaries are less coy. A professional is: 'one showing the *skill*, behaviour or *standards* appropriate in a member of a profession' (Chambers); 'one who belongs to one of the learned or *skilled* professions' (Shorter Oxford); 'one having or showing the *skill* of a professional, someone *highly skilled*' (Oxford paperback); 'a person who does something with *great skill*' (Collins Standard Reference). Professional as an adjective means: '*of a very high standard*' (Chambers Universal); '*extremely competent*' (Collins). Professionalism means 'the *competence* or correct demeanour of those who are *highly trained* and disciplined' (Chambers).

So 'professional' is either a synonym for 'morally superior', or 'highly competent' – or sometimes both simultaneously, as in 'The authority recognises the *professional* responsibility and competence of headteachers in this matter.' (Explanation by the Salford Education Authority as to why it lays down no guidelines on what records schools should keep on their pupils, and to whom whatever records they do keep should be shown.)

We want something to be; therefore it is. We don't want something to be; therefore it isn't. Professional people 'have a high degree of detachment and integrity and, above all, they have a strong sense of responsibility and an exceptional commitment to the interests of their clients which transcends all other commitments.' They have 'the competence and correct demeanour of those who are highly trained and disciplined.' They are 'highly skilled'. And this must be true, not so much because The Times and the dictionaries say it is (who are after all only reflecting what we, the public, think) – but because, having surrendered power to the professional, and not being motivated to reverse the process, it's the only way out of the uncomfortable predicament we would otherwise be in if it *wasn't* true.

* * * * * *

However, if we read the Times leader a little more closely we see that it raises an interesting question: 'They [professional people] have a high degree of detachment and integrity and, above all, they have a strong sense of responsibility and an exceptional commitment to the interests of their clients which transcends all other commitments.' In other words, they are morally superior. The question is, how do they *come* by this moral superiority? But this The Times does not tell me. A previous leader in The Times (October 22 1966) stated that 'money making is thought of as a secondary rather than a primary focus of the professional man's interest', but again the writer does not state *why* he thinks professional men are less mercenary than their non-professional brothers.

The Monopolies Commission in its 1970 report says: 'A seller of professional services is expected to subordinate his self-interest to the client's interest' – but likewise fails to state on what grounds this expectation is based. Neither does the Under Secretary of State, who (in the debate on the Fair Trading Bill) tells the House of Commons that 'the professions maintain standards of ethical conduct beyond those required of the ordinary citizen by the law', tell us how he thinks the professions come to be invested with this ethical superiority. Just the bald assertion: they are.

So if I want to know *why* they are, I'm left to my own resources. Let me therefore look back over the first twenty-seven years of my life – for it was at that age that I became a professional man myself (a solicitor, with a certificate signed by Lord Denning to prove it) – and try to discover what happened to me during those years which didn't happen to Johnny Jones, insurance salesman; which makes me subordinate *my* self-interest to my clients' interests, whereas our Johnny, as like as not, will push whatever policy gives him most commission.

At the age of five (it being wartime), I was sent away to a boarding school in Woolacombe, presided over by two ladies who went under the unlikely names of Auntie Eileen and Auntie Evening, and whose sole purpose in life seemed to be to get their little charges to eat their dinners (*four* slices of unadorned bread and margarine had to be consumed before any jam or Bovril was allowed). Prep. school (again in North Devon) run on naval lines by a retired naval officer; another prep. school (in Sussex) run on military lines by a retired major; public school (in Dorset) run on no particular lines except the conviction that cold showers every morning and cross country runs (when it was too *wet* to play Rugby) were good, if not for the body, at least for the soul; undistinguished 'O' levels, average 'A' levels. Three year law degree course at Cambridge, of which Roman Law predominated the first two – the only item I retained after leaving being the legal formalities for freeing slaves (information I later found invaluable in my first position as an assistant solicitor in a rickety office overlooking Liverpool Street Main Line Station). Three years apprenticeship to a solicitor, during which I ran errands and drafted the occasional conveyance; six months course of lectures and note-taking culminating in the final exam, at which a sufficient number of the previously amassed facts having been regurgitated, a few weeks thereafter Lord Denning put his noble hand to the aforesaid certificate, and the metamorphosis from ordinary man to professional man was complete.

Now these experiences could have made me into a stronger person, or a taller person, or even a more *learned* person (although I believe that apart from my obstinate recall of the legal niceties entailed in freeing slaves, the only permanent effect is a loathing of boiled cabbage and a love of Bovril). But they couldn't have made me into a *better* person. They couldn't have invested me with a high degree of detachment and integrity, a strong sense of responsibility, and an exceptional commitment to the interests of my clients – which the Times leader writer insists that I, as a member of one of the 'established professions', possess. And although it is obviously desirable that I – having as I do the power, in the course of my job, to ruin someone else's life – should possess the 'skill, behaviour and standards appropriate in a member of a profession', the aforesaid 'training' is no guarantee that I have such qualities; nor even that I am any more competent than Harry of the workshop or Harriet of the bookshop. I may or I may not be. My clients have to take their chance.

Some jobs, of course, *do* demand a high level of proficiency before they can even be attempted (surgeon, airline pilot, trumpet player etc.) but this has nothing to do with the difference between professional and non-professional, since such jobs are not necessarily or even primarily professional.

Therefore, as nothing has happened to me to make me morally – or in any other way – different from Johnny Jones, insurance salesman (or Andrew Newton, airline pilot), it follows that nothing will have happened to my fellow lawyers, and the gentlemen who sit on our professional governing body, and presumably my fellow professionals, to make *them* any different either. The difference between professional man and non-professional man is not that the professional has superior morals, nor that he has superior standards; only that he has more power.

And although our Times leader writer is less vulnerable than most, it could happen that he falls on hard times and learns something of the nature of this power; that he acquires some first-hand experience of how a professional man's commitment to the interests of his clients transcends all other commitments. For instance, a routine operation on him or a member of his family could go seriously wrong, and he finds he cannot get beyond the wall of silence and evasion from the hospital; or he is granted a legal aid certificate to sue the hospital conditional on getting a *consultant's* opinion that the hospital was negligent; or he is sent to prison because a substitute barrister – who picked up the papers for the first time an hour before the trial – makes a hash of his defence; or five years after a road accident, which left him crippled, his claim for compensation has advanced hardly at all because his lawyer is incompetent, or has been bribed by the other side's insurance company. In which case he will presumably wish that he had been better informed.

5 *The additional perks of the lawyers*

In the preceding chapters we have examined how, when dealing with professional man, the law makers, judges, commentators and *public* alike, for their various reasons, abandon their normal critical faculties – those critical faculties which they automatically employ in their dealings with ordinary man. And how, as a result, professional man is allowed to regulate his own affairs, maintain his own standards, and design his own system, without interference or question. So far my observations have been on professional man in general, with examples from the four professions which impinge most on everyday life – teachers, doctors, dentists and lawyers. But now we say goodbye to the teachers, doctors and dentists (while thanking them for their company), and turn our attention exclusively to the lawyers.

And here we will see that while the professions in general occupy a privileged position, the legal profession enjoys some additional bonuses as a result of one or two felicitous accidents – some of which we have already touched on.

The lawyers' propaganda machine

Because of the law of libel, any controversial material broadcast, televised or published has first to be vetted by a *lawyer*. Because the legal profession impinges more than other professions on everyday life, it seems to get more coverage in the media. Only a lawyer (or a member of a related profession) is considered competent to comment on legal matters.

These factors make for a powerful propaganda machine. So

while one may come across the occasional piece about this or that *individual* lawyer's chicanery (e.g. in exercising a buy-back clause on a cottage, or in trying to overcharge a client £130,000), the basic issues – the absurdity of the conveyancing system, the cruelty and stupidity of the litigation system – are virtually never touched on. Moreover, on such issues the public is continually fed falsehoods. For example:

(1) On the advantages of going to a solicitor, rather than an unqualified conveyancer who might have disappeared by the time his faulty conveyancing comes to light: 'One thing is for sure; the Law Society will still be there, together with the protection for clients of their compensation fund.' (Homefinder, July 1976). The Law Society's compensation fund does *not* compensate a client in respect of his solicitor's faulty conveyancing, only if the solicitor makes off with his money.

(2) 'If things go wrong you should know that solicitors are subject to all sorts of rules of conduct imposed by both the Law Society and the Courts. . .So if anything goes wrong – and most probably it will not – you can write to the Secretary-General of the Law Society at 113 Chancery Lane.' (Good Housekeeping, March 1981). It is true you *can* write to the Law Society if something goes wrong with your legal matter, just as you can write to the Archbishop of Canterbury about it, but you'd be better off putting the price of the stamp towards a cup of tea.

Incidentally, the piece containing the first quotation was written by a solicitor's wife, and the second was written by a solicitor – details not considered sufficiently important by the respective editors to pass on to their readers.

(3) 'Solicitors provide a professional service for which they accept full responsibility. And this means either putting right mistakes which they might make or compensating clients monetarily.' (Law Society's spokesman, Daily Mail, July 7 1976.) The implication is that if your solicitor makes a mistake, you automatically get compensation. The writer omits to mention that you first have to *prove* the solicitor was negligent in a Court of law – a little formality which could easily take five years, and leave you not only without compensation but bankrupt.

(4) 'Of course a solicitor employs staff to do *some* work for him, which he supervises.' (Law Society's spokesman, Daily Mail, February 15 1978). Two implications here: that unqualified staff do not carry out the whole job themselves, and that they are

always supervised. Both are false, as the Law Society knows – for its Gazette frequently carries solicitors' advertisements for unqualified clerks, stipulating that they 'must be able to work without supervision'.

(5) 'No, you do not 'have' to instruct a Solicitor to deal with your sale. You can handle the contract yourself, if you wish. . .Of course, it is quite legal for you to ignore your Doctor and to saw your own leg off. Legal perhaps, but not very wise. You may have saved the Agent's fees, yes, but that is because he provides a service which you can do for yourself. It is not really a *professional* service; it is more of a trade. . .A Solicitor offers to protect your interests by the exercise of his knowledge and *he backs up his work with a virtual guarantee*. If he fails to do so, you can claim for your loss, either from him direct for professional negligence, or from the Law Society Indemnity Fund.' (*Buying or Selling a House* by Llewelyn, Fellow of Royal Institute of Chartered Surveyors.)

Again the falsehood that if you suffer loss because of your solicitor's bad work you can claim against the Law Society's indemnity fund. Notice also how the author equates doing the conveyancing on your own sale with amputating your own leg, for no more cogent reason, it seems, than that both activities are traditionally done by professionals.

(6) I previously mentioned a BBC radio programme 'Buying a Dream' which recounted how a couple, Bob and Deirdre, bought their first home, and how they already had a solicitor lined up (called Harry!) They refer to him, and the presenter refers to him, as their *solicitor*. Then half way through the programme they have a bit of bother with their building society, which isn't very happy with Harry because – as we learn for the first time – he is not a solicitor at all, but an *unqualified conveyancer* (i.e. someone who is not a solicitor or solicitor's clerk but is in business in his own right as a conveyancer). After this little hiccup, Harry surprisingly reverts to his former status of solicitor in that the presenter continues to refer to him as a solicitor, *and never again as an unqualified conveyancer*. Now it might be that Bob and Deirdre did not know the difference between a solicitor and an unqualified conveyancer, but we may be sure that the BBC does. Evidently the BBC considered Bob and Deirdre an ideal couple for their programme. The only snag was that they had used an unqualified conveyancer, and apparently used him quite successfully. A 45 minute programme on Radio 4 at peak listening time (and

repeated) giving due emphasis to this fact would be a nasty slap in the face for the Law Society, which understandably views these unqualified conveyancers with some alarm. Auntie – the Law Society's lackey – therefore suppresses the fact as best she can, divulging it only in one brief instance when it worked to Bob and Deirdre's *disadvantage*.

(7) 'Whether the accident happens on the roads, at work, or in public or private premises, the victim, if he is blameless, has legal rights. He has the right to sue for damages, that is a monetary award by way of compensation. . .The person responsible for the accident will be ordered to make good that loss. Most claims for damages never reach Court because the victim's solicitor has been able to negotiate with the other side and get a good settlement for his client. A solicitor *by his professional training, skill and expertise* knows what damages Courts are awarding for particular types of injuries, [and] knows when to settle a claim and when not to.' (Evening Gazette.)

Again an advertisement for the solicitors' profession masquerading as unbiased editorial. Again the dissemination of false information – in this instance by the omission of a vital fact: the person responsible for an accident is ordered to pay compensation only if the victim can *prove* in Court that the accident was his *fault*.

(8) 'And you've got to remember that insurance companies on the whole do settle cases quickly when they're good bona fide cases.' (Lord Denning talking about the litigation system, 'Person to Person', Radio 4, June 18 1980.)

The notion that insurance companies – who are in business to make money, and whose income is the amount by which the premiums they get exceed the claims they pay out – act as charities to mitigate the defects of our litigation system, is surprising. I wrote to Lord Denning asking what evidence he had for it. He replied: 'As to your question about insurance companies, I have not any evidence except it is what I have always heard from practitioners in this field.'

It is by such propaganda, masquerading as objective truths, that the public is informed about its legal system. Neither is there any voice to contradict it. Mr. Llewelyn's book – which argues that because you would not amputate your own leg *therefore* you should not attempt your own conveyancing – finds a publisher.

My book, *Conveyancing Fraud*, which shows how solicitors swindle the public out of seven hundred million pounds a year, does not (and I had to publish it myself). Mr. Llewelyn's book is on sale in every branch of every chain book store. Mine is not. Sir Peter Rawlinson is given freedom of the air to explain why barristers are not overpaid (Radio 4, 'It's Your Line'). When Michael Zander gets through and asks an awkward question he is unceremoniously cut off. Lord Denning is similarly given freedom of the air to expound on the English legal system. On the subject of personal injury litigation, he does not say: '*I have always heard from practitioners in this field* that insurance companies on the whole do settle cases quickly when they're good bona fide cases.' He says: 'Insurance companies on the whole do settle cases quickly when they're good bona fide cases.' And he says it to five million people. And five million people believe him.

Because there is nothing to counter this sort of propaganda its power is enormous – so much so that if you asked a hundred people why they go to a solicitor for their conveyancing, probably 90 would reply: 'because if anything goes wrong, you've always got a comeback on your solicitor'; or 'you've got a comeback on the Law Society'; or even 'because you *have* to have a solicitor.' Similarly, if you asked a hundred people what they thought would happen if they were seriously injured in a road accident, 80 would probably reply: 'the other driver's insurance company pays compensation' – with perhaps a quarter of them adding the proviso 'as long as the accident wasn't my fault.'

British Justice is the best in the world

Now for a more subtle form of propaganda. I have suggested some reasons why the public abandons its normal critical faculties in its dealings with professional man. However, in the case of lawyers there is an additional reason. The average citizen respects the law – which he sees as his protection against anarchy. And as in his eyes the law is bound up with the legal system, which in turn is bound up with the lawyers who operate it, his respect for the former permeates to all three. Moreover the law, and the legal system, are somehow bound up with *British Justice* which, as we all know, is the *best in the world*. Whether this is because of our Jury System, devised by Henry II (or was it Alfred the Great?), or our excellence at playing cricket, or the innate superiority of the English character, we're not quite sure. But that the British sense of fair play, when combined with British judges and British barristers, produces British Justice, which is synonymous with incorruptibility and excellence – of this we *are* sure.

I look at the transcript of a BBC 2 Newsweek programme on the legal system (May 24 1979):

Richard Kershaw: 'Good evening. The legal system in Britain is rightly esteemed as a pillar of our democracy, incorruptible and remarkably independent. Most of us breathe more easily, if we think about it, because it's there.'

Now this is not a judge or a lawyer speaking: this is a television journalist whose job is to probe, to find out. No other British institution – not even the monarchy – attracts this sort of comment. And it can be made only because the vast majority of the public agrees with it. The British legal system is a pillar of our democracy and our British way of life; our protection against anarchy on the one hand and tyranny on the other; something to do with Magna Carta (or was it the Tolpuddle Martyrs?) At any rate it's there, and we all breathe more easily because of it.

This notion is so much part of our upbringing that one sometimes hears such views expressed by those whose actual experiences of our legal system one might think would lead them to rather different conclusions. For instance, Checkpoint (February 2 1984) did a programme on a once wealthy businessman whose flourishing steel companies were requisitioned during the war, mismanaged, and left insolvent. He got his companies back after the war, and spent the next forty years in a fruitless battle trying to get compensation through the Courts – which left him ruined physically and financially, even to the extent of being unable to have his shoes repaired. Yet he says: 'We have got the best legal system that man has yet devised.'

Another Checkpoint programme (March 11 1982) described how one Bernard Saltman was arrested for setting fire to his own factory. Although there was almost no evidence against him, and the Judge's summing up indicated an acquittal, a perverse jury brought in a verdict of guilty. His appeal failed and he was sent to prison. His wife explained how as a result of the case they had lost their business, their house, their health, everything. 'But', she said through her sobs, 'I still believe in British Justice'.*

---

* In fact six months later, thanks to the *programme* (and his M.P.) he was released.

Even stranger is the way a writer or commentator can deliver the traditional eulogy on our wonderful legal system, and then let fall a few facts indicating that it is nothing of the sort, without apparently noticing any contradiction. So in a book *The Courts and You* by Michael Cook, the author tells us 'Our judicial system is admired and emulated throughout the modern world' (p.19); and 'The Courts of law are one of your most precious possessions. Without them. . .you would be unlikely to possess anything else' (p.3). But further on in the book the author advises us: 'Avoid litigation. Do a deal. Shake hands. Forget it. But whatever you do, *do not litigate*' (*his* italics). And he gives two reasons for this advice: 'Anyone who embarks on litigation could find that he has a tiger by the tail – the costs its jaws'; and 'It is an accepted medical fact that recovery from an injury can be delayed by the [strain of the] proceedings relating to it.' (p.120.) In other words, says Mr. Cook, the Courts of law are one of your most precious possessions, fundamental to the preservation of your rights; but for goodness sake don't go near them if you don't want to be ruined financially, and further damaged physically.

Lord Benson, in a lecture delivered February 12 1981 (reprinted in the Law Society's Gazette), states: 'The existing order [i.e. the legal system] which has evolved over the years has served the public well.' But a little further on he blandly states: 'Even now very many thousands of people in this country are unable to obtain justice because they cannot afford the costs.'

In another book, *The Bar on Trial* (Robert Hazell), we read that 'the undoubted integrity of English barristers, their sense of dedication to their clients, and their generally high level of professional competence have all contributed enormously to the quality of justice administered in the English Courts' (p.9). But further on the author (who is himself a barrister) tells us of some of the little tricks perpetrated by these men, with their undoubted integrity and their dedication to their clients – or rather perpetrated by their clerks on their behalf, and with their tacit approval:

> 'No clerk gives overmuch consideration to the wishes of the client. . .In the event of a conflict, the clerk's first thought is what action will give least offence to the solicitors concerned; if this means taking Mr. X off a case in order to release him for a more lucrative brief, or to please a firm of solicitors who are regular customers, then this may be done with little thought

for the possible effect on the lay client' (p.107) – which of course may be that the client's case is lost, and his life is ruined.

'The clerks overload their principals with engagements in the hope that where two cases conflict, one will settle or go short, so that the barrister will still be able to do both cases and collect two fees instead of one. If this hope does not materialize, one brief will have to be returned; and *if it is returned at sufficiently short notice* the solicitors will probably have to accept someone from the same set of chambers' (p.120).

Jonathan Caplan in a useful essay* says: 'The assumption that law was necessary led uncritically to the assumption that lawyers too were necessary.' In fact this logic seems to go a step further: the assumption that British Justice is excellent leads uncritically to the assumption that the legal system and the lawyers who operate it must be correspondingly excellent. And while there may be one or two imperfections here and there – perhaps four years *is* rather a long time to wait, and perhaps £20,000 *is* rather a lot to pay in legal costs, for the Court's decision whether or not an accident victim should get compensation for his injuries – these are only peripheral defects, incapable of shaking this basic assumption.

Judges, who make most of the law, are lawyers

Not only are the law Courts operated by lawyers. The Masters, who decide the procedural but often crucial pre-trial issues between the parties, are lawyers. And the judges who preside over the Courts are lawyers. Now, while some commentators have argued that judges are too old, or come from too narrow a social class (in fact a survey showed that of the 55 High Court judges operating in 1964, 48 went to Oxford or Cambridge), as far as I know the fact that they are appointed exclusively from *barristers* has never been questioned. Judges come from barristers just as water comes from a tap, and little thought is given to either phenomenon. Yet it is this fact, more than any other, which has determined the nature of our legal system. I explain.

Broadly the law is divided into two categories: *civil* law – a body of rules the transgression of which gives an individual, who has

---

* In *Disabling Professions* published by Marion Boyars.

suffered from such transgression, a right to *compensation* against the offender; and *criminal* law – a body of rules transgressing which is an offence against the State, which *punishes* the offender.

Now what do judges do? In criminal cases they sum up the evidence for the jury, and decide on the sentence if the accused is found guilty. In civil cases they decide whether the plaintiff has proved his case, and if so, how much compensation he shall be awarded. But they do something else rather more important. They make law. In fact over the years and the centuries they have made far more law than Parliament. The civil law is almost entirely judge made: which means in effect that it has been the judges (not Parliament) who have decided in what circumstances one individual shall have a right to compensation against another; and it is also the judges (not Parliament) who have decided what procedures and rituals the individual must go through to *exercise* that right.

The civil law is divided into different branches, and one of the most important of these is *negligence*. Under this head someone who is injured has a right to compensation against the person who caused his injury, provided he can prove that his injury *was due to that person's failure to take reasonable care or use reasonable skill* – i.e. that it was that person's *fault*. So a driver whose failure to drive with reasonable care results in someone else's injury, and a doctor whose failure to exercise reasonable skill results in his patient's damage, are both negligent; and if such negligence (fault) is proved in Court, they are liable to pay compensation to their victims. This basic law of negligence was originally formulated by the judges in the last century, since when there have been numerous qualifications and refinements – also made by the judges.

For judges play a dual role. On the one hand they are bound to apply the existing law, as decided and laid down by their predecessors, when the circumstances of a case before them correspond with those of a previous case. On the other hand, when a case before them presents a *different* set of circumstances to any previous case, they may extend or qualify the existing law to meet the new circumstances. In practice their powers are less formalized; and whether a judge feels bound meticulously to apply only those decisions or rules laid down by his predecessors, or whether he feels at liberty to extend or qualify those rules, is very much a matter of discretion depending on the personality and character of the individual judge. At any rate the civil law has evolved – and is evolving all the while – through the judges' decisions. And whenever a judge *does* extend or qualify the existing rules in deciding a case, he becomes a law-maker. Let's look at some examples of how judges quietly perform this role.

As we have seen (p. 27), one of the refinements to the law of negligence is that someone suing a professional man must show a *greater* degree of negligence (fault) in order to win his case, than if he was suing a non-professional man. Lord Denning, Master of the Rolls for two decades, and one of the most influential civil judges of all time, expressed this 'refinement' in the following terms: 'The Courts have no hesitation in holding that mistakes made by car drivers or employers are visited by damages; but they make allowances for the mistakes of professional men. They realize that a finding of negligence against a professional man is a serious matter for him.' However in his judgment in Whitehouse v. Jordan in the Court of Appeal, where Denning quashes the award of £100,000 which had been made against an obstetrician in favour of a brain-damaged child, his lordship gives a more specific reason:

> 'Take heed of what has happened in the United States. Medical malpractice cases there are *very worrying*. . .The damages are colossal. The doctors insure but the premiums become very high: and these have to be passed on in fees to the patients. Experienced practitioners are known to have refused to treat patients for fear of being accused of negligence. Young men are even deterred from entering the profession because of the risks involved. In the interests of all, we must avoid such consequences in England. Not only must we avoid excessive damages. We must say, and say firmly, that in a professional man an error of judgment is not negligent.'

In other words, says Denning, it is in the *public interest* that the law of negligence should be modified in favour of medical men. Now this might be a perfectly valid point of view. But it hasn't been *debated* by anyone. It is simply one man's opinion of what is in the public interest – a man, moreover, who has not been elected but has merely been appointed by the Lord Chancellor. But because he happens to be a judge – i.e. because he happens to have reached the pinnacle of the *legal* profession – his opinion of what is in the public interest determines whether Mrs. Whitehouse shall or shall not get compensation in respect of her brain-damaged child. And (unless it is overruled by a higher Court) it unobtrusively seeps into the law, and determines how future Mrs. Whitehouses will fare.

Now whether we like it or not, what a man thinks is in the public interest is generally unconsciously bound up with what is in *his* (or his colleagues') interest. The President of the Law Society thinks that Austin Mitchell's bill to break the solicitors' conveyancing monopoly was against the public interest; the President of the Association of Unqualified Conveyancers, on the other hand, thinks that the bill was *in* the public interest. Ask a hundred publicans whether it is in the public interest to enact tougher anti-drinking and driving laws, and 98 will say no. Ask a hundred taxi drivers, and 98 will say yes. Over the years the judges have tacitly (or in Lord Denning's case explicitly) modified the law of negligence in favour of professional men because 'they realize that a finding of negligence against a professional man is a serious matter for him'. But if judges, instead of being appointed from professional men, were appointed from the *victims of medical mishaps*, we may assume that they would modify the law the other way – so that someone suing a medical man would need to show only a prima facie case of negligence in order to succeed; because they realize that a medical mishap which damages a patient *is a serious matter for him.*

Judges, being professional men, have modified the law of negligence in favour of professional men. And judges, being ex-barristers, they have more particularly modified the law of negligence and contract in favour of barristers – so that a barrister may not be sued for a negligent Court performance, or for breach of contract.

And judges, being ex-barristers, they have been permitted over the years to fashion the entire structure of our legal system.

So that if your cobbler agrees to mend your shoes in time for your holiday but fails to do so, and you have to buy a new pair, you can sue him for breach of contract. That is the law as formulated by the judges a century or two ago. But if your barrister agrees to take your case but doesn't turn up for the hearing because he has accepted a more lucrative engagement elsewhere, as a result of which your case is lost and your life ruined, you can't sue the *barrister* for breach of contract – because you can't *make* a contract with a barrister. That is also the law as formulated by the judges a century or two ago. And if your cobbler ruins your shoes you can sue him for negligence. But you can't sue your barrister if he ruins your personal injury case, which has taken five years to get to Court. And you can't because the judges – who have been barristers for the greater part of their working lives – say you can't.

And if you are seriously injured in an accident, before you are entitled to compensation you must prove in a Court of law that the accident was caused by someone else's negligence. To do this you have to instruct a solicitor (because you will not be able to understand the esoteric language and ritualistic procedures involved); and your solicitor has to instruct a barrister (because only barristers are allowed to address the High Court); and your barrister will argue your case before a judge; and the judge,after listening to your barrister and the barrister for the other side (who will argue that your injury was *not* caused by his client's negligence), will decide whether or not your barrister has proved your case, and therefore whether or not you are to be awarded compensation for your injuries. And you must go through this rigmarole because that is the law; and that is the law because the judges have decided that it shall be the law.

Lawyers in Parliament

At the time of writing (August 1984), out of a total of 561 Members of Parliament for England and Wales, 104 are lawyers – 72 barristers and 32 solicitors. The Prime Minister is a barrister, as is a third of her cabinet; and these figures are probably typical of any government.

There are reasons why the two branches of the legal profession are so well represented. A solicitor is the only professional person who can delegate *all* his work, conveyancing, litigation or whatever, to his staff (whether qualified or not), and stand for Parliament. A tradesman or businessman can do the same but his business is more likely to depend on his personal energies, whereas the solicitor can (if he chooses) provide merely the front, the legal status, and leave his clerks to do the work. As the Law Society's Gazette (June 19 1974) stated: 'There are numerous cases of [solicitors'] branch offices at which qualified solicitors rarely, if ever, attend.'* Barristers are considered particularly suitable to be Members of Parliament since the job of arguing in Court is akin to debating; and although barristers – unlike solicitors – cannot delegate their work, the successful ones command sufficiently high fees to permit some curtailment of their professional activities without them going hungry. In fact their enhanced status as M.P., and increased contacts, probably mean they suffer no financial loss at all.

So governments may come and governments may go, but the Lord Chancellor (a lawyer and permanent member of the cabinet) sits on his woolsack, and some hundred lawyers – the largest single professional group – are, have been, and presumably always will be, Members of Parliament.

The law unconsciously reflects the interests of those who make it – hence the privileged position of the professions in general who are left to regulate their own affairs, while the tradesman and businessman are subject to a barrage of legislation designed to protect the public from the unscrupulous of their number. But the lawyers have been able to secure some special privileges. For example, since 1804 solicitors have been granted the monopoly of conveyancing. Scale fees – which laid down generous rates of remuneration for unregistered property, rather less generous for registered property – were given statutory force, so that solicitors could virtuously explain to their clients that not only were they entitled to charge such exorbitant fees, they were *obliged* to. However, as soon as it became apparent that with the sudden increase in land registration the scales were ceasing to work to the solicitors' advantage, they were promptly scrapped by the Solicitors' Remuneration Order 1972, leaving solicitors to charge what the market would bear. At the time of writing the government is pledged to abolish the solicitors' conveyancing monopoly. We don't know what the actual measures will be, but I doubt they will make any significant difference to the solicitors' position – any more than setting up the Land Registry at the beginning of this century (which was originally designed to enable anyone to buy and sell a house as easily as he can buy and sell anything else) has made any difference; any more than the abolition of the rule that a Queen's Counsel has to be attended in

* A Law Society rule now stipulates that a solicitor's branch office must be *visited* by a solicitor every day.

Court by an ordinary barrister has made any difference to the barristers' position. The rules may be abolished but after centuries of tradition, the practice quietly goes on just the same.

As important as what the lawyers in Parliament have been able to pass is what they have been able to block. The Pearson Commission on personal injury litigation (which was set up because of some disquiet over the Thalidomide case) recommended compensating *road accident victims* automatically, without proof of negligence – i.e. taking them out of the legal system altogether. The Commission reported in 1978. Yet there has been no move to implement any of its suggestions. The commercial equivalent of our personal injury litigation system is our company law system – whereby someone can run up bills for £*x* thousand, but provided he is trading as a limited company he may not be sued. As to this the Jenkins Committee made significant recommendations for reform a quarter of a century ago. Yet at the time of writing, nothing has changed.

The law is made by the judges and by Parliament. And whereas in the last century the judges laid the foundations of one of the lawyers' main pillars of power when they first formulated the law of negligence, Parliament constructed its twin some thirty-five years ago in the shape of the Legal Aid Scheme.

After the war, Attlee's socialist government set about its noble task of making legal and medical services available to all, regardless of ability to pay for them. But as might be expected, the way it achieved the former was rather different to the way it achieved the latter. Rather than attempt to interfere with the lawyers' status it merely subsidized their services. So that under the Legal Aid Scheme someone who has a reasonable case, but whose means are below a certain limit, can pursue a legal action through the Courts in the usual way, and his legal costs will be paid for by the State. Apart from divorce, if someone of limited means has a legal action it will almost invariably be a *negligence* action. That is, he will have been injured in an accident, and will be claiming compensation from the person who caused his injury – his success depending on whether he can prove in Court that it was due to that person's negligence. And as the legal costs of bringing an action in the High Court run into many thousands of pounds, most people who bring such cases to Court can do so only if they are subsidized by the Legal Aid Scheme.

By such a scheme is justice available to all. There's only one snag. Parliament set up a scheme whereby someone of limited means, who has a reasonable case, can get legal aid to bring his case to Court. Now who decides whether the applicant has a reasonable case? And the answer that Parliament predictably gave was that a *Committee of lawyers* decides.

So Legal Aid Committees, composed of solicitors and barristers, were set up throughout the country to determine legal aid applications. The procedure is that the applicant's solicitor submits to the appropriate Committee brief details of his client's case and the evidence to support it; in the light of which the Committee decides whether or not the applicant has a reasonable case (i.e. a reasonable chance of *winning* his case), and therefore whether or not he should be granted legal aid. Before finally deciding, the Committee will often ask the applicant's solicitor to obtain a barrister's opinion, and in fact many solicitors automatically obtain and submit a barrister's opinion with the application. If the Committee grants legal aid, the case proceeds to Court in the usual way; if it doesn't, the case has to be abandoned (unless of course the applicant can finance it himself). However in borderline cases the Committee may grant legal aid *conditionally*. The condition might be that a barrister's opinion shall be obtained at a certain stage of the action, in the light of which opinion the Committee will then decide whether to renew or cancel the legal aid. Or the condition might be that the legal aid covers only one step or series of steps, after which a *further* application has to be made – which will be granted or refused as the Committee then decides. Moreover, even if legal aid is granted unconditionally, it can be withdrawn at any time if some new evidence comes to light which significantly lessens the applicant's chances of success; or if the other party makes an offer of settlement which the applicant's legal advisers consider reasonable in the circumstances. In such event the applicant's solicitor has a *duty* to notify the Legal Aid Committee, which will thereupon cancel the legal aid.

In theory these rules are reasonable in that it is prudent to ascertain, as far as possible, that the applicant has a reasonable chance of success before allowing several thousand pounds or more of taxpayer's money to be expended in financing his legal action. But in practice these rules mean that in the majority of personal injury (negligence) cases, *it is a Committee of lawyers which decides which claims shall be allowed to come to Court*. And as that Committee will usually be guided by a barrister's opinion obtained by the applicant's solicitor, whether or not a claim is allowed to come to Court frequently depends on what *one lawyer* writes in his opinion. So if you or your child are disastrously injured by someone else's fault, you have a potential claim for, say, a hundred thousand pounds. Yet whether your claim ever gets to Court – and therefore, whether you ever get your hundred thousand pounds – may easily depend on what your barrister writes in his opinion, which in turn depends on what facts your solicitor chooses to give him. And you have no control over the latter, and may not even speak to the former. (And we will see the implications of *that* situation by and by.)

* * * * * *

These, then, are some of the little perks enjoyed by the lawyers over and above the other professions.

Privileged as the other professions are, they cannot altogether have their own way. Within the space of a couple of terms William Tyndale, an apparently normal and healthy primary school, disintegrated under the disastrous regime introduced by a new headteacher and his colleagues. The school managers who protested were barred from the school by the teachers. The education authorities, although fully alerted, refused to take any action. Managers, parents and the few dissenting teachers alike seemed powerless to do anything about the situation. Yet as soon as the *press* got hold of the story the game was up, and the education authorities had to submit to a highly embarrassing public enquiry. During an unusually hot summer the headmistress of another primary school (which my children attended) decided to discontinue afternoon school for an indefinite period, and flout County Hall's conditions for so doing. Again the authorities, although informed, took no action. Again there seemed nothing that parents could do, except transfer their children to other schools. Yet the same day as a story about the situation appeared in our local paper, a note was circulated to all parents advising them that school hours would thenceforth revert to normal.

Similarly, although the other professions by and large have

been allowed to impose their own systems, the systems they impose must have *some* regard for the needs of the public they purport to serve – unlike the system the lawyers impose. For instance an official of the Law Society has stated: 'There are numerous cases of [solicitors'] branch offices at which qualified solicitors rarely, if ever, attend.' Privileged as the other professions are, nevertheless you can't have a doctor's surgery at which doctors rarely if ever attend, or a school at which teachers rarely if ever attend, or an operating theatre at which surgeons rarely if ever attend. For instance a barrister with impunity can, and frequently does, see his client for the first time a few minutes before the trial; and the consequent bodged defence may easily result in an innocent man being sent to prison. Tenuous as the sanctions are against incompetent or overbearing members of the other professions, nevertheless medical men and teachers may not act with such cynical disregard for their clients.

To the gullibility and apathy of the public, and the fact that the judges and commentators are for the most part either professional men themselves or their lackeys, add the lawyers' peculiar privileges – a hundred lawyers in Parliament at any given time; the judges, who make most of the law, being appointed exclusively from lawyers; a propaganda machine which in its subtle way would not disgrace that of a totalitarian state; the power to decide which cases will come to Court and which will founder – and you have a potent recipe.

Nevertheless lawyers are subject to one constraint.

Although they respect authority, the British mistrust any form of blatant power, particularly when it comes in official form. Our forbears even went so far as to cut off the head of a king who rashly claimed that he ruled by divine right; and expelled his son, who eventually succeeded him, when he, too, seemed to be getting too big for his boots. Thereafter the British people gradually stripped the monarchy of all its power, and evolved a system whereby the government of the day can be sent packing every five years. Britain is a country where the police do not carry guns, where gangsterism never caught on, where the fascist party is never more than a lunatic fringe. In Britain the bully boy is the baddie, and the goodie is the little guy who stands up to him – hence our favourite screen heroes are Charlie Chaplin, and the cartoon mouse who is forever knocking spots off the cartoon cat.

Britain is a country where blatant power is mistrusted and therefore does not work.

Sir Oswald Moseley's downfall lay in failing to understand this. The lawyers, on the other hand, have understood it very well.

So it has never been illegal for an unqualified operator to do conveyancing, because the lawyers in Parliament, who passed the original Solicitors' Act, realized that such a measure would be repugnant; and that virtually the same result could be achieved by merely making it illegal for an unqualified person (for a fee) to prepare just *one* crucial document – the deed of transfer. So there is no law prohibiting anyone from doing his own conveyancing. We don't make laws like that in England. Instead, a cabal of banks, building societies, estate agents and solicitors – each with their hands in the other's pockets – will put such pressure on those of their applicants who are minded to do their own *purchase* that only a tiny minority will have the strength of mind to persevere. As for the *sale*, the seller's building society will cannily refuse to hand over the actual receipt on completion, in return for the outstanding mortgage money; but instead the seller's solicitor hands over an *undertaking* to send it within 14 days after completion. By interposing this unnecessary little formality, the seller can be made to believe that he *has to have a solicitor* to act for him, because only a *solicitor's* undertaking to send this receipt will be acceptable to the purchaser's solicitor.*

Similarly, there is no law prohibiting anyone from conducting his own case in the High Court. This is one of the Englishman's inalienable rights, for which our forbears fought and bled at Mons (or was it Agincourt?) But anyone who actually tries to do so will find the ritual and documentation so esoteric that he will almost certainly be defeated.

So our Courts do not operate behind locked doors, as the Courts of some countries do. The doors of *our* Court rooms can be pushed open by any newspaper reporter who chooses to do so. The freedom of the press to report Court proceedings is one of our most valuable safeguards, for which our fathers fought the last war (or was it the one before?) But as the newspapers are

---

* Indeed, this was one of the reasons given in the Royal Commission's report for retaining the solicitors' conveyancing monopoly: 'Such undertakings are an important means of avoiding difficulties or delay in conveyancing transactions; it is possible, for example, to receive purchase money on an *undertaking to discharge a mortgage*.' (para.21.25.)

owned and financed by a small clutch of top businessmen affiliated to the establishment, and in any event their material is censored by the lawyers, the British people probably know less about their legal system than the natives of those countries whose Court rooms *are* kept locked.

In Sicily, if a particular group had the power of our legal profession, one imagines that it would simply declare that it held a franchise in perpetuity over all roads, so that each time anyone moved house he would need to take out a personal licence to use the roads leading to his new house – at the cost of £700 a go. Such measures would not work in England. Instead our lawyers point to the legal formalities involved in buying and selling a house, which they claim are so complex that only *they* are competent to deal with them (at a cost of £700). And anyone who demurs will find himself confronted – not by sinister gentlemen in dark shirts and light ties, but by a tut-tutting bank manager or building society clerk, who will be pretty well as persuasive.

In Switzerland, when a particular group has the muscle of our legal profession, it manufactures drugs of dubious properties, and babies' milk powder, which it sells in large quantities to the third world – with vast profits for the companies concerned, but rather less felicitous results for their consumers. For instance, the babies' milk powder (which the manufacturers advertise as being so much more convenient than breast feeding) has to be mixed with water; but unfortunately in the remote outposts of India and similar, where this milk powder is marketed, there isn't always a supply of uncontaminated water available. The 'Man Alive' programme which exposed these practices (May 21 1981) is horrified at such brutal commercialism. In England we go about things in a more civilized way. Our muscle men don't launch aggressive marketing campaigns for babies' milk powder in the third world. Instead they operate a legal system which demands that the victim of a serious accident, in order to get compensation, has to wait four to six years for his case to come to Court; and risk not only getting no compensation at all, but being ordered to pay more than the amount he is claiming, in legal costs.

But whereas the Man Alive programme can point an accusing finger at the particular Swiss companies, and whereas the victims of the mafia presumably have no difficulty in understanding the nature of its power, those who become entangled in the meshes of our legal system (which can be just as injurious to health as babies' milk powder mixed with polluted water) cannot accuse anyone. Because no-one is to blame. No-one is responsible. It's just the system. So it is that my Lord Denning, former Master of the Rolls, to whom I was allowed in a phone-in programme to put a few points showing the cruelty and absurdity of our litigation system, can chuckle and say benignly: 'You're quite right. I sympathize with you, Mr. Joseph, but it's part of our *system* at the moment and I don't see we can alter it' – as if our legal system was written by God on marble tablets, and carried down from the top of Mount Snowdon by the Archbishop of Canterbury.

This, then, is the final ingredient of the lawyers' elixir, without which all their other ingredients would count for nothing: to have us believe that they are merely powerless cyphers, that the legal system wasn't actually *made* by anyone but somehow, like the weather and the Tower of London, it just happens to be there. And being there, there is nothing anyone can do about it.

And believe it we do. So whereas the case of the wealthy solicitor who evicted the poor man from his cottage (by exercising a buy-back clause in a contract) aroused a storm of indignation in the press – the case of Mrs. Whitehouse, who after ten years litigation failed in her negligence action to get compensation for her brain-damaged child, aroused none. The former was seen as an example of the bully boy abusing his power over the little guy; the latter was simply the workings of 'the system'. We cannot see that Mrs. Whitehouse, and the thousands and hundreds of thousands of people in a similar predicament, are equally the victims of the bully boy: that the legal system didn't just happen but has been *made*, and that it is the lawyers who have made it – who have carefully designed every particle of it, from the requirement that an injured person must prove negligence in Court in order to get compensation, down to the practice of the seller's solicitor, on completion, handing over an *undertaking* to send the receipt for the paid-off mortgage rather than the actual receipt itself; from the rule that only a barrister instructed by a solicitor may argue a case in the High Court, down to the last wodge of verbiage on the local search form.

In particular, we cannot see that because the lawyers have been allowed to make the system, and because they are no less mercenary than any other group of men, the occasions when they have decided that we need their services are determined not by the amount of *law* but by the amount of *money* involved. So they dictate that we need their services when we buy a house, when we sell a house, when we get a mortgage, when we pay off a mortgage, when we make a will, when we die (and someone has to administer our estate), when we get divorced (and our estate has to be divided), when we are seriously injured in an accident. In the latter event we are possibly entitled to a large sum by way of compensation. Accordingly the lawyers dictate that in order to obtain our entitlement, we must employ not one but *two* lawyers (solicitor and barrister). In the case of a very serious accident, possibly entitling us to a *very* large sum, we must employ not two but *three* lawyers (solicitor, barrister and Queen's Counsel).

But more important, because we cannot see that the legal system has been made by the lawyers, *we cannot see that the same conflict of interest which obtains between the manufacturer and his customer applies equally to the lawyer and* his *customer*. We understand that whereas the customer wants a car or a pair of socks to last for ever, the manufacturer doesn't want to *make* a car or a pair of socks which lasts for ever, but would prefer his product to fall to bits after a couple of years. But it seems that we cannot understand that whereas the house-buyer wants an efficient conveyancing system, and the accident victim wants an efficient compensation system, the lawyers do not want to *make* an efficient conveyancing or accident compensation system. And that as the lawyers have been allowed to dictate the system, the resulting system suits *their* interests, not the customer's interests.*

So Peter Goldman, one of the Royal Commissioners on Legal Services, can put his name to a report which states that for the purchaser's solicitor to submit a standard form of enquiries to the seller's solicitor, and another standard form of enquiries to the Local Council, is 'generally and in our view properly regarded as part of the normal service to be provided in a conveyancing transaction.' (21.20.) But at the end of the report, in a Note of Dissent, Mr. Goldman can ask the apparently despairing question: 'Why should the actual processes of buying, selling and moving home remain so preposterously cumber-

---

* Significantly, in all the debate on whether the solicitors' conveyancing monopoly should be relaxed, no mention is made of the actual conveyancing *system*, and neither have there been any proposals to alter it in any significant way.

some and diabolically expensive?' (ND 3.4). Mr. Goldman cannot understand that the processes of buying, selling and moving home are so preposterously cumbersome and diabolically expensive because it suits the lawyers, who have devised them, that they should be so. And if Mr. Goldman, erstwhile *director of the Consumers' Association*, cannot understand that this truism applies to the legal system in the same way that it applies to any other commercial enterprise, small wonder that few of his less well endowed fellow countrymen understand it either.

Mr. Goldman is not concerned to express an individual opinion on personal injury litigation – the process whereby an injured person tries to prove negligence in a Court of law as a pre-condition to being entitled to compensation. But presumably his epithets 'preposterously cumbersome and diabolically expensive' are equally applicable to a litigation system in which the average time for a case to come to the High Court is four years (as found by the Royal Commissioners); and the legal costs frequently exceed the amount of compensation in question. And again we cannot see that the litigation system is preposterously cumbersome and diabolically expensive for the same reason as the conveyancing system is: it has been made by the lawyers – and the more cumbersome and expensive the procedures they make, the richer they become.

We have no difficulty in understanding that the more overmanning and restrictive practices there are in industry, the happier are the unions. But we cannot see that the more inefficient our legal system is, the happier are our lawyers; and that conversely, a reasonably efficient system of house transfer and accident compensation *would have no use for lawyers at all.* Shaw's famous aphorism 'All professions are conspiracies against the laity' is quoted with an approving snigger by every intellectual in town, but no-one actually *believes* it.

Because our critical faculties have first been deadened by our educators, then turned to stone by the Medusa-like mystique of the professional, we have let the lawyers foist on us a legal system of scarcely believable inefficiency and absurdity with hardly a protest.

Moreover, once in operation, the system grows its own Medusa head.

I watch the various members of the staff as they come into my room, and proceed to unpack and then repack the office safe in search of a particular package. Ten minutes pass; twenty minutes. I watch the pile of ill-assorted packages on the nearby table growing, as the great iron cavern gradually empties. Yet it never occurs to any of these people – presumably endowed with normal intelligence – to suggest partitioning the safe and indexing the bundles. You don't query the system laid down by authority, because there is nothing you can do about it; and because there is nothing you can do about it, not only do you not query it – you don't even *think* about it.

So while an unjust or absurd individual will be challenged, an unjust or absurd system will as like as not be accepted without a murmur. If when you repay Mr. Blank the money you borrowed he demands an extra £25 for writing out a receipt, you let out a scream of rage. But when you repay your Building Society mortgage, and the Building Society in accordance with its *rules* passes the deeds to its solicitor, who charges you £25 for the receipt, you pay the extra levy with barely a shrug. After all, that's the system. If a national newspaper carried a story of Mr. Blink, arbitrator, who charged £1,500 for giving his decision in a dispute involving £1,000, he would be nosed out by our consumer vigilantes and pelted with rotten tomatoes. But *The Times* can devote a leader to Mrs. Whitehouse's case in which £100,000 was at issue, and laconically let fall the fact that the legal costs came to over £150,000 – and no-one bothers to raise an eyebrow. After all, we all *know* that Court cases cost a lot of money. That's the *system.*

* * * * * *

'Someone's got to be trusted. Let it be the Judges!' exclaims Lord Denning in his Dimbleby Lecture (November 20 1980). 'Someone's got to be trusted. Let it be the professionals', echoes the British public. 'Money making is thought of as a secondary rather than a primary focus of the professional man's interest', writes the Times leader-writer (October 22 1966).

But why should putting a wig on a man's head or letters after his name make him any more trustworthy, or any less mercenary?

For a child, paradise on earth is a place where he can stretch out his hand and have as many sweets as he likes. As the child grows into an adult it seems that his dream alters only in one particular. For sweets substitute money. A nation of fiddlers was how a 'Man Alive' programme once described us, and I opened by recounting some of the little tricks man gets up to, to cheat his fellows – the barman who dips the rim of a glass in a saucer of gin, so the 'gin and orange' although smelling authentic in fact contains only the latter beverage; the car repairer who demonstrates that the customer's perfectly serviceable clutch is slipping and therefore needs replacing; the plumber who pretends he has renewed a section of pipe behind the bath, when all he has done is to give the stopcock a couple of twists, and so on.

But these swindlers are the opportunists. They live by their wits, which means they live precariously. And although some of them are obviously successful in amassing large amounts of money – e.g. the fraudsters who juggle around with limited companies, and measure their gains in hundreds of thousands – they are essentially the *unsuccessful* type of swindler. For what use is a hundred thousand pounds in the bank to someone who fears the postman's tread, the knock on the door; or fearing neither has yet forfeited his self respect? The successful swindler doesn't have to swindle. He merely operates a *system* which has been carefully set up for him, which gives him the same financial rewards without the attendant disadvantages.

So paradise on earth for a taxi driver would not simply be a place where there were perpetual conventions of blind foreigners waiting to be driven from London Airport to the Dorchester Hotel. For a taxi driver to attain his notion of paradise on earth, an elaborate transport *system* would have to be evolved.

And if over the past two hundred years there had been a hundred cab drivers in Parliament at any given time, instead of a hundred lawyers (and a cab driver was a permanent member of the Cabinet); and if judges were appointed from cab drivers, instead of being appointed from lawyers; and if cab drivers had the power to decide which cases would come to Court and which would founder; and if all material had to be vetted by cab drivers before it was published or broadcast; and if we had been brought up to believe that those in the transport business should be regarded with special respect in view of their superior skill and learning, and that British taxis are the envy of the civilized world – then I daresay we would have that elaborate transport system. . .

Apart from walking (which would be very dangerous since there would be no pavements), taxis would be the only available means of transport in the large towns. The taxi driver would have to be accompanied by a *navigator*, that is, someone well versed in the geography of the town, whose job it is to direct the driver. Because oral directions are liable to be misunderstood, these directions have to be in *writing* – so that on a given signal from the navigator, the driver draws into the curb and awaits the navigator's written directions. The reason for dividing the functions of driving and directing, and having a different person dealing with each, is that it enables the driver to concentrate on his driving without having to worry about finding his way. That at any rate is the theory. In practice it means that the expense of the journey is doubled, the time it takes is trebled, and the possibility of error is increased a hundredfold. This is because whereas either driver or navigator on his own might well be capable of reaching the destination with the minimum of bother, together – and each relying on the other – they stand a good chance of making a hash of it. No matter. It is the taxi drivers' and navigators' interests which are paramount, not their customers'.

For a journey of over seven miles, the driver has to be one of an elite body of *senior drivers* (called peaks because of the distinguishing peak of their cap), who not only has to be directed by a navigator, *but accompanied by an ordinary driver as well.* On such occasions the ordinary driver does nothing. A senior driver commands substantially increased fares; and an ordinary driver becomes a senior driver on appointment by the Minister of Transport – himself an ex-taxi driver, and a permanent member of the Cabinet.

The customer may hire a taxi only through a navigator (whose offices are in the more salubrious part of the town), who in turn has to agree the journey and the fare with the driver's manager, called a *negotiator*. There is one negotiator for every dozen drivers, and it is he who decides what journeys his drivers undertake, and for what fares – taxi drivers being such an exalted body of men, they may not discuss their fares with their customers. In fact the customer may not communicate directly with the driver at all, but all communication has to be through the navigator.

Taxis have to be vehicles of a particular design, the number of which are rigidly controlled. Thus the fares are kept high. It is not unusual for a busy 'peak' to earn £1,000 a day when his journeys can be dovetailed, and the ordinary driver who accompanies him is paid a sum equal to half the peak's fee. When the ordinary driver is himself driving, he can earn four or five hundred pounds on a good day. The negotiator's fee is an additional 10% of the total fares of all his drivers – thus the negotiator often gets more than the individual drivers whom he manages. Navigators' fees, on the other hand, are significantly less; but to make up for this, they have acquired the exclusive right to fill in road licence application forms for private cars (permitted outside the towns), for which their authorized fee is £50 per application.* The navigators claim that they have to charge such high fees for this routine clerical work, to subsidize their unprofitable taxi work, so that all in all a reasonably busy navigator earns about the same as a reasonably busy ordinary driver.

Taxi drivers cannot be sued for breach of contract (because they cannot *make* a contract with their client); nor for negligence (because that would make them excessively cautious, and so be against public interest). There was an occasion when someone did try to sue a taxi driver for negligence, but he was given short shrift by the judges – who of course are themselves ex-drivers. Giving judgment, one judge observed that he had only brought the action 'to embarrass the taxi drivers for his own selfish and opinionated ends'; and another judge stated: 'it is of great public importance that taxi drivers should perform their duties free from the fear that any disgruntled client may subsequently involve them in costly litigation. . .Our transport system has gained the admiration of the whole civilized world. There is no country in which urban transport is operated more efficiently or speedily.'

Taxi fares, being so expensive, are beyond an ordinary person's means. Accordingly there is a scheme whereby people can apply for a permit which entitles them to have their taxi fares paid for by the State – either in full, or more usually subject to a weekly contribution from the permit holder, depending on his capital and income. These permits, which are renewable quarterly, are granted or refused by a committee of drivers and navigators. The scheme is complicated, requiring an army of clerical workers to operate it.

---

* Incidentally, there is currently some talk about other 'suitably qualified' persons being permitted to fill in these application forms, as well.

As mentioned, there are generally a hundred or so taxi drivers and navigators in Parliament, and I notice that the current Prime Minister and a third of her cabinet are taxi drivers. Prince Charles is an honorary member of the Council of Navigators; and the President of the Navigators' Society, who holds office for a year, is invariably rewarded with a knighthood, as is the President of the Drivers' Association.

Such would be a taxi driver's notion of paradise on earth.

And for a lawyer, paradise on earth would be an equivalent legal system. Perhaps something on the following lines:

Someone who is injured in an accident (any sort of accident, not just a road accident) is entitled to compensation *only if he proves in a Court of law that the accident was caused by someone else's fault.* To do this he has to consult a certain kind of lawyer called a *solicitor.* The solicitor in turn consults another kind of lawyer called a *barrister*, to whom he relays the facts as given him, with instructions to *advise.* If the barrister's advice is that there is a reasonable chance of proving negligence (fault), in due course the solicitor will send him further instructions to draft a writ and Statement of Claim. This is the document which initiates the Court action, and summarizes – in legal phraseology – the facts whereby the injured party (plaintiff) is alleging that his injuries were caused by the fault of the other party (defendant). When drafted, the plaintiff's solicitor will send it to the defendant's solicitor, who will send it to another barrister, who will draw up a Defence, a document which – in legal phraseology – *denies* that the plaintiff's injuries were caused by the defendant's fault. On top of the Statement of Claim and Defence will gradually grow a mound of further Court documents – request for further and better particulars of Statement of Claim, request for further and better particulars of Defence, further and better particulars of Statement of Claim, further and better particulars of Defence, and so on – each of which documents will be drafted by the parties' barristers on the written instructions from their respective 'instructing solicitors'. Apart from the procedural documents, the solicitor will also instruct the barrister to advise on each new development, as the action proceeds – e.g. whether a certain document should be disclosed, whether the 'further and better particulars' supplied are adequate, what evidence will be required at the trial, and so on.

So it is the solicitor's job to elicit the facts from his client, get the available evidence, and communicate with the other party's solicitor. It is the barrister's job to draft the various procedural documents, advise his 'instructing solicitor' when requested to do so, and finally argue the case in Court. The client may not communicate directly with his barrister, only with his solicitor.

The reason for the division of these functions, and for having a different person dealing with each, is that it gives the client the best possible service in that he consults a local solicitor as he would a 'general practitioner'; and that solicitor, however humble his practice, has access to the finest 'consultant' in the land. That, at any rate, is the theory. In practice it means that the expense of the case is doubled, the time it takes to get to Court is cubed, and the possibility that the crucial facts will never come to light when the case does eventually come to Court is increased a hundredfold. This is because if one person had sole conduct of the case, he would probably understand the issues and bring out the crucial facts. But when two people are dealing with the case, neither of whom has control of it, but the first is able to act only on advice from the second, and the second gives advice only when instructed to do so by the first; and when the one who presents the case in Court is not allowed to communicate with the client, or get the evidence, but has to rely on whatever facts and evidence the other feeds him; and when the two correspond with each other by means of formalistic written communications, with weeks and months between each such communication; and when an average of *four years* separates the accident from the trial – then there is a good chance that the crucial facts will be lost in the formalistic paperwork and ritual procedures which the system spawns. No matter. It is the lawyers' interests which are paramount, not their clients'.

When finally there are no further documents to be drawn up and exchanged, and no further questions to be advised on by the barristers, and no further procedural points to be settled by 'Masters' Summonses', the plaintiff's solicitor will ask the Court office to fix a date for the trial. And when that day finally arrives, the parties, and their solicitors, and their barristers, and their witnesses, and their expert witnesses, congregate at the High Court. And the plaintiff's barrister will try to show that the accident which happened four years ago, and which caused the plaintiff's injuries, *was* the defendant's fault; and the defendant's barrister will try to show that it *wasn't*. Only the barristers are allowed to address the Court.

If the plaintiff's injuries are severe and his claim correspondingly substantial, or if it is an important case from the point of view of the defendant (who in effect will almost invariably be an *insurance company*), the plaintiff or defendant or both will be advised to employ a Queen's Counsel. Queen's Counsel are an elite body of barristers (called 'silks' because of their silken gown), and command substantially increased fees. When a Queen's Counsel is engaged, he not only has to be instructed by a solicitor, but attended by an ordinary barrister who will sit behind him, *doing and saying nothing throughout the trial*. Behind the mute ordinary barrister will sit the equally mute 'instructing solicitor'. Next to the solicitor will sit his clerk. At the other end of the benches will sit the equivalent trio or quartet of lawyers appearing for the other party.

At the end of the day (or more probably three or four days, because barristers are much given to quoting at interminable length from judgements of previous cases) the judge will decide either that the plaintiff's barrister *has* shown that the accident was the defendant's fault, in which case he will order the defendant to pay the plaintiff an appropriate sum to compensate him for his injuries; or that he *hasn't*, in which case the plaintiff gets nothing except a bill for his own and the defendant's legal costs. These costs will be not only for the trial, but for all the pre-trial work and documentation since the action began; and they can easily exceed the amount of compensation in question. The total bill for a personal injury case, where both parties employ a Queen's Counsel, would be in the region of £20,000.

The solicitor engages the barrister through the *barrister's clerk*. The clerk is the barrister's manager, there being one to each set of barrister's offices (*chambers*), and it is the clerk who decides which cases his barristers will handle, and negotiates the fee with the instructing solicitor. Barristers being such an exalted body of men, they must be spared having to discuss such a sordid subject as money – and in fact a directive from their governing body stipulates that it is *not* advisable for them to spend any time in the clerk's room, where the bargaining – and juggling around with cases – takes place.

Barristers must have offices (chambers) in certain prescribed buildings (Inns of Court). Thus by physically controlling the amount of office space from which they may practise, the number of practising barristers can be controlled, and their fees kept correspondingly high. It is not unusual for a Queen's Counsel to earn £1,000 a day. The ordinary barrister who sits behind him (doing nothing) is paid a sum equal to *half* the Queen's Counsel's fee. When an ordinary barrister is himself conducting the case he can earn four or five hundred pounds on a good day. The clerk's fee is 10% of the total fees of all the barristers in his chambers – so the clerk often gets more than the individual barristers under his managment. Solicitors' fees for Court work are significantly less. However to compensate them, they have had (for the past 180 years) a monopoly of *conveyancing*, whereby for the few hours routine clerical work involved in a house sale and purchase (usually carried out by their unqualified clerks) they charge between £600 and £1,000. Thus all in all, a reasonably successful solicitor gets about the same as a reasonably successful ordinary barrister.

Barristers cannot be sued for breach of contract (because any contract is between the client and the solicitor); nor may they be sued for negligence in respect of their performance in Court (because that would be against public interest). Someone did once try to sue a barrister for negligence, but his action was thrown out by the judges – who are themselves ex-barristers. Giving judgment, one judge observed that the plaintiff had only brought the action 'to embarrass the barristers' profession for his own selfish and opinionated ends'; and another judge stated: 'It is of great public importance that barristers should perform their duties free from the fear that any disgruntled litigant may subsequently involve them in costly litigation. Our system of justice has gained the admiration of the whole civilized world. There is no country in which justice is administered more impartially, efficiently or speedily.'

Solicitors, who of course do not argue the case in Court, can be sued for their pre-trial work. But provided they take the precaution of sending the barrister 'instructions to advise' at every turn, and acting only in accordance with such advice, that will generally afford a complete defence.

Because the legal costs of bringing a case to Court are beyond an ordinary person's means, a legal aid scheme has been set up. Under this scheme an injured person whose capital and income are below a certain limit, and who has a reasonable case, can bring his case to Court in the normal way, and the State will pay his legal costs. Whether an injured person *does* have a reasonable case meriting legal aid (and what conditions will be attached to it if granted, and whether once granted it will be withdrawn at any time) will be decided by a Committee of solicitors and barristers.

There are generally a hundred solicitors and barristers in Parliament at any given time, and I notice in passing that the current Prime Minister and a third of her cabinet are barristers. Prince Charles is an honorary member of the Council of the Law Society; and the President of the Law Society, who holds office for a year, invariably gets a knighthood, as does the Chairman of the Bar Council.

Because we retain our critical faculties in our dealings with the taxi drivers, they cannot realize their notion of paradise on earth. Because we jettison our critical faculties in our dealings with professional man, and because of the various accidents which give *legal* professional man his peculiar advantages, the lawyers can. As my reader will have gathered, the above description of our legal system is not fantasy but fact.

* * * * * *

In the first part of this book I have tried to explain why we have the legal system we do. In the second part I will show what it can mean for those people, having already suffered at best a calamity, at worst a tragedy, who inadvertently get caught up in it.

In 1982 in England and Wales there were 85,673 deaths and serious injuries on the roads; and the yearly overall total of deaths and serious injuries caused by accidents (outside the home) is probably three times that figure. Yet although we live in a consumer conscious age, with reports on everything from tomato soup to holidays in the Dordogne, not very much has been written on our litigation system from the *consumer's* point of view. That is to say, not very much has been written on what actually happens when the victim of one of these accidents (or his dependants) consults a lawyer with a view to claiming compensation. Such articles and reports as there have been are written in general terms, and describe the theory rather than the practice. And although there are a few works which do criticize the system* they are written from the academic point of view, and treat 'the client' as an abstract and rather shadowy figure.

Let's remedy this by looking at some true and – as I shall show – typical case histories: and see how our legal system which is 'admired and emulated throughout the modern world' actually works for the man in the street, or for the man with an unconscious child in the street.

---

* E.g. *Lawyers and the Public Interest*, by Michael Zander; *The Bar on Trial*, edited by Robert Hazell.

Part Two

What the legal system can mean for accident victims who inadvertently get caught up in it

6 *The case of Mr. Perkins*

Mr. Perkins was a bandsaw operator employed by a large heavy engineering company. His work – which he had been doing for the previous seven years – was trimming 'castings'.

A bandsaw is rather like a giant chain saw mounted on the floor, with a vertical blade running through a hole in a metal table, on which the operator holds the material to be cut or trimmed. The metal table is therefore an integral part of the machine, equivalent to the base of a sewing machine. The castings were metal discs, one side flat the other curved, and each weighing about three pounds: and Mr. Perkins's job was to trim the surplus metal (left by the casting process) off the discs by slowly revolving each disc against the teeth of the rapidly downward-moving blade, while holding it firmly, flat side downwards, on the metal table with both hands.

On 3rd July 1973, as Mr. Perkins was working a disc, it spun uncontrolled into the path of the moving blade, which hurled it – curved side downwards – back onto the metal table, from which it rebounded, striking him under the chin. He was knocked out, the base of his skull was fractured; and he claims that the accident left him with permanent pain in the region of his left ear, and subject to dizzy spells which made him unable to continue with his previous work.

Mr. Perkins's explanation for the accident was that sometime previously the metal table top had been broken in two by a forklift truck, and had been repaired by welding the two sections together and bolting a metal plate underneath. This had left one part of the working surface of the table top slightly higher than the other. But more important, the bolt holes had gone right *through* the table. Although plugged with weld, the weld had worked loose with the vibration, leaving *several holes in the working surface in front of the blade*. The bits of metal adhering to the discs he was turning against the saw blade would catch in these holes from time to time, causing the disc to stick on the table. On this occasion a particularly obdurate disc he was working got stuck, and refused to budge. And when (wearing thick asbestos gloves as the job demanded) he applied more pressure to release it, it suddenly yielded and spun over *curved side downwards* into the path of the downward cutting edge of the saw – with the result as described.

So is Mr. Perkins entitled to compensation for his injuries, and his inability to continue in his job? Yes (say the rules), if he can prove in Court that they were caused by his employers' negligence; no (say the rules), if he can't. There are various definitions of negligence, but they all boil down to the single proposition: someone proves negligence if he shows that his injury was caused by someone else's *fault*.

Now although the extent of Mr. Perkins's injuries, being latent, are susceptible of dispute, the question of whether or not they were caused by someone else's fault is straightforward. *One simply has to look at the machine*. If indeed the table top did have holes in the working surface – as he claims – that would establish negligence on his employers' part almost beyond question. The bits of metal adhering to the discs he was trimming would obviously catch in these holes, thus making an already potentially dangerous job that much more dangerous; and the Court would almost certainly accept his account of the accident, and that his injuries were therefore caused by the *fault* of his employers in requiring him to work what was in effect a dangerous machine.

So in this case the question of negligence does not depend on any complicated legal points, nor even on any eye-witnesses' statements (in any event there *weren't* any eye-witnesses to the accident), but simply on whether the metal table top in question did or did not have holes in the working surface. One would not expect such a case to take seven years to come to Court, nor that Mr. Perkins would need to engage five successive firms of solicitors to get it to Court – unless perhaps one had some experience of our legal system, and the lawyers who operate it.

Now suppose that although the rules for getting compensation were the same (i.e. an injured person has to prove in Court that his accident was caused by someone else's fault), there were no such things as lawyers. The injured person would either argue his case himself; or else he would go to someone specializing in such work – not a lawyer, but someone having the same status, education and common sense as, say, a reasonably alert assistant manager of a surburban chain store.

What would happen if, on his discharge from hospital, Mr. Perkins consulted such a person – whom we will call *RAMS*? RAMS would telephone the employers and ask to inspect and photograph the metal table (with Mr. Perkins present to identify it), and also collect a couple of typical discs – to which the employers would agree, as a refusal would be tantamount to an admission that the machine was faulty. If the holes in the table top were as Mr. Perkins stated, RAMS would send a duplicate photograph to the employers and warn them to keep the machine intact. He would then issue a writ: and subject to getting medical evidence to support Mr. Perkins's claim that he is suffering unremitting pain and dizzy spells, and to give a prognosis,* RAMS would be ready to argue the case in Court. In fact, assuming the holes were as Mr. Perkins stated, as soon they saw RAMS meant business, the employers (or rather their *insurers*) would probably concede negligence; and either make Mr. Perkins an acceptable offer, or else merely dispute the extent of his injury and therefore the *amount* of compensation properly payable – in which event the case would go to Court, and the argument would be purely a medical one.

But, of course, a claim for personal injuries is of such importance that for the public's protection it may not be handled by an unqualified operator, but only by a professional lawyer – that is, someone who has passed examinations in law, and whose competence and probity are vouched for by his professional governing body.

So on his discharge from hospital Mr. Perkins consults his union's solicitors, and puts his case in their hands.

On 27th November 1973 they write to his erstwhile employers: 'I am acting for the above named in respect of his accident in the fettling department on 3rd July 1973. I am

* Mr. Perkins's hospital note states: 'Diagnosis concussion. Fracture base of skull.'

instructed to claim damages for negligence.' This letter the employers pass to their insurers.

It is important to remember that whereas the nominal defendant in a personal injury case is the employer, driver, or whoever, whose alleged negligence has caused the plaintiff's injury, the *real* defendant is almost invariably his insurance company, who will be liable to pay the actual compensation if awarded. And if it disputes the claim, the insurance company will instruct solicitors to contest it – nominally on behalf of the defendant but in fact on its *own* behalf. In other words, the defendant's insurance company is the substantive defendant, and the defendant himself is merely the shadow.

Now experienced insurers know exactly what to do with such a letter. Ignore it. Two and a half months later (February 7 1974) Mr. Perkins's solicitor writes a further letter, noting 'with some concern' that he has received no reply. This time the employers' insurers do reply, suggesting a discussion, which takes place three months later on May 24 1974. According to the solicitor's note, the insurance company's representative says that he has had a conflicting account of the accident, and wants to see the foreman – after which he will 'come back to me in the near future'. Two months later (July 19) the solicitor, having heard nothing meanwhile, asks the insurers whether they have completed their inquiries; and a month after that (August 13) the insurers reply that they have *not*, but hope to do so 'in the near future'. Further letter from Mr. Perkins's solicitor (November 19): 'I assume that your enquiries have now been completed and if so I look forward to hearing from you again.'

Discussion finally takes place on December 6 1974, when the insurance company's representative tells the solicitor that '*the foreman feels (sic) that the holes in the table top were behind the blade*'* (i.e. that they were not in the *working* surface and so could not have caused the accident). Nevertheless the insurers make an ex gratia offer of £100 in full settlement. In other words, the employers' insurers are saying that they do not accept that the accident was the employers' fault, and consequently they are not prepared to make any real offer of compensation. But notice how they string Mr. Perkins's solicitor along *for over a year* before actually saying so

* From this discussion it would seem that it is agreed that the table top *had* previously been broken in two, and that there *were* bolt holes going right through it.

– during which time the vital evidence can of course disappear. And notice how willingly his solicitor is strung along. Even then it apparently never occurs to him that if Mr. Perkins is saying that the holes in the metal table were in front of the blade, but the insurers are saying that the holes were behind the blade, all one has to do is to *look* at the thing and see who is right.

The solicitor then arranges for Mr. Perkins to be examined by his union's doctor, who (according to Mr. Perkins) seemed more interested in the bandsaw and the circumstances of the accident – asking such questions as 'Was the casting clamped to the table?' 'Was the saw moving when you were loading the castings on the table?' After a while Mr. Perkins bursts out angrily 'You're supposed to be giving me a medical examination, not questioning me about how I did my work.' The doctor notes in his report: 'Throughout the interview he was aggressively assertive, declaring that he had only come for an examination and not to answer questions.'

The doctor's report is unhelpful to Mr. Perkins: 'There is no evidence of remaining structural damage from the injury that I am told this man sustained on 3rd July 1973. I do not believe he has any disablement as a result.' In fact a year previously Mr. Perkins had been examined by the *insurers'* doctor, who had written a similar report; and the union's doctor stated that he had read, and was in agreement with, this earlier report – though who had sent it to him, or why, is not clear.

By July 1975 – two years after the accident – Mr. Perkins realizes his claim is getting nowhere. And after writing to his solicitor in robust terms, telling him what he thinks of him, he instructs other solicitors.

Solicitor No. 2 arranges for Mr. Perkins to be examined by another doctor, whose written opinion commences: 'I have examined the two previous medical reports in connection with the case and other papers, *including a letter written by Mr. Perkins to his previous solicitor* which indicates very clearly his aggressive and almost paranoeic (sic) attitude over his accident and its results.'

In other words, before the examination Mr. Perkins's new solicitor had not only sent the doctor the other two unfavourable doctors' reports, but also a copy of his client's intemperate letter dismissing his first solicitor (which presumably was in the file).

The reason could only be to show the doctor what an aggressive and unreasonable attitude Mr. Perkins had towards his accident, so that the doctor might report accordingly.

The doctor's conclusion, however, is more cagey: 'I cannot entirely dismiss the symptoms [unremitting pain] as hysterical, and it is just possible that there may have been some organic damage to the left temporo-mandibular joint which might trigger off such symptoms.' And he suggests that the opinion of Sir *XY*, leading authority on such matters, be obtained.

Rather curiously, Mr. Perkins's first solicitor (i.e. his union's solicitor whom he had dismissed) asks his second solicitor the present position of his case; and even more curiously, the second solicitor gives him all the details (including the fact that he intends to consult Sir *XY*). Solicitor No. 2 then writes to Sir *XY* with a copy of the latest doctor's report, and asks whether he will examine his client. Sir *XY* replies:

'I am very doubtful of this patient having any success in a legal action. Even if we accept the fact that he has a derangement of his mandibular joint, these are extremely common occurrences in people who have never had an accident. Therefore positive medical findings would be difficult in law to relate to his accident. I would of course see him, but I feel he is rather wasting his money.' Which is rather like saying of someone blinded in an accident: 'since many people go blind who have never had an accident, this person would find it difficult to prove that his blindness was due to his accident.' Notice that although he is a medical man and has not even seen Mr. Perkins, he nevertheless volunteers a *legal* opinion that Mr. Perkins will be unsuccessful in his legal action.

Solicitor No. 2 writes to Mr. Perkins: 'We enclose a copy of a letter we have today received from Sir *XY*. As you see, he states his doubts of your being successful in a legal action *and we must say that we agree*.' Mr. Perkins replies that the various medical specialists have all given conflicting opinions, and he instructs the solicitor to apply for legal aid and issue a writ without further delay. He concludes his letter even more pertinently: 'The faulty machine which caused the accident, and also the casting which hit me, *have never been examined* and I believe that anyone who is representing me should make some investigation about them.' But solicitors do not always appreciate their clients making pertinent points, and on receiving Mr. Perkins's letter Solicitor

No. 2 tells him that he is no longer prepared to act for him. He has had the case for almost a year, and it is now June 1976 – nearly three years since the accident.

So Mr. Perkins instructs Solicitor No. 3 – or rather his wife does on his behalf: 'We have been suffering extreme difficulties because he has not been able to do his regular job and the social security has not been kind to us . . . and I am very concerned over his present state of health. I am leaving this unfortunate case in your kind and sympathetic care.' In this letter she also tells the new solicitor that the machine in question has been sold to another company in the same town, whose name and address she gives him (which Mr. Perkins learned from one of his former workmates).

Solicitor No. 3 promptly issues a writ – which has to be done within three years of the accident, or the claim is barred.* And he also applies for legal aid. But although he knows that to get legal aid the applicant has to show some prima facie evidence of negligence, the solicitor makes no attempt to inspect the machine (or arrange for someone else to do so and give a report). Instead he sends the Legal Aid Committee copies of the *previous correspondence* between Mr. Perkins's first solicitor and the employers' insurers. Mr. Perkins's application for legal aid is consequently refused – on the grounds that this correspondence indicates that the employers maintain that the holes in the metal table were *behind* the blade (and so could not have caused the accident), '*and the applicant has not submitted any evidence to contradict this.*'

The solicitor writes to Mr. Perkins suggesting an appeal against the refusal, stating: 'We should have to answer this point in great detail.' Yet he *still* makes no attempt to inspect the machine. Consequently the appeal is dismissed for the same reason: 'You have not provided any evidence to confirm what you say about the work table having holes in the working surface. . . .

---

* I stated previously that the writ and Statement of Claim are drawn up by a barrister. This is true when they are incorporated in the same document. But when there is some urgency (as in this case when the time limit for issuing the writ is approaching), the writ may be issued separately – in which case it is drawn up by a solicitor, as it merely contains a dozen or so words setting out the *general* nature of the plaintiff's claim. And the *Statement of Claim*, which sets out the detailed facts whereby the plaintiff is alleging that his injuries were caused by the negligence of the defendant – which is invariably drawn up by a barrister – can follow any time up to a year later.

There is no further right of appeal.' Mr. Perkins has now instructed three solicitors in succession who apparently have not been able to grasp the scarcely complicated fact that if you are acting for someone who is bringing a negligence action, which turns on whether or not a certain metal table top had holes in the working surface, the first thing you must do is *inspect* – and arrange for someone to photograph – the table top in question.

The Legal Aid Committee's final refusal of Mr. Perkins's legal aid application was in October 1976. As he is not dropping the case he therefore has to pay the legal fees himself. He has already paid £50 (to cover the legal aid application) to his current solicitor, who now asks him for a further £300 – which he rather ambiguously states that he needs 'on account of costs and disbursements before the trial.' £350 in 1976 might be the equivalent of £700/£800 at the time of writing: not a large sum as legal fees go, but a hefty sum for an unemployed factory worker to find.

On receiving the £300 the solicitor delegates the case to his clerk, and the clerk instructs Counsel* to advise, and to draw up Statement of Claim. It is by such 'instructions' (which are always in writing) that the solicitor (or his clerk) relays the relevant facts to Counsel. The following is an extract:

> 'Mr. Perkins says that it was the table that caused the accident. It had been cut in half in a previous incident and then welded back together, with the result that it was unstable with many holes in it, and the right hand side was about ¼" higher than the left and was therefore not level. He asserts that this caused the casting to stick on the table, although the foreman says that the holes were behind the saw blade and therefore did not play any part in the accident. Mr. Perkins says that the holes were in front of the blade, but in any event he does not know whether it was the holes or the instability or unevenness of the table which actually caused the accident, or it may be a combination of all of them. The factory has since closed and Mr. Perkins believes the machine has been sold to Messrs X of [gives address], but it is not known whether they actually have this table in use. If they do not have it, the whereabouts of the table are now unknown.'

---

* 'Counsel' and 'barrister' are synonymous. Up to now I have used the word 'barrister' as it is more colloquial, but from now on I will use the word 'Counsel', which is how a solicitor describes him.

In due course Counsel drafts Statement of Claim; and at the same time gives a non-committal written opinion, of which the following is the nub:

> 'I can understand the importance of having a smooth even surface for rotating the casting as it is presented against the saw blade. However, I think the difficulty will be in satisfying the Court that the accident occurred in the manner described by the Plaintiff, particularly in the absence of any supporting evidence. As the machine has not been preserved by the Defendants, if they have any photographs they should be asked to reveal them forthwith. I regard the prospect of establishing liability [negligence] at no higher than 50%.'

Notice what has happened to a few simple unequivocal facts after being percolated through three not very interested legal gentlemen. Mrs. Perkins initially tells the solicitor in a letter that the machine in question has been sold to another company in the same town, whose name and address she gives him. The solicitor hands the file to his clerk, probably saying something like: 'The defendants have sold the machine to another company but whether or not they've still got it I don't know.' The clerk tells Counsel: 'Mr. Perkins *believes* the machine has been sold to Messrs X of — but it is not known whether they actually have this table in use. If they do not have it, the whereabouts of the table are now unknown.' Counsel – no doubt skimming through his instructions – evidently understands this to mean that the whereabouts of the machine *are* now unknown, because he states that the difficulty is the *absence of any supporting evidence*, and suggests that Mr. Perkins's erstwhile employers should be asked if they have any *photographs* of the machine.

Then again, Mr. Perkins knows exactly how the accident occurred, and at the outset he gave his solicitor a written statement:

> 'I held each casting with both hands flat on the table, turning it anti-clockwise against the blade to remove the excess metal. Some three years before my accident a forklift truck damaged the machine table and in fact broke it in half. Following this the two sections were welded together. Furthermore, holes were drilled to join the two broken parts together by means of a plate underneath. There were a number of these bolt holes in

the machine table in the area where the workman operated, on which the castings would catch from time to time. This particular casting had a sharp piece of metal protruding from it, which caught in one of the holes on the machine table. On trying to release it, it suddenly sprang up, hit the blade, rebounded and hit me on my chin.'

This unequivocal statement becomes, in the clerk's Instructions to Counsel: 'Mr. Perkins says that the holes were in front of the blade, but in any event he does not know whether it was the holes or the instability or unevenness of the table which actually caused the accident, or it may be a combination of all of them' – which if true would make his case far more difficult.

Mr. Perkins's case is basically simple. He claims that his accident was caused by the presence of holes in the working surface of the table of the machine he was required to use. But notice how in the hands of his lawyers, this simple situation has become hopelessly confused and complicated; and notice in particular how the obvious and immediate requirement – to inspect and photograph the table top – has somehow got lost.

To understand why this happens one has to understand the nature of a solicitor's office.

The primary purpose of a solicitor's office, like any other commercial enterprise, is to make money. Mr. Perkins, an unemployed factory worker who has dismissed one firm of solicitors and has been dismissed by another, is not the most inviting of commercial prospects. In fact he represents the bottom of the market. Nevertheless, solicitors don't like refusing work, and if legal aid can be obtained Mr. Perkins's case is jacked up to the lower middle market. Unfortunately legal aid, if granted, is not retrospective but covers only *future* work. Thus the legal costs of making the actual legal aid application have to be paid by the client himself. Moreover in this case the writ has to be issued immediately, else the claim will be barred. So the solicitor initially takes £50 from Mr. Perkins – which would probably be as much as he could immediately find. Now £50 (perhaps the equivalent of £100 today) does not buy much legal work, and would just about cover the initial interview with the solicitor (who at that time charged £25 an hour for his time), issuing the writ and Court fee, and filling in the legal aid application form. It would certainly not cover, in addition, inspecting and reporting on the table top – for which a solicitor would normally instruct a third party, as he would not reckon to visit a factory in the outskirts of the town himself. So the solicitor submits the legal aid application *without* a report on the table top, no doubt thinking he has done his best in the circumstances, or more probably not thinking very much about the matter at all.

When the legal aid application – and the appeal – fail, the case is irredeemably at the bottom of the market. Nevertheless the solicitor cannot very well refuse to continue to act for Mr. Perkins. So he takes £300 on account of costs (probably the most Mr. Perkins can scrape together), and hands over the case to his clerk.

Now litigation files – even those on which little progress has been made – tend to accumulate masses of documents; and the longer the case goes on, the more documents there are. This particular file when I collected it, and presumably when the clerk took it over, was the typical jumble of loose letters, statements, industrial tribunal claims forms, pay slips, legal aid forms etc., in no sort of order, some of which had inexplicably been copied half a dozen times. Of course if the clerk was alert, able and intelligent he would sort the file out, separate the relevant from the irrelevant, put the correspondence in date order and clip it together, read it all through (starting with Mr. Perkins's statement of how the accident happened); and he would then realize that the first thing to do is to inspect the machine table top. But then if he was alert, able and intelligent he probably would not be a solicitor's clerk in the first place – who isn't paid very much, and can never be more than a go-between between client and Counsel, however able he is. So the clerk doesn't sort the file out or read it through, but probably relies on his employer's verbal instructions, when handing him the file.

Having worked in several solicitors' offices myself, and having taken over from my various principals several similarly 'down market' litigation files, I can readily imagine the conversation: 'I'd like you to take this one over. Factory accident case. We're acting for the employee. Claims that when he was trimming some castings one of them flew up and hit him, because the table he was working on had been broken in two and was unstable. You'll find a statement somewhere in the file. You'll see he's already had two firms of solicitors before us. Legal aid was refused because of insufficient evidence of negligence. I think you'll find the defendants have sold the machine to another company, but whether or not they've still got it I don't know. Frankly, I don't think much of his chances on the evidence, but he insists on going on, and we've got £300 on account which will cover us for the time being. Anyway, now we're in funds you'd better take Counsel's opinion, and get him to draft Statement of Claim.'

So when the clerk states in his Instructions to Counsel: 'Mr. Perkins. . .does not know whether it was the holes or the instability or unevenness of the table which actually caused the accident, or it may be a combination of all of them', Mr. Perkins knows precisely what caused the accident. It is the *clerk*, who has never seen Mr. Perkins and has not read the file properly, who does not know.

Two weeks after getting Counsel's opinion, the clerk sends the defendants' solicitors* the Statement of Claim (which has been drafted by Counsel). And pursuant to Counsel's advice, he asks them whether their clients have got any *photographs* of the machine. A month later they reply – not altogether surprisingly – that they have not.

Meanwhile Mr. Perkins, who was sent a copy of Counsel's opinion, suggests to his solicitor (as he had suggested to his previous solicitor) that he should look at the machine for himself. And on 27th January 1977 the clerk writes to the defendants' solicitors: 'We believe your clients know the whereabouts of the table, and will you therefore let us have facilities to inspect the same.' A curious letter this, because Mrs. Perkins had already told the solicitor, and the solicitor's clerk had in turn told Counsel, the name and address of the company which had bought the machine from the defendants. Anyway let's trace the milestones of this particular marathon, from the time when Mr. Perkins's solicitor's clerk first tumbles to the idea that the machine, with its allegedly holey table top, should be inspected (27th January 1977, seven months after his firm took over the case), to when such inspection actually takes place.

27th January 1977. Solicitor's clerk writes to defendants' solicitors asking for facilities to inspect machine.

2nd February. Defendants' solicitors reply, giving name and address of company which bought machine (which solicitor's clerk already knew), and state that the company is agreeable to an inspection.

---

* The insurers appointed solicitors to act for the defendants after the writ was served.

11th March. Solicitor's clerk writes to Mr. Perkins asking when it will be convenient for him to view the machine, to which Mr. Perkins replies 'any Wednesday afternoon' (having now got a temporary job).

19th April. Solicitor's clerk writes to Mr. Perkins, stating that the defendants' insurers have increased their offer from £100 to £500, plus all his legal costs, which he urges Mr. Perkins to accept: 'This offer was arrived at after much negotiation and argument on our part, and in our opinion is a very sound offer indeed and ought to be accepted to save the time, trouble and expense of going to Court on an action which Counsel has intimated you may not win at all.' (Counsel's opinion, of course, was on the assumption that the machine was *unavailable.*) No mention is made in this letter of the proposed inspection, but notice that the improved offer comes when an inspection of the machine seems imminent. Mr. Perkins refuses offer.*

2nd June. Solicitor's clerk writes to defendants' solicitors: 'We now wish to inspect the machine with the assistance of *our engineer* and a photographer. We believe you have no objection, but please confirm that you are agreeable to this before arrangements are made for a mutually convenient inspection.' Another curious letter. The defendants' solicitors have already indicated that they have no objection. In any case, as the machine is now neither owned by them nor on their premises, the defendants' permission is unnecessary.

16th June. Defendants' solicitors reply that it must be a joint inspection with a representative of their firm, and their clients' engineers, present. They also ask the name of the engineer whom the plaintiff proposes to instruct.

17th June. Solicitor's clerk contacts a firm of *consulting engineers* with a view to them inspecting the machine when a convenient appointment can be made.

July/August. The date which the solicitor's clerk suggests clashes with the engineer's holiday; the date which the engineer suggests is inconvenient for the defendants' solicitor, and so on.

13th September 1977. The learned and professional gentlemen finally congregate at the given address to see whether the metal

---

* Most personal injury cases are, in fact, 'settled out of Court'. That is, at any time before the case actually comes to Court the defendant makes an offer which the plaintiff accepts in full settlement of his claim, and withdraws his legal action.

table top of the bandsaw, which Mr. Perkins was operating when he met with his accident over four years previously, had holes in the working surface. And they find (surprise, surprise) that the original metal table top has been replaced with a new one.

Apparently at some unspecified time after the present owners bought the machine from the defendants, a mobile crane had dropped a heavy load onto the table, damaging it beyond repair, so a new steel plate table top had been fitted.

The engineer instructed by Mr. Perkins's solicitor, on his behalf, nevertheless gives his report:

> 'We were unable to inspect a casting of the type your client was trimming at the time of his accident, but according to his statement which you sent with your letter of instruction, we understand your client alleges that the casting he was trimming jammed in a hole in the surface of the table. We are clearly unable to comment on the condition of the table since as enunciated *it was not available for inspection and has been destroyed*. The present owners, however, agree that it had been welded together. Accepting your client's description that it was full of various holes, we would readily agree that this would give rise to difficulties in offering the component to the saw blade. . .but we cannot say that its condition is likely to induce the ejection of components. . .and we equally cannot say that this gave rise to a forseeable risk of injury in the manner which befell your client. Whilst it is conceivable that the component may be ejected, it must be borne in mind that this could occur in a multitude of directions only a few of which would give rise to injury. Accordingly on our understanding of the circumstances of the accident we would not in this respect consider the defendants to have been negligently responsible for your client's misfortune, but that it ought properly to be attributed to pure mischance.'

Notice how, although the engineer admits he has not seen the faulty table top, nor any of the castings, he nevertheless takes it upon himself to give a *legal* opinion that Mr. Perkins's employers were not negligent, and a fatuous legal opinion at that* – just as

---

* Stripped of its highfaluting language, the gist of the engineer's opinion seems to be that as there are so many directions in which a casting rebounding on the metal table could fly up *without* hitting the operator, the fact that on this occasion it *did* hit the operator was just bad luck, and not due to the employers' fault in providing a faulty table.

the learned consultant Sir *XY*, without having seen Mr. Perkins, volunteered his *legal* opinion that he had no case.

As stated, the reason given why the original metal table top was not available for inspection – and mentioned in the engineer's report – was that a mobile crane had dropped a heavy load on it, damaging it beyond repair. Mr. Perkins's solicitor (who now takes the case back from his clerk) makes no enquiry into this strange mishap, but in a letter dated November 8 1977 renews his efforts to get Mr. Perkins to accept the defendants' insurers' offer, and abandon his legal action:

> 'Unfortunately the table in question, which no doubt contributed to the accident, is no longer available and was not available for inspection on 13th September 1977. The defendants do, however, admit that the table had been welded together. Enclosed is a copy of the report and opinion of the Consulting Engineer *who is an extremely experienced man and his opinion is highly regarded*. . .You will see that in his opinion the circumstances of this accident were not reasonably forseeable* by your employers, and if that is correct they could not be held to be negligent. In those circumstances we must advise you that we do not consider that your prospects of success are very good and. . .we have no evidence to support your case save your own evidence. Therefore we must advise you that the offer of £500 and your costs is one which you should accept, because we feel that the likelihood of your succeeding is remote, and you may recover nothing at all and be ordered to pay your own costs and the costs of the defendants which will undoubtedly exceed £1000. We repeat that it is our advice that you should accept the offer of £500 and costs.'

And he writes Mr. Perkins three further letters, repeating this advice. While it must remain a matter of conjecture why the medical consultant and the engineer – the two experts whom Mr. Perkins's solicitors consulted on his behalf – seem to be so anxious to dissuade him from continuing his legal action, there are cogent reasons why his own solicitor should be. The first is common to all down-market personal injury cases: if the plaintiff

---

* Academic lawyers define negligence in terms of whether the accident was 'reasonably foreseeable' by the defendant, but this is only another way of defining *fault*. E.g. if a car driver caused an accident because his brakes unaccountably failed, you can say either that he was not negligent because the accident was not reasonably foreseeable, or because it was not his fault.

accepts the defendants' insurers' offer, a bothersome not very profitable case magically becomes a straightforward profitable one – because the insurers' offer invariably includes, in addition, payment of *all the plaintiff's legal costs*. Secondly, if the case goes to Court the solicitor's mishandling of it might come out, and he might – horror of horrors – be publicly criticised by the judge. And now that the original table top has been destroyed, Mr. Perkins's solicitor has an even more compelling reason: he risks being sued for negligence in that he did not inspect the machine until *fifteen months after taking over the case* – by which time the vital evidence had disappeared.

However, Mr. Perkins is even less inclined to give up. He has the layman's obstinate faith in British Justice, believing that whatever difficulties and delays he has encountered, if only he can get his case before a *British Judge* the truth must emerge, and he will be awarded proper compensation for his shattered life. Accordingly he instructs his solicitor to bring the case to trial. The solicitor demands a further sum on account of costs. And when Mr. Perkins reminds him of his earlier letter indicating that the £300 (which he paid) would be sufficient to take the case to trial, and urges him to take some positive action, the solicitor tells him to get other solicitors to act for him. It is now March 1978, nearly five years since the accident.

Mr. Perkins instructs Solicitor No. 4 who asks Solicitor No. 3 for the papers. But Solicitor No. 3 refuses to hand them over until his bill – in which he is claiming a further £265 – is paid. Indeed he threatens to sue Mr. Perkins for this sum. This is a common impasse when a disgruntled client instructs other solicitors. Five months later Mr. Perkins writes to the Law Society (local branch) complaining that Solicitor No. 3 has bungled his case, left him unrepresented, and is refusing to release the papers to another solicitor. The Vice-President of the local branch of the Law Society writes to Solicitor No. 3:

'I enclose a copy letter I have received from Mr. Perkins, a former client of yours. I am sure you will appreciate that I have to investigate these complaints with a view, if possible, to getting the difficulties resolved between the parties. It would help if you could give a reply suitable to send on to the client and send a second copy for my file. Sorry to trouble you. Kind regards.'

The solicitor duly sends the Law Society a three page letter in reply, explaining that the case was 'extremely complex' and 'the accident involved our client using a bandsaw attached to a table which our client said *was unstable and that this caused the casting to jam against the saw* and then to fly up and hit him on the head. . . . Legal aid *was refused on the merits of the case*.' How, in the light of Counsel's opinion, they tried to explain the difficulties to the client, who did not understand them or wish to understand them. '*Efforts were then made by us to trace the bandsaw and table.* Unfortunately the factory had closed since the accident and the table and bandsaw had been disposed of to another company. We were able, with the co-operation of the Defendant's insurers, to trace the bandsaw but unfortunately the table seemed (sic) to have disappeared. Having found the bandsaw we instructed Consultant Engineers to inspect the same and report. . . Unfortunately the Consulting Engineer was not able to say that Mr. Perkins would be able to show negligence, and was not prepared to accept that the accident happened in the manner alleged. . . .Accordingly we advised him that he should accept the defendants' offer of £500 and costs, and that we no longer considered that there was any merit in his case at all, and that if he insisted upon pursuing the matter to trial we should want further monies on account of costs. . .' and so on.

The Vice-President of the Law Society writes to Mr. Perkins: 'Enclosed herewith a copy of a letter I have now received from [your erstwhile solicitors] which I hope explains the position to you.'

The Law Society currently gets 9,000 complaints a year about solicitors (according to the President in a letter dated April 19 1984). Apart from the tiny minority involving misappropriation of clients' money or breach of the Solicitors' Accounts rules, it deals with these complaints in the same way as it dealt with Mr. Perkins's complaint. That is to say, it sends the solicitor a copy of the client's letter of complaint, and it sends the client a copy of the solicitor's reply. Because the Law Society does not requisition and go through the file, or make any investigation into the client's complaint, the solicitor's reply can contain whatever falsehoods he pleases. For instance, legal aid was not refused 'on the merits of the case' (i.e. because Mr. Perkins's claim had no legal merit), but because the solicitor had not bothered to get the necessary supporting evidence. The solicitor did not have to trace the bandsaw: at the outset Mrs. Perkins *told* him the name and address of the company which had bought it. The client never said the accident occurred because the table was *unstable* (which would be difficult to prove), but because it had *holes* in it (which would have been simple to prove), and so on.

However, in November 1978 Solicitor No. 3 does release the papers, and Solicitor No. 4 takes over.

Solicitor No. 4 works in a very large office boasting over a dozen partners. He sees Mr. Perkins to discuss the case, takes £115 from him on account of costs, and in January 1979 sends Counsel (a different Counsel) instructions to *advise in conference.* This is how the solicitor describes Mr. Perkins's accident in these 'instructions':

'Mr. Perkins claims that when working on a bandsaw a piece of casting flew off and struck him on the chin, which caused him lasting injuries. Mr. Perkins maintains that the accident arose out of the employers' failure to provide a safe system of work, and failure to provide him with satisfactory equipment to do the job in a safe manner.' And the solicitor asks Counsel to advise 'our client who is determined to have his day in Court whatever the cost, despite the apparent lack of any supporting evidence in his favour.' The solicitor points out that Mr. Perkins has already had three previous solicitors, and warns 'that Counsel may well experience difficulties with the client.' He ends his instructions by asking to have a private meeting with Counsel beforehand – for what purpose he does not state.

We saw how in Solicitor No. 3's 'Instructions to Counsel to advise', Mr. Perkins's clear and concise account of how the accident occurred became imprecise and confused. But notice how, although Mr. Perkins's statement is still in the file, Solicitor No. 4's account in *his* Instructions to Counsel is even more nebulous – the accident was caused by 'the employers' failure to provide *a safe system of work, and failure to provide him with satisfactory equipment to do the job in a safe manner.*' Neither was it a *piece* of casting which hit him, but the casting itself.

Now although with the destruction of the original table top Mr. Perkins's case is seriously weakened, there are still significant facts to support it. For instance the defendants do not dispute that the original table top *had* been broken in two and welded together, and that there *were* bolt holes going right through it (albeit they claim that these were behind the blade, see p. 154).

Moreover if, as Mr. Perkins claims, these bolt holes were in *front* of the blade – that is, in the working surface of the table top – then its destruction by a mobile crane dropping a heavy load onto it was a singularly convenient mishap for the defendants. So a statement by the crane driver – and his presence in Court – to explain how he came to press the wrong button just at that moment is a fairly obvious requirement. And if Mr. Perkins does lose his action for want of evidence, it is also fairly obvious that he has an action for negligence against one or more of his previous solicitors for their failure to inspect the machine (or, in the case of Solicitor No. 3, until it was too late).

Yet none of these points occur to Solicitor No. 4, who does not even mention in his Instructions to Counsel the crucial fact that the table top had been broken in two. Nor do they occur to Counsel, who after the conference merely notes: 'I confirm that in conference I advised the Plaintiff that I thought his chances of success were slim, and that we could not call our engineer.'

However after the conference, which takes place in March 1979, the solicitor broaches a more important subject – his costs. He writes to Mr. Perkins asking for a further £250 on account, adding 'if you were to bring in a total of £400 it is unlikely that I will require very much more from you.' Mr. Perkins pays the £250 (bringing his total payment to Solicitor No. 4 to £365). Solicitor No. 4 – who is leaving the firm – then hands the file to a partner, after dictating a note:

'This is a High Court personal injury matter and you will note from the file that we are *approximately* the fourth set of solicitors to deal with the matter. Mr. Perkins is convinced that the defendants owe him damages although he has indeed got a very weak case. . .We have now been given sufficient costs for us to take the matter into Court and brief Counsel, although Mr. Perkins has been advised that further costs will be payable to us. . .The file is very large and there is a lot of correspondence which will have to be gone through at some time before the trial.'

From his 'Instructions to Counsel to advise' the *solicitor* evidently has not gone through the file except in the most cursory manner. The partner, to whom the solicitor gives the file, in turn gives it to a clerk, who some weeks later hands it to another clerk. In fact after the original solicitor left the firm in May 1979, the references on the correspondence and notes indicate that five different people in turn dealt with the case in one capacity or another during the remainder of that year. And from their various notes to one another it seems that they are not completely *au fait* with the situation (or even in some cases their own native language). For example:

'The Person to whom is dealing with matter from S—. As soon as a letter comes in from defendants' solicitors consent to us setting down the action out of time two bundles of the pleadings need to be prepared, all pleadings on top of file, sorted more or less into bundle of originals and a bundle of photocopies, they need putting into date order. . .I think Counsel if Mr.— [name spelt wrongly]' (18 June).*

'This is a particularly massive file and I have spent and 1¼ looking through it without becoming any wiser except to agree with the opinions expressed that Mr. Perkins will lose his action.' (16 August).

'When papers returned from Counsel, if they still have them, when returned I suggest that they are sent on to [another Counsel]† . . . the other things without going through the file to tell whether or not [first Counsel's] note has in fact been dealt with. If necessary J— to have a word with me once papers have come back from Counsel. Must be chased up. N.B. Checked with Counsel's chambers and they say that we *have* received the papers back' (15 October).

'Paid out so far £15. We have received £365. There should be a writ somewhere.'

In November Mr. Perkins complains once again to the Law Society about the apparent lack of progress on his case, and that he is being asked to pay yet more money on account of costs. The solicitors reply to the Law Society: 'The difficulty in this matter is that Mr. Perkins persistently refuses to accept legal advice [i.e. that he has no case], and the reports of the experts employed by him. He is now insisting that the case is placed 'before a Judge'. It is accepted that this is his right, but without legal aid he must be prepared to pay for it and to accept the time and effort involved in pursuing it.'

* This note refers to 'setting down for trial', one of the two processes which have to be done before the Court gives a hearing date, and entails lodging at the Court office two sets of 'pleadings' – i.e. writ, statement of claim, defence etc. (The other process is lodging 'Certificate of readiness for trial', which is done subsequently.) Notice that S— evidently prefers to dictate instructions to his unknown successor, rather than do it himself.

† Mr. Perkins was dissatisfied with Counsel's performance at the conference in March, and insisted that *another* Counsel be instructed.

However the difficulty is happily resolved the next month (December 1979) by someone in the firm deciding that the £365 which Mr. Perkins paid on account is now pretty well spent on the work done to date (plus £54 for Counsel's conference fee), and curtly demanding a further £400 'to ensure that our costs for conducting the matter are reasonably secured, failing receipt within 14 days we shall apply to be removed from the record as your solicitors.'

Mr. Perkins being unwilling to pay such a sum (and according to his wife being 'hardly able to bear up under the pain and strain'), exit Solicitors No. 4. Even their modest achievement, during the year they had the case, of lodging two sets of 'pleadings' at the Court office drew a response from the clerk of the Court: 'The bundles of pleadings are not in sequence. Please attend at the listing office and put both bundles in order.'

And so, finally, to Solicitor No. 5. He takes £350 from Mr. Perkins, files 'Certificate of Readiness' at the Court office, and in February 1980 sends Counsel (a different Counsel) Instructions to advise in Conference, and argue the case in Court on Mr. Perkins's behalf. This is how the solicitor describes Mr. Perkins's accident in these instructions:

'Mr. Perkins bases his claim on the fact that the table he had to work on, despite complaints, was full of holes so that the casting jammed in that. However as your instructing solicitor understands, he attempted to free this casting without first turning off the saw [which would have been impracticable each time a casting stuck as the machine had an overrun of 40 seconds], with a result that upon the casting jumping free it fell against the saw and spun away and struck him on the chin.'

Again, how imprecise this is, compared to Mr. Perkins's written account. No mention of *why* the table had holes in it; or *why* the casting jammed in one of the holes; or *how* it came to strike him on the chin. These are vital details because Counsel gets his facts primarily from the solicitor's 'instructions'; and if the solicitor presents Counsel with a woolly picture, that most likely will be the picture which Counsel presents in Court. But more significantly, the solicitor goes on to tell Counsel what he thinks of Mr. Perkins's case:

'Mr. Perkins has made it quite clear that he wished to have his day in Court and have a Judge to decide the case *even after having been advised by myself and [previous Counsel] that there was almost no chance of success.*' The solicitor does not tell Counsel the points in Mr. Perkins's favour – presumably because he has not gone through the file in any detail, with its jumble of ill-sorted and mostly irrelevant documents accumulated over the past six and a half years. And faced with such a vague description of the accident, and with the solicitor's own comment that the client has almost no chance but just wants his day in Court, Counsel is unlikely to take much interest in the case either.

Although with the destruction of the original table top Mr. Perkins's case has been seriously weakened, there are still significant points in his favour which, if properly argued, could still result in his winning his case (i.e. satisfying the judge that his accident was the employers' fault). Let's summarize them:

1. It is not disputed that the metal table top had previously been broken and had been welded together, and had bolt holes going right through it. The employers claim that these holes were *behind* the blade and so could have played no part in causing the accident; Mr. Perkins claims that the holes were *in front of* the blade.

2. Mr. Perkins had been doing this job for seven years and was presumably a reliable and experienced workman. His explanation of the accident is convincing: the bits of metal adhering to the castings which he was turning against the saw blade would catch in these holes and cause the casting to stick on the table; and when, wearing thick asbestos gloves, he tried to release a particularly obdurate casting which had got stuck, it suddenly yielded and spun over into the path of the saw blade, which hurled it down onto the metal table from which it rebounded, striking him on the chin.

Although there were no eye-witnesses of the accident, the defendants' foreman's explanation – in the accident report book – was that Mr. Perkins loaded the castings onto the side of the working surface (preparatory to trimming them) *with the saw still going*, and one of them caught in the blade and rebounded. This is a less likely explanation, as an experienced workman, who had been doing the job for seven years, would be unlikely to be so careless.

3. The destruction of the metal table top by a mobile crane dropping a heavy load on it is a strange mishap, calling for further investigation. (For instance, did it occur during the eight

months between Solicitor No. 3's first request to inspect the machine, and when the inspection finally took place?)

Yet the solicitor mentions none of these points in his Instructions to Counsel – which are the final instructions before the actual trial. However, at the conference, Mr. Perkins (who was accompanied by his wife) was able to put some of the points to Counsel direct, and seemed satisfied that he understood them. Counsel decides that only one medical witness should be called – the doctor who gave the cagey report (see p. 156); and the solicitor arranges an appointment for Mr. Perkins to be examined by him again, before the trial.

A date for the trial is subsequently given, and on the morning of the appointed day (June 13 1980) Mr. and Mrs. Perkins present themselves at the High Court, as directed by their solicitor, where they meet their Counsel. But not the one with whom they had had the conference, and who they were told would be handling the case – but a much younger gentleman, whom they had never seen before. The original Counsel had apparently been held over in another case.

'With shock and dismay we went into the Court with a Counsel we had met for the first time that very morning. The other side's Counsel conducted, dominated, and even seemed to try the case. Our Counsel said very little. When he was called on to make his closing speech he said: '*My Lord, I do not know enough about this case to make a speech. I can only say that in view of the nature of the accident the firm was in breach of its statutory duty.*' Then he sat down.'* According to Mr. and Mrs. Perkins, he put none of the points supporting their case to the Court – which is hardly surprising since his 'brief' (Instructions to argue the case in Court) did not mention any of them, and he had probably picked up the papers for the first time that morning.

At 1 p.m., after a little over two hours, the case which had taken seven years to get to Court was over. The Judge sums up and gives judgment:

'The Plaintiff was employed as a bandsawyer when on 23 June 1973 a casting jumped up and hit him on the chin. The Plaintiff says there were holes in the table and pitmarks as a result of it

---

* Counsel's feeble performance even drew a comment from Mr. Perkins's medical witness, who, in a letter to the solicitor acknowledging his fee, observed 'Mr. Perkins did have an unfortunate deal in the absence of the Counsel who had been preparing the case.'

having been repaired, and as a result the component became stuck. When he released it with his left hand, it came into contact with the saw blade. I am unable to find the Plaintiff has made out any sort of case. I accept entirely the evidence of the Defendants' foreman, and I am wholly satisfied there were no holes from the bottom drilled right through that could result in an accident. I am satisfied that it was a perfectly adequate table which continued in use at the Defendants' factory until they sold it, and at the other works until something dropped on it. *Not a shadow of a case has been made out. Judgment for the Defendants together with costs.'**

So the Judge, after listening to the conflicting verbal evidence of Mr. Perkins and the defendants' foreman, decided that there were no holes in the working surface of the metal table, and that therefore Mr. Perkins's accident was not due to his erstwhile employers' negligence (i.e. was not their fault), and that therefore he gets no compensation.

To obtain this decision cost some six or seven thousand pounds. Mr. Perkins's total legal costs came to around £1,500 – an unusually modest total for a High Court action, presumably because his various solicitors geared their demands to what they thought an unemployed factory worker could pay. His opponents' legal costs which he was ordered to pay – as the losing party invariably is – came to £3,331. And the services of the Judge, Court officials, use of Court building etc. cost the taxpayer probably another thousand or two.

So Mr. Perkins, by seeking compensation for his accident, ends up not only without a penny compensation, but £1,500 worse off – and only his infelicitous financial circumstances save him from being worse off to the tune of four or five times that sum. Because he lived in a Council flat and had no assets, the defendants did not try to enforce their order for costs. Had he been buying his house on mortgage one may assume that his *own* legal costs would have been approximately the same as the defendants'; and the defendants could have recovered their costs by selling his house and putting him and his family into the street. This is a risk that any litigant who owns his house but does

---

* This extract is taken from a note in the file. As there was no question of an appeal, no transcript of the trial was obtained. Notice that the learned judge has got the date of the accident wrong. It was 3rd July 1973.

not get legal aid, and who does not have a few thousand pounds or more in his pocket, has to take. But his fruitless battle for compensation over seven years has probably cost him more than the £1,500 he has had to pay in legal costs.

As mentioned, the doctor who had given the earlier 'cagey' report examined Mr. Perkins again prior to the trial, and gave another report (dated May 29 1980):

> 'He complains of extreme tenderness in the left ear and behind the ear and says he still cannot lie on his left side in bed. . .It is clear from the hospital notes that he had a fracture of the bone of the skull involving the temporal bone in the region of the temporo-mandibular joint. . .His main complaint is of the continuing tenderness in and behind the left ear. . .It is difficult to construe this as an entirely organic condition, and there must be a strong functional or hysterical element since it is not possible to equate the area of tenderness and hypersensitivity with an anatomical lesion. It would appear that his complaint is largely functional or hysterical although it was determined by his accident.'

In other words the doctor is saying that after seven years from the accident, he can find no *physical* cause for Mr. Perkins's continuing pain, and that although it was originally triggered off by the accident it must now have a psychological basis. As is stated in *The Courts and You* by Michael Cook, a book in the Law Society's 'It's your law' series: 'The strain of the [legal] proceedings and of the trial itself can be considerable. It is an accepted medical fact that recovery from an injury can be delayed by proceedings relating to it.'

And presumably the strain of the legal proceedings, and the consequent delay in recovering from the injury which gave rise to them, will increase in proportion to the incompetence of the lawyers handling the injured person's case.

When *Which?* wants to know how well or badly car repairers do their job, it plants a car, with some deliberately induced faults, for servicing on fifty unsuspecting garages in turn, and monitors the results. But neither the Consumers' Association (publishers of *Which?*), nor the Royal Commission which spent £1.25 million in purporting to investigate the legal profession, would think of subjecting *lawyers* to an equivalent test – that is, planting a fictitious accident victim on fifty unsuspecting solicitors, and seeing how he got on after three or four years.

Until such a survey is carried out, I suggest that the experiences of Mr. Perkins – who consulted five firms of solicitors in succession, who between them consulted four barristers – will serve to be going on with:

Solicitor No. 1 (Mr. Perkins's *union's* solicitor). Handled case from its inception in July 1973 to July 1975. Neither inspects the machine and its integral metal table top – the holes in which allegedly caused the accident – nor applies for legal aid, nor issues writ. Merely carries on a desultory correspondence with the defendants' insurers.

Solicitor No. 2 (July 1975 to June 1976). Neither inspects machine/table top, nor applies for legal aid, nor issues writ. Tries to get Mr. Perkins to abandon his claim on the strength of a *legal* opinion of a medical consultant who had never even seen him.

Solicitor No. 3 (June 1976 to March 1978). Applies for legal aid without submitting evidence to support application – i.e. without inspecting and reporting on table top. Ditto appeal against refusal of legal aid. Gives inaccurate account of alleged cause of accident in 'Instructions to Counsel to advise'. Does not inspect machine/table top until 15 months after taking over case, by which time original metal table top has been replaced with a new one. Tries to get Mr. Perkins to abandon claim on the strength of an obviously biased, even fatuous, engineer's report. Falsifies facts in his answer to Mr. Perkins's complaint to the Law Society.

Solicitor No. 4 (November 1978 to December 1979). Gives imprecise/inaccurate account of accident in his 'Instructions to Counsel to advise in conference'. Fails to mention in such instructions facts/evidence supporting Mr. Perkins's case, but instead tells Counsel that there is *no* supporting evidence. After the solicitor who was originally dealing with the case leaves firm, Mr. Perkins's file is shunted backwards and forwards among five different members of the firm, none of whom take any interest in it.

Solicitor No. 5 (January 1980 to June 1980). Gives imprecise/inadequate account of accident in his Instructions to Counsel. Fails to mention in such instructions facts/evidence supporting

Mr. Perkins's case, but instead tells Counsel that 'there was almost no chance of success' but that Mr. Perkins 'wished to have his day in Court'.

Counsel No. 1 (instructed to advise by Solicitor No. 3). Although he is told name and address of company which bought the machine from the defendants, he does not advise the solicitor at once to *inspect* machine/table top (but instead advises solicitor to ask if the defendants kept any *photographs* of it). It was primarily the failure to take this obvious step which was to prove fatal to Mr. Perkins's case.

Counsel No. 2 (instructed to advise in conference by Solicitor No. 4). Does not consider facts/evidence supporting Mr. Perkins's case (which would have been apparent from the documents which the solicitor submitted with his instructions). Instead tells Mr. Perkins that his chances 'were slim'.

Counsel No. 3 (instructed to advise in conference and argue case in Court by Solicitor No. 5). Listens to Mr. Perkins's points at conference and seems to grasp the issues, but fails to attend the trial. Instead sends along an inexperienced junior as substitute.

Counsel No. 4 (last minute substitute for Counsel No. 3). Represents Mr. Perkins in Court. According to Mr. and Mrs. Perkins puts none of the facts/evidence supporting their case to the Court or to the witnesses. According to Mr. and Mrs. Perkins admits he does not know enough about the case to make a final speech. His feeble performance even draws a written comment from Mr. Perkins's medical witness.

This, then, is how down-market personal injury litigation is handled, not just by the nine solicitors and barristers whom Mr. Perkins happened to consult, but probably by over half the solicitors and barristers in the country.

Meanwhile Mr. Perkins still cannot believe that he does not have some sort of remedy, and he again complains – this time not to the Law Society but to his Member of Parliament, Mrs. Jill Knight M.B.E. After investigating the matter she replies:

'. . .There was never much hope that you would win the case, and you will know that this was the legal advice you received from several lawyers. It really is important to follow the advice of one's solicitors. . .It was precisely because it was felt your case could not succeed that you were not able to get legal aid, and that too really should have warned you not to proceed. It was a great shame you did not accept the offer which the firm originally made, again as your solicitors advised. . .Of course it was later withdrawn, which meant that you got nothing – which honestly was your own fault.'

* * * * * *

If any reader is interested in querying the authenticity of any of the events in the foregoing narrative, and cares to write to me (address on rear cover) enclosing stamped addressed envelope, plus the current cost of photocopying, I will send the relevant copy documents.

Meanwhile, a few of them are reproduced in the appendix immediately following.

R REF. AC/P.19/76 11th March, 1977

UR REF.

ear Mr. P s,

re: Accident

Further to this matter, we are now trying to arrange a ite inspection at the premises of imited, of Street, . We would be obliged f you could inform us of a convenient time when you will be ble to attend to view the table, along with our Mr. Bird and he Solicitors for the other side. We are also going to arrange or a photographer to be present to take photographs of the table.

Will you please communicate with this office and inform us f a convenient day in the week which you will be able to attend n an appointment and what time.

We await to hear from you.

Yours faithfully,

UR REF. AC/P.19/74 8th November, 1977

OUR REF.

ear Sir,

re: Accident

We have now obtained the Consulting Engineers' report nd opinion, following their inspection of the machine, namely he bandsaw, on the 13th September, 1977 when although you were equested to attend you did not attend. Unfortunately the table n question, which no doubt contributed to the accident, is no onger available and was not available for inspection onthe 13th eptember, 1977. The Defendants do, however, admit that the table ad been welded together.

Enclosed is a copy of the report and opinion of the Consulting ngineer, who is an extremely experienced mad and his opinion is ighly regarded. Please consider what he says carefully and you ill see that in his opinion the circumstances of this accident ere not reasonably forseeable by your employers and if that is orrect they could not be held to be negligent because they can nly be responsible for occurrences which would have reasonably een forseeable to them prior to the accident.

In those circumstances we must advise you that we do not onsider that your prospects of success are very good and in the ight of this opinion from Mr. of Messrs. , & we have no evidence to support your case save your own evidence. he Defendants will call their own expert engineer, who will no doubt ave advised them similarly as Mr. has advised us.

Therefore we must advise you that the offer which was made to ou to settle this case in the sum of £500.00 and your costs is one hich you should accept because we feel that the likelihood of you

Continued..........

Subject R. H. P s

MESSAGE **Date** 21.11.1979

You will have received the letter drafted by Jim ; I now attach a letter which we have received from Mr. P s today (20th November) enquiring as to the position.

I would like to reply in robust terms telling him that a further £500.00 on account of costs must be provided within 14 days otherwise we shall consider our instructions at an end and make an application to the Court to be removed from the record as his Solicitors on the grounds that he is unable to provide the necessary security for our costs.

MPT

This is the final stage of a game which is a variation of 'pass the parcel'. Best played in a large firm of solicitors, it consists of one of the partners taking on a down-market personal injury case; taking as much on account of costs as the client's circumstances permit; and then passing the file to another member of the firm, who passes it to another, and so on. When nine months later (no progress having been made meanwhile) the client starts asking awkward questions such as: 'What's happening on my case?' he is asked for a further sum on account of costs, which he won't be able to pay. The solicitors then get shot of the case on the grounds that 'the client is unable to provide the necessary security for our costs'.

7 *The case of David Johns*

On 19th September 1973, during the lunchtime play period in the school playground, David Johns (aged 8) dropped his handkerchief. As he bent down to retrieve it, Ian (also aged 8), who was holding a bit of broken car aerial about a foot long with a jagged point, swung round and accidentally struck him in the eye with it.

David was taken to the headmaster's office and the headmaster telephoned his mother at her place of work, telling her that there had been an accident, and that she should come to the school. When she arrived three-quarters of an hour later (for she worked on the other side of town), David was sitting by himself in the back of the headmaster's car, holding a pad to his eye. The headmaster then drove mother and son to the hospital, which was half an hour's drive away. Within ten minutes of arrival David was seen by a consultant eye specialist, who injected antibiotics in an attempt to prevent infection – the eye having been badly lacerated. The same day the eye was operated on, but to no avail. Infection had set in and a few days later the eye had to be permanently removed.

A playground accident on an otherwise ordinary Wednesday morning, and a child has to live the rest of his life disabled. As my reader will remember, he does not automatically get any compensation: only if he can prove in Court that his injuries were the result of someone else's negligence (fault). Moreover, in this case it would be no use proving the accident was *Ian's* fault – because he wouldn't have any money to pay compensation. For

David to get compensation he has to show that his accident was either wholly or partly the fault of the school or its staff, or the Education Authority.

So on David's discharge from hospital, early October 1973, mother and son call on the senior partner of a local firm of solicitors which had handled the purchase of her Council house a few years previously – the sort of gentleman whom you, O reader, might well consult should you ever find yourself in Mrs. Johns's position.

They tell him the above facts (David's recollection of the accident being understandably hazy), and Mrs. Johns also tells him something of her financial situation, from which it is evident that she will need *legal aid* to bring legal proceedings, and the legal eagle gets to work. On 23rd October he writes to David's parents as follows:

> 'Dear Mr. and Mrs. Johns. We are pleased to say that both Mrs. X and Mrs. Y [the two playground supervisors on duty at the time of the accident] have called at our office quite voluntarily and have discussed with us David's accident. Unfortunately what they tell us does not assist us in making a claim against the Council. Mrs. X was inside the school at the time, and although Mrs. Y was outside in the school playground, she did not at any time prior to the accident see the boy concerned with the car aerial. Our last remaining source of enquiry therefore, must be to try and find out where the aerial itself came from and in this connection we are trying to see the boy concerned, we will, of course, keep you informed. However, we did think that you would like to know that both Mrs. X and Mrs. Y were both very much concerned at David's accident. . .but as we have said before, really their evidence is of no assistance to us. Yours faithfully.'

This letter gives us quite a lot of information about the mental acumen of its author. And if I were the parent of a disabled child relying on such a person to get my child compensation for his injury, none of it would I find reassuring.

The solicitor has evidently pinned his chief hope on the playground supervisors volunteering information to 'assist us in making a claim against the Council' – i.e. the Education Authority – which they are hardly likely to do, since not only are they employees of the Authority but the most likely culprits of any negligence, if negligence there was.* And because the supervisor who was outside tells him that she did not see the boy with the bit of broken aerial, the solicitor is apparently satisfied that there was no question of negligent *supervision* of the playground; and that the only chance of proving negligence will be to show that the school or Education Authority should have prevented the bit of broken aerial from being on the school grounds in the first place.

A contemporaneous note which he made of the interview confirms this view:

> 'At the time of the accident Mrs. X was actually inside the school and the only 'nanny' outside the school *in the yard* was Mrs. Y. . . I questioned Mrs. Y about the circumstances in the playground before the accident and I am quite satisfied that she did not see the other boy with the car aerial or whatever impliment (sic) it was, and that if she had seen him with it she would have taken it away. *The only line of investigation that now seems worthwhile persuing (sic) as far as I can see is where the impliment came from and if its source (sic) could have been prevented e.g. if the impliment had been thrown over the school wall if it could have been discovered before the boy found it.* To this end I think we must try and see the boy who caused the injury.'

It does not occur to the solicitor (just as it did not occur to Mr. Perkins's first three solicitors) to *look* at the thing he is dealing with – in this case the school playground, which is a ten minute drive from his office. Had he done so he would have seen that the playground area is a generous expanse of ground comprising a tarmac rectangle measuring 150 feet by 70 feet, set in (and in no way separated from) a flat grassy area, where the children also played, measuring – at its furthest extremities – 200 yards by 100 yards. The whole is surrounded by a low open-boarded perimeter fence, two sides of which abut a public footpath. So had the learned solicitor made that ten minute car journey, he

---

* An employer is vicariously liable for the negligence of its employees. So the Education Authority would be liable for the negligence of the playground supervisors or any of the school's staff, and would have to pay any compensation awarded – for which it would, of course, be insured. Alternatively, the Education Authority might be liable for negligence in its own right, e.g. for failing to provide enough supervisors. So if I am run over by a company's lorry, the company might be liable either vicariously by virtue of the negligence of its employee, or by virtue of its *own* negligence if it had failed to maintain the vehicle properly.

would have seen at once that there would be no question of the Education Authority, or the school, being able to *prevent* a sharp bit of metal a foot long from being lobbed onto the school grounds, and therefore picked up by a child, at any time. And he would also have seen that *one supervisor* was inadequate for children of that age group (7 to 11) in that expanse of ground. But because he doesn't make that ten minute car journey, he's toying with evidence which can *never* prove negligence, while ignoring that which possibly can.

The solicitor writes to Ian's mother requesting an interview with her son (to ask him where he found the implement), which she refuses. But she tells him that certain boys who witnessed the accident had made statements to the headmaster. Mrs. Johns also tells him of these statements, and that the parents of the boys in question were agreeable to him being given copies. But she hears nothing further.

Now the solicitor knows that to succeed in her claim, Mrs. Johns needs evidence of negligence – and that she also needs some prima facie evidence to get legal aid. But as this case is evidently not one which he sees as meriting a great deal of his time and attention, he does not try to *get* any evidence. He does not look at the playground. He does not interview the boys who saw the accident – nor even bother to get copies of the statements which he has been told they made to the headmaster. Neither did he get statements from the two playground supervisors whom he *did* interview. On the other hand he does not want to tell Mrs. Johns that she has no case,* lest it turns out that she does have. In other words, he is in the traditional dilemma of a busy solicitor landed with a down-market personal injury case – which dilemma he solves in the traditional way. That is, he puts the file in his filing cabinet and forgets about it.

When four months later (February 1974) Mrs. Johns telephones to ask what is happening, he digs the file out and writes to her on 21st February:

> 'We refer to your telephone message to our office the other day concerning the progress of David's case, and also your application for Legal Aid. The position is that we have drafted

---

* I refer to it throughout as *her* case, although technically it is her son's case.

and submitted a case for the Opinion of Counsel* and we are awaiting the result of this. We cannot apply for legal aid at this stage until we have the result of Counsel's Opinion.'

He has, of course, done no such thing: but he hands the file to his junior partner to take over, who hastily dictates 'Instructions to Counsel to Advise' – which he sends Counsel on *22nd February*. So from now on it is the junior partner who is dealing with the case.

In these 'Instructions to Counsel to Advise' the junior partner relays David's very hazy account of the accident and his mother's account of its aftermath (as summarized in the opening two paragraphs of this chapter). He tells Counsel that there was a supervisor in the playground – but not that there were *two* supervisors on duty, one of whom had gone inside at the time of the accident. Neither has he or his colleague taken up Mrs. Johns's suggestion to get copies of the statements of the boys who saw the accident. Instead he suggests to Counsel that as potentially dangerous objects (bottles, cans etc.) are habitually thrown into the school grounds from the public footpath, it might be arguable that the Education Authority should have cleared the grounds of debris each morning before playtime. And he asks Counsel to advise on the prospects of Mrs. Johns winning a negligence action against the Education Authority, by reason of the presence of a dangerous implement on the school grounds, 'or under any other head'.†

However, in his written opinion Counsel does consider the possibility of negligent supervision, as follows:

'There is evidence that there was a person in charge of the children at the material time, and to show negligence it would be necessary to show that she was not reasonably vigilant. This

* 'Submitting a case for the Opinion of Counsel', 'instructing Counsel to Advise', 'taking Counsel's Opinion', are synonymous. Significantly the solicitor chooses the most pompous alternative. 'When there is a gap between one's real and one's declared aims one turns instinctively to long words [or pompous phraseology] like a cuttlefish squirting out ink.' (Orwell – Politics and the English Language, *Collected Essays.*)

† The solicitor adds another possible head of negligence for Counsel's consideration, viz. the headmaster's delay in getting David to hospital. But as the consultant's report subsequently exonerated him (see p. 88), this aspect was dropped.

involves considering what there was to be seen. As I understand it, this whole transaction was a matter of seconds and not preceded by any fight or struggle that would have drawn anyone's attention to the possibility of violence being done. . . A broken piece of aerial is not a conspicuous object nor one the purpose of which is to cause injury. If Ian merely had it in his hand, a supervisor might have seen it without appreciating what it was, or the possible consequences. It might even be mistaken for a ruler or a pencil. *On this supervision point it seems to me that this case is analogous to Newton v. East Ham Corporation (1963) in which a boy of four was injured by another boy throwing a bit of coke; a supervisor was present but her attention was elsewhere. It was held that she was* not *negligent, there being no obligation to provide efficient supervision to watch all parts of the playground at once.*'

This is an example of how splitting the role of legal adviser into two or three people, fine in theory, works in practice. Senior partner takes on a down-market personal injury case. He sees the client, writes a few letters, and then as the case is neither very interesting nor lucrative, he hands it over to a junior colleague (often a clerk but in this case another solicitor). Second solicitor relays the facts as he understands them (either from the file or verbally from his colleague) to Counsel – the specialist – with instructions to advise, thinking that he is thereby doing his job perfectly adequately. Counsel writes an apparently plausible opinion on the facts as given him, thinking that the solicitor will have mentioned *all the relevant facts* in his instructions, and that therefore he need not enquire further. In other words, each member of the team relies on the other, and the crucial facts fall through the gaps between them.

For instance, the original solicitor interviews the two playground supervisors on duty, who tell him that one of them had gone *inside* at the time of the accident. But this fact never gets to Counsel, who is merely told in his Instructions to Advise: 'At the time of the accident there was a school 'nanny' in the play area whose job it was to supervise the children at play.' Counsel assumes from this that *one supervisor was adequate*, without enquiring what *size* the play area was, how *many* children were in it, *where* the supervisor was standing in relation to the accident – none of which facts has he been given.

As to how the accident happened, the solicitor has not interviewed or got statements from any witnesses, so he merely relays David's very hazy account: that as David bent down to pick up a handkerchief 'Ian swung round at this point and hit David with something in his right eye [which turned out to be] a piece of broken aerial.' Counsel, for his part, does not suggest getting statements from the other boys in the playground to see if they can give any more detailed information, but again assumes that he has been given all the relevant facts – and that therefore the accident was the result of an *isolated* act on Ian's part, over in 'a matter of seconds'; and analogous to a previously decided case where a boy in a playground threw a piece of coke at another, and the Court held that the playground supervisor had *not* been negligent.*

As to the other suggested head of negligence – that the school or the Education Authority should have kept the grounds clear of potentially dangerous objects such as a bit of broken car aerial – Counsel says:

> 'If the aerial were found by Ian in the school grounds, then it would be arguable that the proposed Defendants were in breach of their duty to keep the school grounds clear of any matter likely to become dangerous in the hands of children. At present, however, the position under this head is open since there is no *evidence* that the aerial came from the school grounds. . .Ian could give the best evidence on this, but I understand that his parents are reluctant to allow him to be interviewed. If there is any further evidence I shall be glad to consider it but. . .at present I cannot hold out any great hope to David's parents. All I can say is that the gravity of the case certainly justifies further investigations.'

Here Counsel seems to be implying that the school has an *absolute* duty to keep its grounds clear of dangerous objects, and that David has an arguable case provided it can be shown that that is where Ian *did* find it. In fact this is not so. The 'duty' of the school and its staff in this respect is the same as in any other respect: to take reasonable care or (in this context) to exercise reasonable

---

* You will of course realize the crucial difference, when considering whether a playground supervisor was negligent in failing to prevent an accident, between an accident which was the result of an *isolated* act, and an accident which was the culmination of a *series* of potentially dangerous acts.

vigilance. And, of course, no amount of vigilance on the part of the school could prevent a bit of broken car aerial from being lobbed over from the public footpath at any time.

So because Counsel does not enquire further as to how the accident occurred, nor into the geography of the playground, but is content to apply a few dubious academic principles to the solicitor's palpably inadequate version of the facts, Counsel's Opinion – so far from shedding any light on the matter – merely compounds the original solicitor's error. That is, it dismisses the possibility of negligent or inadequate supervision of the playground at the time of the accident; and holds out that the only hope of establishing negligence is by virtue of the presence of a potentially dangerous implement on the school grounds (as to which further evidence is required to show that is where Ian *did* find it).

On getting Counsel's Opinion – which he does in March 1974 – the solicitor submits an application for legal aid, together with Counsel's Opinion, to the Legal Aid Committee. Now as we have seen, depending on the strength or weakness of the applicant's prima facie case, the Committee can either grant legal aid unconditionally to cover all the steps up to and including the actual trial; or it can refuse the application. But it may also grant legal aid conditionally; or it may limit the legal aid to cover just *one step*, after which a further application has to be made. In fact it is this latter type of legal aid which Mrs. Johns receives, in May 1974. In view of the guarded terms of Counsel's Opinion, and the fact that her solicitor has not submitted any evidence of negligence to support her application, she is granted a legal aid certificate limited to making *further enquiries* on the lines Counsel suggested. Incidentally she herself has to make a contribution of £250 to the legal aid fund by means of twelve monthly instalments, which has been assessed by reference to her and her husband's income and capital (which includes the house they are buying).

Accordingly, following the implications of Counsel's Opinion, the solicitor instructs an *enquiry agent* to try and establish that Ian *had* found the implement on the school grounds, and also to find out how often the grounds were cleared of dangerous objects. The enquiry agent tries to see Ian to get a statement, whose parents again refuse; but he gets elaborate statements from the school caretaker, and two groundsmen employed by the Education Authority, as to their weekly grass cutting and rubbish clearing activities. And the solicitor submits these statements to the Legal Aid Committee, and the Legal Aid Committee grants another 'limited' legal aid certificate to enable Counsel's *further* opinion to be taken; and on September 25 1974 – slightly over a year after the accident – the solicitor sends the enquiry agent's report and the caretaker's and groundsmen's statements to Counsel, with 'Instructions to Further Advise'.

But he also sends Counsel something else.

Mrs. Johns, having heard at the outset that certain boys who witnessed the accident made statements to the headmaster (which information she passed on to her solicitor who ignored it), she herself writes to the Education Authority asking for copies. She is told that these statements are with the Authority's solicitors and that any approach should be made through her own solicitor, which information she again passes on to him. And this time her solicitor does apply for and receive copies, as follows:

(1) 'We were playing 'chaseys'. Ian saw this thing and picked it up. *He was sticking it in the ground and flicking it up like that. He was just chasing after us and flicking mud with the thing playing 'chaseys'* . . . David came over to Ian. I was walking towards the playground. I turned when David shouted 'Ow!' I saw him sitting holding his eye.' (Paul Fidgeon.) (Presumably by 'the playground' he means the tarmac rectangle, the incident having occurred in the grassy area beyond.)

(2) 'I saw Paul Fidgeon, Christopher and Ian playing with something. *Ian was digging in the ground and flicking mud up.* David came near. . .and Ian accidentally *flicked it up.*' (Paul Waterhouse.)

(3) '*Ian was larking about flicking muddy water at other boys with the aerial*, and on David coming up he turned and caught his eye with the aerial.' (Neil.)* (Prior to playtime it had been raining heavily and evidently there were puddles around.)

(4) 'Ian and David were *bending down together*. I saw that Ian had something in his hand and as he stood up *he brought his arm up and caught David in the face with the object* that he was holding in his hand.

---

* This actual statement was not passed on to the solicitor (because Neil's father did not want his son involved in a Court case), but was presented in summary form by the father.

. . . I ran up to see what had happened to David and I saw that blood was coming from his eye which was also *covered with grass and mud.* I saw the object that Ian had thrown away, it was about 12 inches of car aerial.' (Christopher.)

Three of these statements mention that Ian was flicking up mud with the bit of aerial; two state that he was flicking the mud at the other boys; two state that he was *chasing* or larking about with the other boys; and one states that Ian and David were bending down together, and that after being struck David's eye was covered with grass and mud. David's own recollection is that he was struck while bending down to pick up a handkerchief he had dropped.

So from these statements, and David's own account, we can now get a fairly clear indication of how the accident happened. Ian (aged 8), having found a bit of broken car aerial, for a merry prank had been chasing after the other boys, digging the aerial into the ground and flicking them with mud, *the digging and flicking obviously being one simultaneous action in view of the nature of the implement*, and his playmates were running away from him. However David, bending down to pick up a handkerchief, temporarily offers a more stable target. Ian therefore bends down beside him, sticks the aerial into the ground, and smartly brings it up in order to flick David with mud. But because David's face is near the ground at that moment, he unfortunately catches his eye with the implement as well.

Now whatever the various legal definitions of negligence may be, they all boil down to the single proposition: the plaintiff proves negligence if he shows that his injuries were caused, either wholly or partly, by the defendant's *fault.* And in the vast majority of personal injury cases this is not decided by any complicated legal propositions, but is simply a matter of common sense. So it is common sense that if David's accident had been the result of an *isolated* act on Ian's part – e.g. if Ian had suddenly picked up the implement off the ground and lunged at David (or if he had picked up a bit of coke and hurled it at David) – then the accident would not have been anyone's fault,* because there would have been virtually nothing that any supervisor, however vigilant, could have done to prevent it. Equally it is common sense that if David's accident was the culmination of a *series* of potentially dangerous acts on Ian's part, such as a supervisor in a reasonably

* Except Ian's, who is not worth suing as he wouldn't have any money.

sized playground doing her job reasonably well should have been alerted to, then David's accident *would* be someone else's fault. It would either be the fault of the supervisor who should have been alert to the danger in time to prevent it, or the other supervisor who went inside leaving the playground inadequately supervised, or the school or Education Authority for not providing an adequate number of supervisors for such a large play area, or the school or supervisors for not limiting the area in which the children were allowed to play.

So the boys' statements, together with the other available evidence, indicate a strong prima facie case of negligence: a vast play area, the children obviously not confined to the tarmac rectangle; a boy aged 8 chasing the other boys, digging a broken car aerial with a jagged point into the ground and flicking them with mud, which escapade finally results in one of his playmates (also aged 8) losing an eye; two playground supervisors on duty, one of whom had gone *inside* at the time of the accident, the other apparently neither seeing the accident nor the events leading up to it; and although the duration of Ian's mud flicking activities is not mentioned in any of the statements (not surprisingly, since they were taken on behalf of the *defendants*), the fact that at least three boys were aware of them suggests minutes rather than seconds. (And had Mrs. Johns's solicitor tied up a few loose ends, e.g. had he asked the supervisor, whom he interviewed, to mark on a rough plan of the playground *where* she had been standing at the time of the accident, had he asked the other supervisor *why* she went inside, had he himself got statements from the boys in the playground – then a strong prima facie case of negligence might well have been converted into an almost unanswerable one.)

But although presented with copies of the boys' statements, Mrs. Johns's solicitor appears not to realize their significance. For although he sends these statements to Counsel with his Instructions to Further Advise (dated September 25 1974), he does not *mention* them in such instructions, but concentrates instead on the various items of rubbish which the groundsmen say they used to find on the school grounds. Neither does learned Counsel appreciate the significance of the boys' statements, for in his Further Advice, which is dated October 9 1974, he merely observes: 'There is nothing in the most recent information to induce me to change my view that the evidence is not likely to prove that the play area was negligently supervised.'

However, because of the groundsmen's statements as to the amount of rubbish they habitually found on their weekly grass cutting and clearing operations (this school being one of several they attended), and because Paul Fidgeon's statement indicates that he *saw* Ian pick the aerial up, Counsel feels more hopeful of establishing negligence by virtue of the presence of a potentially dangerous object on the school grounds – which he says is 'the only live issue'. Accordingly, in his Further Advice, Counsel advises the solicitor to engage an enquiry agent to make a search of the school grounds *on seven successive days* to ascertain the amount of rubbish deposited during a typical week, with a view to showing that the system of *weekly* clearing was inadequate. And he also advises that Paul should make a further statement confirming that he saw Ian pick 'the thing' up on the school grounds. Note that Counsel, who has obviously read Paul's statement, advises getting Paul to give this further and quite useless information; but not the information which might establish negligence beyond question – viz. *for approximately how long before the accident had Ian been chasing the other boys, digging the aerial into the ground and flicking them with mud?*

So pursuant to Counsel's Further Advice, it's back to the Legal Aid Committee to obtain a further 'limited' legal aid certificate to cover the further investigations and the further statement. And the limited legal aid certificate having been granted, the further investigations and further statement are duly made; and the solicitor submits the further report (which itemizes all the rubbish the enquiry agent observed on the school grounds over a week), and the further statement, to Counsel; and on February 27 1975 Counsel submits his 'Still Further Advice'.

His conclusion is that: 'As it by no means follows that a properly conducted search would uncover *everything*, and any more frequent search would bring little benefit in terms of reducing the risk. . .there are no reasonable prospects of this action succeeding, and I am quite firmly of this opinion.'

So in his third written opinion, a year and a half after the accident, Counsel finally states that the presence of a bit of broken car aerial on the school grounds does not amount to negligence – a conclusion which would be obvious to anyone who actually looked at the place in as many seconds. While at the same time both Counsel and solicitor have dismissed the evidence of negligent or inadequate supervision, which has been thrust under their noses.

On receiving Counsel's 'Still Further Advice', the solicitor dictates a note to his senior partner (who started off dealing with the case):

> 'I have written to Mr. and Mrs. Johns asking them to come in and discuss the matter. We have now had Counsel's Further Advice which says that the case has no chance of success . . . Obviously the situation is that we must report this to the Legal Aid Committee and it is clear that the Legal Aid Committee will wish to discharge the existing legal aid certificate and will refuse to issue a full Certificate to proceed with a writ. It is probable *if I ring the Secretary of the Legal Aid Committee* that he will arrange for a hearing for Mr. and Mrs. Johns to put representations to the Legal Aid Committee as to why the legal aid certificate should not be discharged, although in my opinion this is a matter of form, and it will be discharged.
>
> The only practical course of action open to them is to take the matter up themselves and to pay for proceedings, which is obviously going to be very expensive and bearing in mind the weight of opinion from Counsel is likely to be abortive. *Certainly we would need very strong deposits of cash from Mr. and Mrs. Johns before we could even instruct Counsel*, and the likelihood is they would be responsible for the other side's costs. Perhaps you would have a word with me before you see them.'

Notice how establishing that Mrs. Johns has no case, and getting her legal aid discharged, seems to have assumed a greater urgency than either of the solicitors exercised in pursuing her case. Why, for instance, does he have to *telephone* the Secretary of the Legal Aid Committee, and why will he need *very strong deposits of cash* before he would even instruct Counsel to take the first step in the action – i.e. draft the writ and Statement of Claim?

Mrs. Johns, however, is unwilling to accept that she has no case, and she asks for a second opinion from a *Queen's Counsel.* So the solicitor applies for a further limited legal aid certificate to cover this, which is granted – and on May 29 1975 the solicitor submits *Instructions to Queen's Counsel to Advise.* Or rather (from the reference on the letter) his clerk does. Not surprisingly, the clerk's 'instructions' show no greater understanding of the common sense points involved than that of his two principals. His instructions, moreover, betray a certain difficulty with his own native language:

> 'It would be pointless for Instructing Solicitors to go into any great detail in these instructions as to the details of the accident and their views as all matters are adequately dealt with in the previous instructions to Junior Counsel but briefly the matter has been approached in three ways. Initially it was considered that the question of supervision and whether this was adequate. Then was considered [the headmaster's failure to take David straight to hospital]. Finally it was considered that the position with regard to foreign objects in general which appear to have accummulated (sic) to some marked degree on this school playing field and which appear to have been a regular hazard, if not to the pupils, then to the equipment of the gardener attending to the cutting of the field. It is the opinion of Junior Counsel that generally the prospects of successing (sic) do not warrant an action being brought and has advised accordingly. Mr. and Mrs. Johns desire that the opinion of Queen's Counsel be obtained and Instructing Solicitors will be pleased if Counsel will so advise.'

With these Instructions the clerk sends all the previous Instructions to Counsel to Advise, the three previous Counsel's Opinions, the caretaker's, groundsmen's and enquiry agent's reports, and *two* of the four boys' statements (Paul Fidgeon's and Neil's).

Four months later (September 24 1975) Queen's Counsel submits his written opinion, his conclusion being that Mrs. Johns has no prospect of showing negligence – either by reason of the potentially dangerous implement being on the school grounds, or inadequate supervision of the children at playtime – 'and I can only advise that the legal aid certificate be now discharged'.

On the first head, the reasons he gives are the obvious ones already mentioned. On the second, he assumes (like the other Counsel) that the accident was the result of an isolated act, and that the system of supervision was adequate:

> 'Turning now to the accident, it is not entirely clear what happened but when a number of children – there is no indication as to how many – were playing outside after lunch,

with a school nanny keeping a general eye over them, Ian found a broken car aerial about a foot long and began to play with the aerial and whilst he was doing so David came near him. The aerial which was in Ian's hand then caught David in the right eye.'

Notice again what happens to facts when they are shunted about among several learned legal gentlemen. The solicitor, in October 1973, interviewed the two playground supervisors on duty, and elicited that one of them had gone inside at the time of the accident. Four months later, in his partner's Instructions to Counsel to Advise, this becomes: 'At the time of the accident there was a school 'nanny' in the play area whose job it was to supervise the children at play.' And two years later, in Queen's Counsel's Opinion, it has become 'A number of children were playing outside after lunch, *with a school nanny keeping a general eye over them.*' Yet whether or not the 'nanny' *was* keeping a general eye over them is – or should be – exactly the point at issue.

Notice also how Queen's Counsel says that it is not entirely clear how the accident happened. For some reason he has not been given a complete set of the four boy witnesses' statements, but he has been given *two* of them:

'He [Ian] was sticking it in the ground and flicking it up like that. He was just chasing after us and flicking mud with the thing playing 'chaseys''; and 'Ian was larking about flicking muddy water at other boys with the aerial'.

These two statements – combined with David's own account that he was struck as he bent down to pick up a handkerchief he had dropped – give a very clear indication of how the accident happened. They also cast considerable doubt as to whether at the time a supervisor *was* 'keeping a general eye over' the children. It would seem that Queen's Counsel, who nowhere in his Opinion mentions these statements, *has not read them*, but that they remained buried under all the verbal rubbish – previous solicitors' Instructions and Counsel's Opinions, legal aid certificates, caretaker's and groundsmen's reports etc. – which he was sent.

The solicitor (that is, the senior partner) sends Mrs. Johns a copy of Queen's Counsel's Opinion, with the warning that he will have to send a copy to the Legal Aid Committee which, he says, will almost certainly cancel her legal aid. And he adds that if she continues her case, 'bearing in mind *the importance of the case to the Council's insurers* and the fact that two barristers' opinions are against you, the Insurance Company will certainly fight the matter. . .and if you were to lose the costs would certainly be WELL in excess of £1000 and probably they would run into SEVERAL thousand pounds. . .We feel that you should have a meeting with both our partners so that you can be in no doubt as to the present legal position.'

At this meeting both partners try to persuade her to abandon the case, one of them warning her that even if she won initially, the Council (i.e. the Education Authority) could take the case up to the House of Lords. According to a note she made at the time, 'I left his office in tears. The pressure was unbelievable.'

Mrs. Johns, however, still does not accept that she has no case, and now decides (perhaps belatedly) to study the evidence herself. She knows that certain boys who saw the accident made statements, and she writes to her solicitor asking for copies, adding: 'I have mentioned these statements to you at various times but have never ever seen them.' She also asks for a copy of his Instructions to Queen's Counsel to Advise. The solicitor sends her copies of the boys' statements, but explains that he cannot send a copy of his Instructions to Queen's Counsel as it 'has in fact been returned to the Legal Aid Committee.'*

On receiving the copies of the boys' statements, Mrs. Johns at once realizes their significance, and she asks the solicitor why he never sent them to Queen's Counsel – assuming that he did not because the Opinion nowhere refers to them.

He replies that Christopher's statement was not sent to Queen's Counsel – he does not mention Paul Waterhouse's statement which also was not sent – 'because it was corroborative evidence only as to the accident and does not really help the case in any way from a legal point of view other than in that connection.' And he says that his firm can no longer continue to act for her. 'The reason for this is quite simply that we feel that you have lost confidence in our services, particularly after the last conversation. We are dealing in this case *with an extremely complicated point of law* and what advice is relevant and what is not

* When I collected the file it contained the original Instructions to Queen's Counsel *and* a copy. The solicitor's reluctance to send Mrs. Johns a copy is presumably because it would show that Queen's Counsel had not been sent all the boys' statements (because Instructions to Counsel always list accompanying documents).

relevant is a matter for our advice, and we simply cannot continue to conduct the case when you question us on matters of law which are difficult to explain.'

Meanwhile, on December 12 1975, the solicitor wrote to the Legal Aid Committee:

> 'We now have Queen's Counsel's Opinion that there is no realistic prospect of obtaining damages *and that the legal aid certificate can be discharged*, and we enclose herewith a copy of his Opinion. We have explained this view to our clients who are very reluctant to accept the situation. We have explained to them that we are under a duty to bring the matter to your attention and that almost certainly you will discharge the legal aid certificate. . .The nature of the incident is such that *there is no clear picture as to exactly how the incident occurred*. The parents believe that Queen's Counsel was unable to form a clear picture of the incident due to the fact that all the statements had not been supplied by us to him. In fact the only statement [which was omitted] does not advance the cause in the slightest degree. . .'

Predictably enough, given the two unfavourable Counsel's Opinions, and the solicitor's letter, the Legal Aid Committee withdraws Mrs. Johns's legal aid. Or rather, as it was originally only a 'limited' legal aid certificate, the Committee refuses to extend it further, which comes to the same thing. Mrs. Johns appeals against this decision, which appeal she conducts herself–as she had no time to get other solicitors between the date she received the solicitor's letter telling her he would no longer act for her, and the date of the appeal. But her appeal is dismissed.

She complains to her Member of Parliament (William Rodgers) that her solicitor had not sent vital statements to Counsel, and as a result of Counsel's consequent unfavourable Opinion her legal aid has been cancelled. After getting the solicitors' version* the M.P. replies to Mrs. Johns:

'Your solicitors have obviously acted very conscientiously on

---

* How we took Counsel's Opinion which unfortunately was against our client but 'in view of the seriousness of the accident we persuaded the Legal Aid Committee to allow a further opinion from a Queen's Counsel to be taken as we felt there might possibly be a chance of bringing proceedings even though existing case law was against our client', but unfortunately Queen's Counsel's Opinion was also against our client etc. etc.

your behalf. The question, however, as far as Legal Aid is concerned is whether there is a reasonable chance of your action succeeding against the Education Authority. This is not a matter that either you or I can judge. *It is a question of law for the lawyers.* Counsel's advice showed that on the basis of precedent it was unlikely that your action would succeed. . .I wholly understand your sense of frustration, but it is necessary to consider very carefully whether an action which might cost some thousands of pounds can usefully be brought.'

Mrs. Johns, in some desperation, writes to another M.P. who has a reputation for being concerned with medical and legal injustice, but who cannot help except to assure her that she 'couldn't have a better Member of Parliament than Mr. Rodgers.' End of Part One. We'll take a break and continue the narrative in a couple of minutes.

* * * * * *

Meanwhile let's look at one or two general points. David Johns, aged 8, lost his eye in a playground accident at school. Now it could be that the accident was no-one's fault;* or it could be that the accident was someone's fault, but there is no evidence to prove it. In either case there would be no question of David getting any compensation. An accident victim gets compensation only if his accident was due to someone else's fault *and* he can prove it in Court. So if one sunny morning you or your wife or your husband or your child is disabled as the result of an accident, it's just the luck of the draw which determines whether any compensation is payable. A capricious system. Now as accident victims go, David seems to be one of the lucky ones. Prima facie his accident *does* seem to be someone else's fault, and there is quite a lot of evidence to prove it.

Yet Mrs. Johns cannot get the case to Court – or even take the first step towards getting it to Court – because her solicitors are mishandling it. But intelligent and articulate as she is, *there is nothing she can do about it.* Dividing the legal profession into solicitors and Counsel makes it virtually impossible for either to be impugned. If Mrs. Johns complains about her solicitors they will reply that they took *Counsel's Opinion* at every turn, and

* Other than the little lad who actually did the damage, which is irrelevant as he would have no money to pay any compensation.

followed his advice to the letter. Therefore, ipso facto, they did their job perfectly properly. On the other hand she cannot impugn Counsel, firstly because she has no contact with him (and may not even *speak* to him); secondly because she is in the dark as to what facts and evidence he has been fed – solicitors' Instructions to Counsel being an esoteric document not normally seen by the client, perhaps analogous to a doctor's report to a consultant. Even when, with unusual perception, Mrs. Johns realizes what has gone wrong – that the solicitor has not submitted to Counsel, or that Counsel has not properly considered, the boys' statements – there is *still* nothing she can do about it; because the only people she can complain to (her Member of Parliament, the Legal Aid Committee, the Law Society) will automatically accept the professionals' assessment of the situation, rather than her's. After all, we are dealing with questions of *law*, and what is relevant and what is not relevant is a matter for the *lawyers* to decide.

Notice how, when she starts asking her solicitor pertinent questions, as to *why* he did not submit the boys' statements to Counsel, he takes refuge behind his professional status: the case involves 'an extremely complicated point of law', and because she has the temerity to question his handling of it she must find other solicitors.* Notice also that whether or not she gets legal aid – and most people can only bring a case to Court if they do – depends on *Counsel's Opinion*. The oracle must give his favourable opinion, so that public funds are not squandered. Which gives the oracle a lot of power without, it seems, any commensurate responsibility.

So having consulted a reputable firm of solicitors who have obtained four Counsel's Opinions, Mrs. Johns's case has advanced not at all. Her legal aid has been finally terminated; and even if she decides to proceed with the case and finance it herself, she will find the two adverse Counsel's Opinions still weighing heavily round her neck. Moreover it is now nearly two and a half years since the accident, and the first step in the legal proceedings has not even been taken. The more time that passes, the less her chances of ultimate success will be – because witnesses' memories dim and their evidence is the more easily challenged; and of course the witnesses themselves may disappear. This,

---

* If you remember, this was how Mr. Perkins's Solicitor No. 2 reacted when Mr. Perkins suggested that he should *look* at the machine in question.

then, is how Mrs. Johns's basically simple case, which turns on two or three not very complicated facts (the size of the playground, the number of supervisors, how long before the accident Ian had been chasing and flicking his playmates with mud with a bit of broken car aerial) has fared when the legal system is run by lawyers, the *professional* gentlemen.

Let's consider for a moment how her case might have fared if it wasn't: if there were no such things as lawyers, but on his discharge from hospital David and his mother had called on *RAMS*. Remember RAMS? – someone with no qualifications, but with the same status, education and common sense as a reasonably alert assistant manager of a surburban chain store, who has set up in business to do the job of assembling the evidence and presenting personal injury cases in Court.

In a revealing letter to the Legal Aid Committee explaining why he needs to instruct an enquiry agent, Mrs. Johns's solicitor said 'We feel that this is a case where a certain amount of on the spot research is required, and this cannot really be undertaken by ourselves.' And if you remember, when Mr. Perkins's Solicitor No. 3 finally got round to the idea that the machine should be inspected to see if the holes in the metal table top were behind or in front of the blade, he instructed a *consulting engineer* rather than look at the thing himself. Even a 'good' solicitor who was dealing with a run-of-the-mill personal injury case, which needed someone to go out of the office to get some evidence or interview a witness, would not, I think, normally do it himself, but would probably send his clerk. In other words, the solicitor is a man of status who sits in his office dictating his letters and his Instructions to Counsel; and the actual evidence either has to come to him, or if it doesn't he instructs someone else to get it. But because RAMS *has no status* he gets whatever evidence he needs *himself*. And because he has not had his head stuffed with academic legal conundrums for three years, he will see his client's accident in practical rather than in academic terms. Thus, unlike the learned solicitor, he realizes that if he is dealing with something, the first thing he must do is go and *look* at it.

So after seeing Mrs. Johns, RAMS at once drives to the school, photographs the play area, and makes a rough plan of it. And because he looks at the thing he is dealing with, he sees at a glance (without Counsel or anyone else having to tell him) that the school cannot possibly be blamed for the presence of a bit of broken car aerial a foot long in the school grounds; but that any negligence on the part of the school or its staff would have to have been in the *supervision* of the children during playtime. Therefore he needs to know *how* the accident happened – as to which David is very hazy. So he gets from David or his mother the names and addresses of the children most likely to have seen the accident, and interviews them and gets statements *probably that same evening* – i.e. before the *school* approached them. On getting their statements he realizes, again without anyone having to tell him, that there is a reasonable chance of proving negligent supervision. And when he has interviewed and got statements from the two playground supervisors on duty, one of whom had gone *inside* at the time of the accident, he would know that it was a good chance.

Thus within a couple of days RAMS will have got the three bits of evidence he needs (the geography of the play area, the witnesses' statements, the supervisors' statements) to argue Mrs. Johns's case in Court – which two solicitors and two Counsel, shunting the papers backwards and forwards amongst each other, have failed to get in two and a half years. Her case is that Ian's escapade of chasing his playmates, digging a bit of broken car aerial into the ground, and flicking them with mud with it, had gone on for longer than it should have done if the play area had been reasonably well supervised; and that as a result of the negligent or inadequate supervision David lost his eye. (This is not to say that RAMS would necessarily have *won* the case – which would depend on the actual evidence the witnesses and supervisors gave, how they stood up to cross-examination, and what view the judge took. As long as the *basic* rules remain, whether an accident victim gets compensation must always be a lottery, however efficiently his case is presented.)

Being of the same status, RAMS would charge the same as a freelance carpenter or painter, i.e. currently about £50 a day. So for two days preparing the case and a day arguing it, he would charge in the region of £200. Thus not only does he not need to take Counsel's Opinion at every turn, with all the delay and obfuscation that that entails, but Mrs. Johns does not have to get legal aid to employ him, with all the delay and botheration that *that* entails.

Of course RAMS might be incompetent. But there are several

reasons why he is less likely to be incompetent than a solicitor. Firstly, common sense would be his stock-in-trade, whereas the solicitor's academic training, and his litigation (and conveyancing) ritual dance, are the very negation of common sense.* Secondly, this would be his *sole line of business*, whereas the average family solicitor relies primarily on conveyancing, probate and divorce for his income, and merely dabbles in personal injury litigation when occasion requires. Thirdly, unlike the solicitor, he does the job himself from start to finish – gets the evidence, does the thinking, and finally argues the case in Court – so he would derive some satisfaction from doing it properly. Fourthly, he would not be able to shelter behind any professional mystique or Counsel's Opinion. Nevertheless if RAMS *was* incompetent it would not be so disastrous, for his clients would be better able to deal with him. As he has no status the client can treat him as an equal. Thus at the first meeting Mrs. Johns would ask him how he intends to proceed; and because there is no Counsel's Opinion or legal aid to be obtained, there is no reason for any delay. So if he has not interviewed the witnesses or whatever within a couple of weeks, Mrs. Johns knows he is messing her around – so she can dismiss him and instruct another RAMS. And as word got around that the vast majority of personal injury cases involved little more than common sense, there would be nothing to prevent Mrs. Johns and her ilk arguing their own cases themselves.

But I digress. Court cases are so important that for the public's protection they may not be presented by the unqualified operator, but only by the professional – that is, someone who has passed examinations and whose competence and integrity are vouched for by his professional governing body. So if Mrs. Johns wishes to proceed with her case, she has to instruct another firm of solicitors; which she does in January 1976.

* * * * * *

It takes a few months for the second solicitors to get hold of the file, the first solicitor having sent it to a firm of costs draftsmen to

---

* I develop this theme in Part 2. For the moment suffice it to say that the purpose of the solicitor's academic training – whereby he learns to recite the Rules against Perpetuities backwards – is to *prevent* him wondering whether there is anything slightly ridiculous in him, a highly paid professional man, having to ask Counsel whether, e.g., David Johns has a negligence action in respect of a playground accident.

draw up his bill. But eventually it is handed over in May 1976.

Having studied the papers, which include the four boys' statements and the previous solicitor's note of his interview with the playground supervisors, the second solicitor advises Mrs. Johns against proceeding with the negligence action. However, he suggests making an application under the Criminal Injuries Compensation Scheme – a scheme whereby the victim of a *crime of violence* can apply for compensation to the Criminal Injuries Compensation Board. But to be a crime at all, the perpetrator has to *intend* to cause injury. As on the evidence Ian clearly did not intend to cause any harm but was merely engaged in a childish prank, it is difficult to see why the solicitor should have suggested this course.

The application to the Criminal Injuries Compensation Board, for which the solicitor engages a Counsel on Mrs. Johns's behalf, is heard in November 1976 and – predictably – dismissed. Meanwhile the negligence action has remained in abeyance, except that the solicitor has issued a writ (which has to be done within three years of the accident, see footnote on p. 157).

December 1976. It is now over three years since the accident, and despite having had to pay £100 for the latest legal escapade (as well as having had to pay £250 in contributions to the legal aid fund in respect of her former solicitors' services), Mrs. Johns still insists on proceeding with the negligence action. Now that her legal aid has been withdrawn she will have to pay her legal costs herself, which the solicitor requires her to begin paying by weekly instalments.

So, the writ having been issued, the next step is for the solicitor to instruct Counsel to draft *Statement of Claim*. And as this is a different Counsel, the solicitor sends him copies of the boys' statements, and a summary of the facts of the accident as follows:

> 'David joined a group of other children when an incident occurred and David received an injury to the eye and subsequently lost the sight of that eye. It now transpires that one of the children had found on the grass, part of a car radio aerial and that subsequently that aerial came into contact with David's eye and the injury was sustained. Counsel will note that there is with the papers an opinion of Queen's Counsel.

Notwithstanding the advice from previous solicitors, previous Counsel, Queen's Counsel, and present instructing solicitors, the parents insist on bringing the action and have been made fully aware of the risks involved. Counsel may find himself in some difficulty as to pleading negligence in this matter, and unfortunately Instructing Solicitors are not going to be too helpful in that respect. So far as can be seen from the incident, the only allegation that can be made was that there was perhaps a lack of care on behalf of the Authority in failing to regularly inspect the playing fields. . .The second prong would appear to be lack of supervision by the 'nannies' who are apparently employed to supervise the children outside the school. There is some indication that the nanny was not present when the incident occurred.'

Notice how, for some reason, every detail in this account has been blurred or distorted. Whereas David's right eye had to be removed, Counsel is told David *lost the sight of that eye*. Ian hit David in the eye with a bit of broken car aerial becomes: *It transpires that one of the children found part of a car aerial and that subsequently that aerial came into contact with David's eye*. The nannies are *apparently* employed to supervise the children. There is *some indication* that the nanny was not present when the incident occurred.

The next year (1977) is taken up with the formal steps of preparing the case for trial.

February 4, Plaintiff's Statement of Claim, which has been duly drafted by Counsel, is sent to the solicitors acting for the Defendants.*

February 24, Defendants' Defence – which simply denies that the accident was caused by the negligence of the Education Authority or its employees – is sent to the Plaintiff's solicitor.

May 31, Summons For Directions, at which a Court official makes an order for each side to serve the other with a list of any relevant documents (e.g. medical reports, photograph of the aerial etc.) in their possession.

November 8, Plaintiff's solicitor files 'certificate of readiness' at the Court.

January 1978, the Court office notifies the parties' solicitors of

* I.e. the Education Authority which, if you remember, is vicariously liable for the negligence of its employees.

the date of the trial – February 9 1978.* This is when the case will be heard in the High Court; and the judge, after listening to the evidence and argument of Counsel for both sides, will decide whether David's accident four and a half years ago was or was not due to the negligence of the Education Authority or its employees; and how much compensation the Authority should pay David, if he decides that it was.

Meanwhile Mrs. Johns's solicitor has instructed Counsel to 'advise on evidence'. This is a standard step whereby the solicitor asks Counsel what evidence (documents, witnesses etc.) he, the solicitor, should have available at the trial – and Counsel duly 'advises on evidence'. On the question of witnesses, Counsel states that David will be required to give evidence, and: 'the question of supporting witnesses should however be discussed with Mrs. Johns so as to ascertain which of the boys would be likely to make the best impression as a witness, and *his presence* should be secured at the trial.' Counsel has not followed up the solicitor's remark in his previous Instructions, that 'there is some indication that the nanny was not present when the incident occurred.' For he neither enquires *what* indication there is of this rather crucial fact, nor suggests that the two 'nannies' who were on duty at the time should be required to give evidence at the trial. As for the four boy witnesses, Counsel has been given copies of their statements – and their's is the vital evidence which alone can establish negligent supervision. Yet Counsel seems to be suggesting that only *one* of them will be needed, and which one should be left to Mrs. Johns to decide. Neither has Counsel ever suggested, nor apparently has it occurred to the solicitor, that these boys should be interviewed and asked to make fuller statements; and in particular asked for *how long* Ian had been chasing the other boys, digging the aerial into the ground, and flicking them with mud – their statements, which had been taken on behalf of the defendants, not surprisingly omitting this vital point.

Nevertheless, despite the half-hearted way in which Mrs. Johns's legal team seems to be prosecuting her case, it now appears that – four and a half years after the accident – it is

* Normally the date of trial is nine months after the case is 'set down for hearing'. That this date is much sooner is probably due to the parties' solicitors stating that the trial would take only a few hours.

actually going to come to Court.

As often happens at this juncture, the defendants, through their solicitors, make an offer of settlement – £1,000 plus legal costs.* This offer is made on the telephone to Mrs. Johns's solicitor on January 19 1978; and confirmed by the defendants' solicitors in a letter of the same date, which stipulates that a condition of the offer is that '*there will be no attendant publicity whatsoever, and that all allegations of negligence are withdrawn.*'

The solicitor discusses this offer with Mr. and Mrs. Johns† on 24th January 1978, and makes a note of the discussion:

'As I feared, it seems that this offer merely encourages them to continue with the litigation. I pointed out quite clearly that the end result would mean no damages for David and a heavy bill of costs. It would be in David's interests to accept £1,000. I gave them until Friday to let me know what their instructions are on the matter, and thereafter I must proceed to trial.'

In fact at this meeting Mr. and Mrs. Johns unequivocally rejected the offer, but as the solicitor insisted that they think about it and let him know, they confirmed their rejection by telephone two days later. A telephone note on the solicitor's file dated 26th January states: 'Mrs. Johns phoned. They have discussed the offer and decided *not* to accept. Proceed to Court.'

Accordingly, having previously served them with subpoenas (at the insistence of Mrs. Johns),‡ on 26th January the solicitor writes to the parents of the four boy witnesses notifying them of the date of the Court hearing – 9th February – and advising them that their respective sons should be outside the Court office at 10.15 a.m. that day. And on 31st January the solicitor sends Counsel final Instructions ('brief') to argue the case in Court on David's behalf; and arranges for Counsel to see David and the four witnesses for a final 'conference' just before the Court hearing.

---

* See footnote on p. 163.

† Hitherto Mrs. Johns has taken the initiative, her husband remaining in the background and giving her such support as he could. Incidentally, he still suffers from a stress induced medical condition, dating from his son's accident, whereas his wife escaped apparently unscathed.

‡ In his brief to Counsel the solicitor stated: 'The Plaintiff has insisted that the children should be subpoenaed although Instructing Solicitors have indicated that this is not necessary.'

Whereas Counsel will already have been given the facts of a case in his various previous instructions, he is a busy man dealing with numerous other cases; and the solicitor's 'brief to Counsel' should be a comprehensive summary of all the facts and evidence which Counsel will present in Court to establish his client's case. In this 'brief' the solicitor describes the accident in much the same way as in his previous instructions: 'A group of boys appear to have met and one of the boys had in his possession a car aerial. There was some skylarking and David was struck in the eye. The result is that the eye has had to be removed.' Again nothing about the *nature* of the skylarking as evidenced by the four boys' statements; nothing about the fact that one of the two playground supervisors on duty had gone *inside* at the time of the accident; nothing about the *size* of the play area, and the fact that one supervisor would be inadequate.

However, Counsel has been briefed; the four boy witnesses have been subpoenaed and notified of the date of the trial; and on 9th February, the appointed day, Mr. and Mrs. Johns and David go to the Court, where they meet their solicitor.

But there were no witnesses, and no-one from the other side.

'We asked him where were our witnesses but he didn't reply. Then our barrister came, whom we had never seen before. He asked 'What's your decision on this offer?' We told him we weren't accepting it and wanted to go to Court. He said 'I'll let you think it over.' We replied we didn't need to think it over. He said 'You're putting me in a dilemma. You think it over'; and went away, and returned after what seemed like 20 minutes but may have been less. He again asked 'Well, what about it?' and we again replied that we didn't accept, and wanted to go to Court. He then said: 'Well in that case we'll remove you as your son's next friend,* and we'll accept the £1,000 on his behalf, and you'll have to get another barrister and solicitor to fight our decision.' We were in this small room by the Court. Our solicitor never said anything. It was very hot in there. After some time Cec [Mr. Johns] suddenly stood up and shouted: 'Bugger it, all right I'll

* Where the plaintiff is an infant the action has to be brought through his '*next friend*' – usually one of his parents – who is his representative, and who makes the decisions on his behalf.

accept. But he'll never go back to that bloody school again.' '*

In fact, unknown to Mr. and Mrs. Johns, the previous day the solicitor had sent letters to all the witnesses' parents as follows:

'We confirm the recent telegram. Certain negotiations have taken place and your son's attendance at Court on Thursday is not required.'

Also on that day he had lodged a Summons applying for a Court Order to remove the father as David's 'next friend' (if the parents persisted in their refusal of the defendants' offer), together with an affidavit which he had sworn in support of such application. The gist of this affidavit was that in view of the opinion of the parents' legal advisers (past and present) that there was no chance of winning the case, the parents were not acting in their child's interests in refusing the defendants' offer of £1,000; and that the father should therefore be removed as his child's 'next friend', and some other person should be appointed to accept it on David's behalf.

Now there have been instances where a child's 'next friend' in legal proceedings has been removed. But this rarely happens. And when it *has* happened, the person seeking to remove the 'next friend' is almost invariably a relative of the child, who considers that the 'next friend' is not pursuing the child's case with proper diligence, and is therefore prejudicing the child's interests. Of course it might be that an infant plaintiff's case is so weak, and the defendants' offer to settle out of Court so generous, that the parents' legal advisers might well feel that if the parents do not accept then it would be in the child's best interests to remove them as decision makers. But such an extreme action (which would have very dangerous implications) has never, I think, been taken in such a situation. In any case that is not the situation here.

So why does Mrs. Johns's solicitor prepare to take such an

---

* Any out of Court settlement where the plaintiff is an infant has to be 'approved' by the Court. Although intended as a safeguard, the Court almost invariably rubber stamps the agreement which the infant plaintiff's Counsel tells the judge has been reached between the parties – which is what the Court does on this occasion. Indeed, short of the judge requisitioning the plaintiff's solicitor's file and spending a couple of days going through it, it is difficult to see how it could be otherwise.

extreme step when, so far as David is concerned, there is only £1,000 at issue – scarcely a king's ransom for the loss of an eye?

And why is he suddenly so concerned on David's behalf that he files at the Court, a summons and a three and a half page affidavit – by far the longest document he has produced hitherto – to get the father removed as 'next friend', when he has shown such singular lack of concern on David's behalf in his actual *handling* of the case over the previous two years? For instance, although at the outset he was given the four boy witnesses' statements, he never drew Counsel's attention to them, or tried to interview the boys to get fuller statements. Although these statements as they stand show exactly how the accident occurred, and that it occurred in a way which prima facie indicates negligent supervision, in his Instructions to Counsel he describes the accident in the vaguest terms ('one of the boys had in his possession a car aerial. There was some skylarking and David was struck in the eye'). He tells Counsel 'there is some indication that the 'nanny' was not present when the incident occurred', but does not follow up this vital fact; nor interview the two playground supervisors; nor require them to give evidence in Court; nor bring to Counsel's attention the size of the play area, and the fact that one supervisor would be inadequate to supervise it on her own, and so on.

The timing of his strange initiative raises a third question. The defendants' solicitors made the offer to him by telephone on 19th January and confirmed it by letter the same day. The parents refused the offer at the discussion with him on 24th January which (because he insisted they go away and 'think about it') Mrs. Johns confirmed in a telephone call on 26th January – as to which there is a note in the file. The solicitor therefore knows on 26th January that the parents have definitely refused the defendants' offer. Why, therefore, does he not *at once* make the application to remove the father as 'next friend', instead of making arrangements for the trial to go ahead (writing to the four witnesses' parents to have their sons at the Court, delivering the brief to Counsel), and *then* deciding to remove the father as 'next friend', and cancel the witnesses' attendance? Or to put the question another way, the parents having finally refused the defendants' offer on 26th January and the solicitor having accordingly made arrangements for the case to be heard in Court, what happened between 26th January and 8th February to make him change his mind, decide that the case shall not after all come to Court, and cancel the witnesses' attendance?

It seems that the solicitor himself has anticipated this question, in that in his affidavit he puts the date of the defendants' solicitors' telephone call, when they first made the offer, as '*on or about 26th January 1978*'; and judiciously omits mention of Mrs. Johns's telephone call of 26th January when she finally refused the offer. So we have a fourth question. Why does the solicitor say in his affidavit that the defendants' solicitors' telephone offer was made 'on or about 26th January 1978' – and one only uses the expression 'on or about' when one is not sure of a date – when he knows the exact date, and that it was 19th January 1978?

As far as I can see, there are only two possible answers to these questions. One is that the solicitor is fearful that his slovenly manner of prosecuting his client's case will be exposed if the case goes to Court, and he is prepared virtually to force his client to settle out of Court to prevent that happening. This, however, I think is unlikely, because even at this late stage he could still interview the boys; and Counsel could still make out quite a good case on their evidence, plus the size of the playground. Indeed there would probably still be time to contact and subpoena the two playground supervisors.

The other explanation, which I think is more likely, is that the gentlemen ultimately responsible for paying the compensation in such cases – that is, the reinsurers with whom the defendants' insurance company itself insures the risk (just as a bookie hedges his bets) – were fearful that if David's parents succeeded in their action against the Education Authority, it might encourage other parents whose children had accidents in schools up and down the country, and who would not otherwise think of so doing, to take similar action. Remember the condition of the offer – that *'there will be no attendant publicity whatsoever'*? So a few thousand to Mrs. Johns's solicitor, probably in the shape of some exceptionally lucrative business (and perhaps a little something for learned Counsel), to prevent that happening, would be a prudent expenditure. In other words, the solicitor has been bribed. Or more probably the initial bribe, which was responsible for him trying to sabotage David's case in a passive way from the outset, was dramatically increased at the last minute to induce him to sabotage it in a rather more active way. So when on 8th February, the day before the trial, he wrote to the parents of the four boy witnesses: '*Certain negotiations have taken place* and your son's attendance at Court on Thursday is not required', his choice of words was – in the circumstances – suprisingly apt.

* * * * * *

If any reader is interested in querying the authenticity of any of the events in the foregoing narrative, and cares to write to me (address on rear cover) enclosing stamped addressed envelope plus the current cost of photo-copying, I will send the relevant copy documents.

Meanwhile a few of them are reproduced in the appendix immediately following.

INSTRUCTIONS TO LEADING COUNSEL TO ADVISE ON LIABILITY - Legal Aid Reference No. 8/4/74/2461N

On the 19th September 1973 David J who is aged 9 and attending the Junior School where he was a pupil. There was an incident when he was hit in the eye by a broken piece of car radio aerial. The resulting injury and infection which set in caused the need for the removal of that eye.

It would be pointless for instructing Solicitors to go into any great detail in these instructions as to the details of the accident and their views as all matters are adequately dealt with in the instructions to Junior Counsel but briefly the matter has been approached in three ways. Initially it was considered that the question of supervision and whether this was adequate. Then was considered the question of whether, had the child been taken straight to the hospital, and not as was the case, kept at the school for prolonged period, whether the infection requiring the removal of the eye would have been avoided. Finally it was considered that the position with regard to foreign objects in general which appear to have accummulated to some marked degree on this school playing field and which appear to have been a regular hazard, if not to the pupils, then to the equipment of the gardener attending to the cutting of the field.

It is the opinion of Junior Counsel that generally the prospects of successing do not warrant an action being brought and has advised accordingly.

The next friend of the infant plaintiff desires that the opinion of leading Counsel be obtained and instructing Solicitors will be pleased if Counsel will so advise.

he Area Secretary,
he Law Society,

12th December, 1975.
LH/CAM

ear Sir,

Certificate No. 8/4/74/2461N

---

s you know we represent David J in connection with an incident
hich occurred at the Junior School on the 19th September, 1973.
s a result of this incident David who at that time was 9 years old
eceived an injury to his eye which ultimately resulted in its
urgical removal. As you will see from the papers Legal Aid has
een granted for various preliminary purposes and finally to obtain
he opinion of Leading Counsel. We now have the opinion of Mr.
Q.C. to the effect that there is no realistic
rospect of obtaining damages and that the Legal Aid Certificate
an be discharged and enclose herewith a copy of Mr. 's
pinion.

e have explained thisview and the present situation to our clients
ho are very reluctant to accept thesituation. We have explained
o them that we are under a duty now to bring the matter to your
ttention and that almost certainly you will discharge the Certificate
ut at the same time allow Mr. and Mrs. J the opportunity of
ppearing before the Committee to advance reasons why the Certificate
hould not be discharged. We trust that this opportunity will be
fforded to Mr. and Mrs. J .

he nature of the incident is such that there is no clear picture
s to exactly how the incident occurred. The parents believe that
ueen's Counsel was unable to form a fullyand clear picture of the
ncident due to the fact that all the statements had not been
upplied by us to him. In actual fact the only statement that has
ot been to Mr. is a statement of Christopher Foxton, one
f the boys involved which in our opinion does not advance the
ause in the slightest degree.

This is Mrs. Johns's solicitor's letter to the Legal Aid Committee, as a result of which her legal aid certificate was cancelled. Note that the solicitor says 'there is no clear picture as to exactly how the incident occurred'. The four boys' statements (in his possession) do give a clear picture how the incident occurred (see p. 187/8). The solicitor also tells the Legal Aid Committee that only one statement – Christopher Foxton's – was not sent to Queen's Counsel. In fact Paul Waterhouse's statement was not sent either.

Our Ref. INS/JA

19th January 1978

Dear Sirs,

Re: County Council and D.C. J
Without Prejudice

We confirm today's telephone discussion with your Mr. when we informed you that our clients have had the benefit of Counsel's Opinion who considered that this case could be defended successfully

Nonetheless the Insurers are prepared to make an ex gratia payment to your client's son. The amount they have instructed us to offer is £1,000 plus a contribution of £650 towards the Plaintiff's costs.

We must inform you that this offer is final and is not capable of negotiations nor is the question of costs.

The offer is made on the distinct understanding and undertaking by your client that in the event of it being accepted there will be no attendant publicity whatsoever, that all allegations of negligence are withdrawn and that this is an ex gratia offer made without any admission of liability or fault.

Will you be good enough to let us know your client's intentions within the next ten days which is when the Civil Sittings start as we do not wish to deliver a Brief if the claim can be disposed of.

cont/....

7. On or about the 26th January, 1978 I received a telephone call from the Defendant's Solicitors indicating that they had instructions from their Insurance Company clients to put forward an offer of £1,000.00. damages in settlement of the Plaintiff's claim on an ex gratia basis, together with the sum of £650.00. contribution towards the Plaintiff's costs. I contacted the Plaintiff Mr. Cecil J and in the presence of his wife the following day I advised them of the offer and asked for their instructions. I indicated to them that the offer should be accepted in view of the grave danger that if the action was

N THE HIGH COURT OF JUSTICE 1976 J. No. 307

UEEN'S BENCH DIVISION

ETWEEN:

DAVID J
(An infant suing by his father and next friend
CECIL J) Plaintiff

and

EDUCATION AUTHORITY Defendants

LET THE SOLICITORS to all parties attend before the Honourable Mr. Justice Cantley sitting at the Crown Court, 9th day of February, 1978 at 10.30 a.m. in the forenoon on the hearing of an application on the part of David J a minor for an Order that Cecil J be removed from his Office as the next friend of the Plaintiff David J on the grounds set out in the affidavit annexed hereto and that the Court do give consideration to the appointing of a next friend in place of the aforesaid Cecil J .

For such Order as the Court in its discretion thinks fit

....

Served this 8th day of February, 1978

SOLICITORS FOR THE PLAINTIFF

8 *The case of Tessa Andrews*

On 19th March 1962 Tessa Andrews, aged 8, was struck on the side of the head by a van as she was crossing or preparing to cross the road. At the time of the accident she was holding the hand of a younger girl who was unhurt. Part of Tessa's skull was shattered, and her resulting brain damage was permanent and disastrous.

Her father – a jeweller in a small way of business – instructed a large city firm of solicitors with a view to claiming compensation for negligence. At a preliminary meeting with the litigation partner he outlined how, as he understood it, the accident happened; and also gave some leads as to how he thought negligence on the part of the van driver might be proved.

The litigation partner (as I think is customary in large firms) delegated the case to one of his 'managing clerks'.

Over the next few months the clerk obtained a hospital report, and the police report of the accident – the police having arrived on the scene almost immediately. He also obtained statements from two bystanders mentioned in the police report, who did not see the accident and could give no relevant information. On 7th September 1962 he wrote to Mr. Andrews stating that because no-one *saw* the accident, 'it will be a matter of very great difficulty' to establish negligence on the part of the driver – which my reader will remember is a pre-condition to an accident victim, however disastrously injured, being entitled to compensation.

Mr. Andrews reiterated in a letter the points he had made at the initial meeting:

1. At the time of the accident there were a lot of children

around on their way home from school, and this particular road is always lined with parked cars. Therefore the driver should have taken special care.

2. The force with which Tessa was hit ('to smash her skull in pieces') indicates that the van was being driven too fast.

3. The fact that only the right hand side of Tessa's head was hit, and the rest of her suffered no bruises or even scratches, shows that she was hit as she merely put her head out between two parked cars to see if it was safe to cross, and that therefore the van was being driven too close to the parked cars.

4. At the time of the accident Tessa was holding the hand of a younger girl whom she regularly collected from school, and who was not injured in any way. Moreover, although no-one actually saw the accident, a man had noticed the two girls walking slowly hand in hand in front of him, apparently looking for a safe place to cross the road; and as he passed them (a few seconds before the accident) the elder one had cautiously stepped off the kerb between two parked cars.* Thus the evidence of these two witnesses – younger girl and passer-by – would indicate that Tessa did not suddenly run into the road.

5. The roadworthiness of the van should be checked.†

In addition to these points, the police report of the accident, obtained by the solicitor's clerk, contained another crucial piece of evidence. Commencing at the spot where Tessa had been hit, there was a single continuous tyre mark on the road, 39 feet long, which had been made by the van's offside wheels. At its commencement this tyre mark was 10 feet 4 inches from the nearside kerb (i.e. the kerb which Tessa had stepped off), and at its termination it was 16 feet from the nearside kerb.

This tyre mark, and its position, has a fourfold significance: (a) as it was a *single* mark, it indicates that only one side of the van's brakes were fully effective; (b) if the van's *offside* wheels were 10 feet 4 inches from the nearside kerb at the spot where Tessa was hit, the van must have been driven dangerously close to the line of parked cars at this point (which corroborates the other evidence that she was hit as she merely put her head out to see if it

---

* It was this person (who was *not* one of the bystanders mentioned in the police report) who broke the news of the accident to Tessa's mother – who lived nearby – told her what he had observed, and left his card.

† The police do not automatically check a vehicle involved in an accident unless it is a fatal one.

was safe to cross); (c) as the tyre mark *commenced* at the point of collision, the driver must have seen something to make him brake some 40 feet* *before* the collision; (d) assuming the tyre mark had no pronounced curve in it, it indicates that the driver did not swerve, since he altered course only by 5 feet 8 inches over the distance of 39 feet from where the tyre mark commenced to where it terminated.

The solicitor's clerk, however, attaches no significance to the police report and the tyre mark. And he is equally dismissive of Mr. Andrews's points, curtly replying to his letter: '*If, as you suggest, your daughter put her head between two stationary vehicles, this in itself would suggest that a very considerable part of the blame for the accident must rest on her.*'

Meanwhile the driver's insurance company, without any admission of liability, makes an ex gratia offer of £1,000 in full settlement, which Mr. Andrews refuses. He writes to his solicitor's clerk:

> 'I definitely will not accept this offer and ask you to go ahead and get the case to the High Court. My daughter is a mental wreck for life. She has passed through every type of neurological and intelligence test, and according to Dr. Vaughan of Guys Hospital she has the intelligence of a 3½ year old, and she is permanently epileptic. But she could be educated to a certain extent in Switzerland or America. I therefore ask you to issue a writ and hope the Court will give substantial compensation to enable me to do the best possible for her. As it is, my wife is suffering tremendously with her nerves since Tessa has been home, and it won't take long before she reaches the state of a mental collapse. . .I want the justice of the Court which I am prepared to accept, win or lose. I will then feel I have done all in my power to help my family, which after all is my duty.'

Like Mr. Perkins, Mr. Andrews has heard that British Justice is second to none. But the solicitor's clerk disregards his instructions, and in March 1963 (a year after the accident) instructs

---

* Average *thinking* time – i.e. from when a driver sees something to make him brake to when he actually starts applying his brakes – is ⅔ of a second, during which time a vehicle going at 30 m.p.h. travels 30 feet; plus 13 feet from when the brakes are first applied to when they reach their maximum efficiency so as to cause a tyre mark – or brake mark – on the road.

a *Queen's Counsel to advise* – although Mr. Andrews has not asked him to, and there has been no suggestion of legal aid.

In his 'Instructions to Counsel to Advise' the clerk makes no mention of the tyre mark; nor does he mention any of Mr. Andrews's points, which he has not followed up. He has made no investigation as to the van's roadworthiness; and although he sends Counsel the police report, and statements which he obtained from the two bystanders who can give no relevant information, he has not approached the two witnesses who *could* give some relevant information – the girl whose hand Tessa had been holding, and the passer-by who had noticed Tessa cautiously stepping off the kerb. In fact the bulk of his 'Instructions to Counsel to Advise' is taken up with the insurance company's offer:

> 'There have been some 'without prejudice' discussions between Instructing Solicitors and the solicitors acting for the driver's insurance company.* Liability on behalf of the motorist has been categorically repudiated, but the insurance company have put forward an offer of £1,000 purely as an ex gratia payment to express their sympathy for the child's misfortune. The father is exceedingly reluctant to accept this offer and it is somewhat difficult to make him understand that before the defendant is liable the plaintiff has to establish negligence. . .'

In a preliminary note, Counsel says that before he can give an opinion he needs to see photographs of the street, and a surveyor's plan on which the police should mark the position of the child in the street. But although he has been sent a copy of the police report, Counsel does not mention the tyre mark. Nor does he suggest making a mechanical inspection of the van. However he does say that when the additional material he has requested is to hand, he will require a consultation.

The clerk, having obtained photographs of the street, and a surveyor's plan marked as requested, he sends them to Counsel with a note stating:

'Instructing Solicitors are being *very heavily pressed* by the solicitors for the Insurance Company to come to a decision as to

---

* You will remember that although the nominal defendant is the driver, the *real* defendant is his insurance company; and it is the insurance company who instructs solicitors to defend the claim.

the acceptance of the offer which has now of course been outstanding for some considerable time. Counsel will therefore please advise as a matter of urgency whether this offer should be accepted.'

And without the suggested consultation taking place (at which Mr. Andrews could have put his points direct to Counsel), Queen's Counsel writes his opinion on a single side of foolscap paper:

'The case is obviously very weak and it is only too clear that the Defendant's case will be: 'Suddenly and without warning the child emerged from the cover of a stationary vehicle. Nothing could have saved her and I was in no way negligent.' There will be no-one to contradict him . . . I am reluctant to advise acceptance [of the offer] but I must say that it seems to me that the only chance of establishing negligence would be out of the mouth of the driver himself . . . *On the whole I feel it is right for me to say that the offer should be accepted.*'

This opinion is dated 1st August 1963, and a month later the solicitor's clerk writes to Mr. Andrews:

> 'We have now obtained an Opinion from Mr. – Q.C. who is probably the most experienced Barrister in accident cases. All the information in our possession was placed before him. Indeed at his request further information was sought from the police and every scrap of information available was placed before Counsel. We now enclose a copy of his Opinion from which you will see that somewhat reluctantly he advises that the offer should be accepted because the case is so very weak. *The solicitors acting for the Insurance Company are getting rather impatient and have intimated that if the offer is not accepted soon it may be withdrawn, in which case nothing will be forthcoming. In these circumstances we must urge you most strongly that the offer should be accepted.* Please let us have your instructions as soon as possible.'

Mr. Andrews replies that, as he previously stated, he will *not* accept the offer, and he once again urges the solicitor's clerk to proceed with the case as speedily as possible. The clerk answers even more forcefully:

> 'We must point out to you in the clearest possible language that if you commence proceedings we are of the opinion that they will fail. Not only is this our opinion but also the opinion

of the most experienced Q.C. in this field. If you lose, not only will there be NOTHING for your daughter, but you will be responsible not only for your own legal costs but the costs of the other side, and the total sum involved could be very considerable. On the other hand, if the offer is accepted there will be £1,000 available which . . . *we are quite certain is the best obtainable in the circumstances. This offer will not be kept open very much longer and we must again urge you to let us have your instructions to accept it.*' (Letter dated 11th September 1963.)

Now why does Mr. Andrews's solicitor's clerk urge him to accept the insurance company's offer of £1,000, for his disastrously brain-damaged child, in such forceful and dogmatic terms? And why has he not followed up any of Mr. Andrews's leads: e.g. why has he not interviewed the two witnesses – the young girl whose hand Tessa had been holding, and the passer-by – whose evidence would indicate that Tessa did not 'suddenly and without warning' run in front of the van? And why has he not arranged for a mechanical inspection of the van? And why has he not put any of Mr. Andrews's other points to Counsel? And why has he not inquired as to his client's financial circumstances and applied for legal aid? And why does he go to a *Queen's* Counsel (whose opinion of course carries far more weight), when for an initial opinion one would normally go to an ordinary Counsel? Turning to Counsel's opinion, why does 'the most experienced Queen's Counsel in this field' not notice the crucial evidence of the single tyre mark, and its position, contained in the police report – a copy of which he has been sent? And why does he not suggest getting a mechanical report on the van, or even asking a few pertinent questions as to its maintenance? And why does the consultation he originally suggested not take place? We'll leave these questions in abeyance for the moment.

Meanwhile it is one and a half years since the accident, and Mr. Andrews's domestic circumstances do nothing to allay his frustration with his solicitors. He complains to the Law Society that they are refusing to carry out his instructions to bring Tessa's case to Court, and are putting undue pressure on him to accept the insurance company's derisory offer. The Law Society relays Mr. Andrews's complaint to the litigation partner, who replies:

'Unfortunately after the most careful enquiries we were unable to obtain any evidence whatsoever which indicated the driver was in any way to blame. It would appear that this most unfortunate child stepped out into the path of a motor car (sic) giving the driver no chance to avoid her. However the Insurance Company made an offer of £1,000 as a gesture in view of the serious nature of the child's injuries. . .and we suggested to Mr. Andrews that the opinion of Queen's Counsel should be obtained as to whether this offer should be accepted. To this Mr. Andrews agreed albeit without any enthusiasm. After careful consideration Counsel advised that on balance the offer should be accepted.'

The Law Society duly relays the solicitor's reply back to Mr. Andrews; and at the same time adds its own comments: 'If *Queen's Counsel* is of the opinion that the prospects of success if you commence litigation are not great, and that therefore £1,000 is a suitable figure at which to arrange a settlement, *I do not understand why you are not prepared to accept it*.'

Mr. Andrews, however, is not prepared to accept it; and in October 1963 he dismisses his solicitors and instructs another firm. Although his firm has been dismissed, the managing clerk for some reason is still concerned with the insurance company's offer, for in his letter to the new solicitors (with which he sends them the file) he says: 'There is a matter of considerable urgency. . .some time ago the insurance company through their solicitors made an ex gratia offer of £1,000. . .and they have been pressing us for some time for a reply to the offer, indicating that otherwise it may be withdrawn. *Counsel's Opinion on the advisability of accepting this offer accompanies these papers*.'

Mr. Andrews gives his second solicitors the same leads as to proving negligence as he had given the first; and at first they seem to be more than willing to take the case. They say that there is a good chance of success, agree at once to apply for legal aid, and take details of his financial position to fill in the legal aid application form. But then something evidently occurs to make them re-appraise the position. For on 13th December 1963 – without having applied for legal aid – they write to him saying that in view of *Queen's Counsel's Opinion* that the insurance company's offer should be accepted, 'the offer should be put before the Court for their consideration, as it may be that in the circumstances the Court thinks the case should be settled on the terms suggested.' In other words, Mr. Andrews's second solicitors are saying that because of Queen's Counsel's Opinion, Mr. Andrews must have a preliminary Court hearing to decide whether he should be *allowed* to proceed with his child's claim. Why, having agreed to take the case, they now adopt this bizarre attitude is perhaps another question to be added to our list. Mr. Andrews refuses the solicitors' suggestion. They in turn refuse to continue to act for him.

After nearly two years since the accident, despite having instructed two firms of solicitors, not even the first step towards getting the case to Court has been taken. Mrs. Andrews is now on the verge of collapse, and Mr. Andrews has had to give up his work to look after Tessa full time at home (there being no institution available in view of her aggressive behaviour). And for good measure his first solicitors, having presented him with a bill for £120 which he cannot pay, have instructed a firm of debt collectors who are threatening him with legal proceedings. Like so many others before and after him, Mr. Andrews in seeking British Justice – the envy of the civilized world – finds that he has strayed into the nightmare world of Kafka.

Nevertheless he struggles on, gets the legal aid application forms, and himself submits an application for legal aid. His application is refused for reason E on the form – that the applicant has not shown reasonable grounds for pursuing the claim. As the Legal Aid Committee asked to see all his correspondence with his previous solicitors, it seems that the Queen's Counsel's Opinion that the insurance company's offer should be accepted is still dogging his footsteps.

Mr. Andrews lodges notice of appeal against this refusal, and instructs a third firm of solicitors. He tells his new solicitor of the two witnesses, and the various leads which could be followed up to show negligence on the part of the van driver, as he had told his two previous solicitors. Solicitor No. 3 gets the papers (including the police report) from Solicitor No. 2, and engages a different Counsel to argue the appeal – whom Mr. Andrews meets prior to the hearing in order to go over the various points. And Mr. Andrews scores a significant victory. A *conditional* legal aid certificate is granted.

The condition is that after the various procedural steps have been taken by the plaintiff's and defendant's respective solicitors preparatory to the trial, but before the case is 'set down for hearing' (i.e. officially put in the queue of cases which are going to trial), *Counsel's further opinion must be taken* and submitted to the Legal Aid Committee. In the light of that opinion the Committee will then either allow the case to go to trial, or else revoke the legal aid – in which event the case will have to be abandoned. This is a common condition, the philosophy being that learned Counsel will be in a better position to assess the plaintiff's case *after* the various procedural steps have been completed; and if Counsel then considers that the plaintiff's chances of success are doubtful, public funds should not be wasted in continuing to subsidize his case.

It is now June 1964, and after the legal aid is granted Solicitor No. 3 hands the matter over to his clerk who henceforth deals with the case. Nevertheless for convenience, and because he represents and acts in the name of his solicitor employer, I will continue to refer to him as a solicitor. So after the legal aid cetificate is granted, Solicitor No. 3 instructs Counsel to draft writ and Statement of Claim – the first procedural step in a legal action. Counsel says that before he can do so he needs to see an up to date medical report; and the solicitor writes to the relevant Consultant on 4th August 1964, but hears nothing. He sends reminders on 10th September, 8th October and 5th January 1965. Probably the doctor – Dr. Vaughan – never received the letters, since the solicitor addressed them to 'Dr. Vaun'.

Meanwhile the expiration of the three year limitation period, within which the *writ* has to be issued or the claim is barred, is drawing ominously near. However on 12th February 1965 the solicitor does issue the writ (which on its own is a simple document, see footnote p. 157), and serves it on the defendants' solicitor.

Up to now the *defendants'* solicitor has kept in the background. But now he has received the writ, he writes to Mr. Andrews's solicitor (23rd February 1965): 'We are aware that there were solicitors instructed in this matter before you, and we did in fact have a discussion with them. We do not know whether you would wish us to have a discussion with you before costs are incurred. We do not know whether you have been fully informed *as to what transpired.*'

A meeting does take place in March 1965, although there is no note of what was discussed. But for whatever reason, Mr. Andrews's solicitor takes no further action on the case for the remainder of that year; and although Counsel, who eventually received the Consultant's report, drafted the Statement of Claim, the solicitor does not serve it on the defendants' solicitor.

Towards the end of the year Mr. Andrews, worried that he has heard nothing for the last nine or ten months, writes to his solicitor asking what progress has been made. He gets no reply. He writes again on 23rd January 1966, and the solicitor replies: '*We are unable to say at the present time when the case is likely to be heard, but we will have the matter set down for hearing as soon as possible.*' As he has not obtained any of the necessary evidence, nor even served the Statement of Claim, he is nowhere near the stage of setting the matter down for hearing. His aim presumably is to fob Mr. Andrews off, rather after the manner of a builder who assures a worried client that he will get the roof on as soon as possible, when he has no plans to dig the foundations.

On 27th January 1966, pursuant to a telephone call from the defendants' solicitor, Mr. Andrews's solicitor instructs Counsel to Advise as follows:

'Instructing Solicitors have commenced proceedings in this matter and delivered a Statement of Claim [untrue; he hasn't]. The Defendants' Solicitors telephoned us saying that they are unable to understand why the Plaintiff was granted a Legal Aid Certificate in respect of the proceedings. Instructing Solicitors are informed that they made their offer of £1,000 not with an admission of liability, but because their client had some sympathy with the injuries sustained by the child. They feel, however, that if it is our client's intention to persue (sic) the claim, they must withdraw the offer of £1,000 and deny liability. *They have also stated that they feel they will have to report the matter to the Legal Aid Committee with a view to having the Legal Aid Certificate discharged.* We informed them that in the circumstances we would obtain further advice, particularly in view of the fact that it *could be prejudicial to the infant.* In the circumstances will Counsel please advise thereon.'

Why the solicitor feels he needs to go to Counsel for advice when the defendants' solicitor resorts to such crude tactics is not clear; but at any rate in a conference (on 3rd March 1966)

Counsel* advises him in robust terms. On 4th March 1966 Mr. Andrews's solicitor writes to the defendants' solicitor:

'We fully adviced (sic) Counsel of your opinion in these proceedings but he has adviced (sic) that the offer of £1,000 made in this matter be rejected. He has also asked for leave to instruct a Queen's Counsel to act with him and persue the case to trial. In the circumstances *we now enclose herewith our Statement of Claim* and must call on you to file your defence in due course.' (Although in this instance it is a solicitor's clerk rather than a solicitor who is dealing with Mr. Andrews's case, as we have seen from the two previous chronicles, the only difference so far as the quality of the work is concerned is that a solicitor must necessarily have passed 'O' level English.)

So four years after the accident, the Statement of Claim is finally served on the defendants' solicitor. Tactic A, which is a favourite with insurance companies – making a derisory offer, with the perpetual threat that if the plaintiff pursues the claim the offer will be irrevocably withdrawn – although it seemed to come within a whisker of succeeding, has failed. The defendants' solicitor now resorts to tactic B.

29th March 1966. Letter from defendants' (insurance company's) solicitor to plaintiff's (Mr. Andrews's) solicitor: 'We thank you for your letter of 4th March and acknowledge receipt of Statement of Claim herein. Before we go to the expense of another medical examination we are wondering whether there would be any useful purpose served by us having a general discussion with you. We did see you a long time ago and nothing has happened for some considerable time. We are still prepared to have a talk with you with regard to the matter generally. You know our views on the subject. Perhaps you would let us know whether you think any useful purpose would be served by such discussion, when we will call on you accordingly.'

30th March. Plaintiff's solicitor to defendants' solicitor: 'It may

* This is a different Counsel to the previous one who, as often happens, has dropped out of the picture. In all there will be four different Counsel who will have acted on Mr. Andrews's behalf at various times. No. 1, the Queen's Counsel who gave the original opinion that the defendants' offer should be accepted. No. 2, the (ordinary) Counsel who attended the legal aid appeal and drafted the Statement of Claim. This pair has now dropped out. No. 3, the (ordinary) Counsel whom the solicitor is now consulting, and who stays with the case. No. 4, another Queen's Counsel who has not yet come on the scene.

be of some assistance if a further discussion could take place. In these circumstances we look forward to hearing from you.'

1st April. Defendants' solicitor to plaintiff's solicitor: 'In the circumstances if you would favour us with an appointment our representative will call on you accordingly.'

4th April. Plaintiff's solicitor to defendants' solicitor: 'We would suggest 14th April for the appointment which we trust is convenient.'

7th April. Defendants' solicitor to plaintiff's solicitor: 'We would prefer to call on you 13th or 15th April.'

12th April. Plaintiff's solicitor to defendants' solicitor: 'Unfortunately 13th and 15th April are inconvenient. We would suggest any time next week. We await hearing from you further.'

15th April. Defendants' solicitor to plaintiff's solicitor: 'We will telephone you with a view to fixing a mutually convenient appointment in due course.'

28th June. Plaintiff's solicitor to defendants' solicitor: 'We would refer to your letter of 15th April when you intimated you would be telephoning to make an appointment. We should be obliged if arrangements could kindly be made for a further discussion to take place.'

30th June. Defendants' solicitor to plaintiff's solicitor: 'The writer has been heavily pressed over the past few weeks but will endeavour to get down to see you one day next week.'

1st July. Plaintiff's solicitor to defendants' solicitor: 'The writer is on holiday for the next fortnight. No doubt arrangements can be made for a discussion immediately thereafter.'

5th July. Defendants' solicitor to plaintiff's solicitor: 'We thank you for your letter of 1st July and look forward to your further communication accordingly.'

6th July. Plaintiff's solicitor to defendants' solicitor: 'We thank you for your letter of 5th July and would advise you that the gentleman dealing with this matter is absent from the office until 18th inst. when your letter will be placed before him and no doubt he will communicate with you further in due course.'

12th July. Defendants' solicitor to plaintiff's solicitor: 'We are obliged to you for your letter of 6th July and look forward to your further communication.'

The meeting eventually takes place in August, although as with the previous meeting, there is no note of what was discussed.

In fact the events of the previous year seem to be repeating themselves.

On 14th October 1966 Mr. Andrews writes to his solicitor enclosing some copy letters showing the difficulty he is having in getting Tessa into any sort of institution or home suitable for her needs; and asking what progress has been made on the case. The solicitor does not reply. On 22nd January 1967 Mr. Andrews writes him a more despairing letter: 'A year ago you wrote to me that you were having the case set down for hearing but I have had no indication from you when this is likely to be. Please tell me which Court it will be so I can myself ask when the case is likely to come up, as I presume you have no time to do so. You must realize how concerned I am about this case as it is now nearly five years since the accident. I am waiting with great anxiety to hear from you very soon.'

The solicitor replies on 23rd January 1967 again fobbing him off: 'We acknowledge receipt of your letter of 22nd inst. and confirm acknowledgement of your letter of 14th October last with enclosures. We feel that in order to take any *negotiations* further will require an up to date medical report in this matter. To this end we have already been in correspondence with Mr. Vaughn to ascertain the position. . .we are pressing matters to the best of our ability but do not feel that the matter can be taken further until an up to date examination has been arranged to see if this coincides with your own opinion.'

It is now five years since the accident which caused his child permanent brain damage. Yet none of the three firms of solicitors successively instructed by Mr. Andrews has got statements from any of the relevant witnesses (policeman who made the post-accident report, passer-by, younger girl); nor a report on the mechanical condition of the van; nor a report on the tyre mark mentioned in the police report. In fact in five years, the only step which has been taken is to serve the writ and Statement of Claim on the defendants' solicitor. Even this is a doubtful achievement since the Statement of Claim (as drawn by Counsel No. 2) omits the allegations that the driver was driving *too near* the line of parked cars, and that the brakes were faulty.*

In this instance it is Solicitor No. 3's clerk who has been dealing with the case – although for convenience I have referred to him as a solicitor. As I shall show in due course, a large proportion of solicitors and their clerks who handle these sort of cases are hopelessly incompetent, having had no relevant training, having no aptitude for or interest in their job, and being subject to no sanction however badly they do it. Is Solicitor No. 3's clerk – who has had the conduct of Mr. Andrews's case for nearly three years – merely one of these, or is there another explanation for his apparent ineptitude? For the answer let's look at his next letter (22nd March 1967) to the Legal Aid Committee, which has submitted a routine enquiry as it has heard nothing since legal aid was granted nearly three years previously.

> 'In this matter we have had the opportunity of seeing Counsel on several occasions. The position is that proceedings have been commenced and a statement of claim has been delivered. The Defendants' Solicitors take the view that the offer of £1,000 is quite adequate in view of the complete denial of liability. We have now received a number of documents from Mr. Andrews relating to his daughter and are going back to Counsel to discuss the matter further. *Counsel is very concerned as to the offer which has been put forward in the light of the absence of evidence to show negligence on the part of the motorist.* The Defendants are still prepared to pay £1,000 in settlement of any claim . . . which the father of the infant is not prepared to accept. If Counsel advises *in the light of the further documents obtained* that the offer should be accepted we will refer the matter back to you, and in the light of Counsel's Opinion *it may be necessary for a summons to be issued to the Master in view of the fact that Mr. Andrews is not prepared to accept the offer.'*

In this letter, a facsimile of which is reproduced in Appendix C, the writer's meaning is just beneath the surface; and the recipient has to do just a little scratching to uncover it, as follows:

---

* These omissions could be fatal since the Statement of Claim must state precisely *in what way* the plaintiff is alleging that the defendant was negligent, so that the defendant (and his advisers) know exactly what is going to be alleged against him at the trial. So if the Statement of Claim merely alleges (as it does) that the driver drove too fast, failed to keep a proper look out, and failed to stop or swerve, then the plaintiff will not be allowed to argue at the trial that the driver drove too near the parked cars or that his brakes were faulty.

Our Counsel (with whom we are constantly in touch) thinks that the defendants' offer of £1,000 should be very seriously considered in view of the absence of any evidence to show negligence on the part of the motorist. The offer is still open. We have just received a number of documents from our client, Mr. Andrews, which we are going to refer to Counsel and which we anticipate will make him advise that the defendants' offer should be accepted; in which case it will probably be necessary to issue a Master's Summons to remove Mr. Andrews as his child's 'next friend', as he will never agree to accept.

This letter is not the work of an incompetent but an artful person. The reason for its oblique style is that most of the facts the writer wishes to convey are lies, and not being sure of his ground he is feeling his way rather cautiously. The last time he was in touch with Counsel was over a year ago, and Counsel never expressed any concern over the defendants' offer 'in the light of the absence of evidence to show negligence on the part of the motorist'. On the contrary, Counsel unequivocally advised that the defendants' offer should be rejected – and the solicitor's clerk wrote to the defendants' solicitor on 4th March 1966: 'We fully advised Counsel of your opinion but he has advised that the offer of £1,000 be rejected.'

As to the documents which he has received from Mr. Andrews – which he indicates will probably cause Counsel to advise acceptance of the defendants' offer – these are merely letters which Mr. Andrews sent him the previous October, showing the difficulty he was having in getting Tessa placed in a suitable institution. In his 'Instructions to Counsel to advise in Conference', which the solicitor's clerk submitted a few days after his letter to the Legal Aid Committee, he refers to these documents as follows: 'Mr. Andrews has provided us with documents from various institutions and hospitals showing the extreme difficulty which he has had in endeavouring to have Tessa placed, and also photographs showing Tessa before and after her accident.' These 'documents' therefore have no bearing on whether the defendants' offer should be accepted; or if they do, they would make such offer *less* rather than more acceptable. Indeed, it is difficult to think of any documents which Mr. Andrews could have possibly sent his solicitors which would prompt Counsel to advise that the insurance company's offer of £1,000 for his hopelessly brain-damaged child should be accepted.

The object of the solicitor's clerk's letter to the Legal Aid

Committee is to answer its routine enquiry and, as the Committee exercises a loose supervisory jurisdiction over legal aid cases, to prepare it for his forthcoming strategy. The letter also indicates what the strategy is. The solicitor's clerk is going back to Counsel to try and persuade him, on the pretext of having received some further documents, to write an Opinion that the defendants' offer of £1,000 should after all be accepted. The father will not agree, so he will be given the Johns treatment. A Master's Summons will be issued, supported by Counsel's Opinion (and presumably the previous Queen's Counsel's Opinion), to remove Mr. Andrews as his child's next friend; and someone else will be appointed to accept the defendants' offer on Tessa's behalf.

And why such strategy on the part of Mr. Andrews's own legal adviser when in view of the available (albeit hitherto ignored) evidence of the van driver's negligence, Tessa has a good chance of winning her case in Court? And why the lying letter to the Legal Aid Committee? Two more questions to be added to the pile, to which I think we can now give the probable answer.

The compensation for such a disastrously damaged child, if the case came to Court, could well be in the region of a quarter of a million pounds in today's money (which sum, of course, would be payable by the reinsurers). On the other hand a few thousand to the plaintiff's legal advisers (or some of them), and maybe the case need *not* come to Court but can be settled for an ex gratia payment of £1,000. In other words, Solicitor No. 1 and Queen's Counsel instructed by him 'to advise', and Solicitor No. 3's clerk, *have all been bribed.* (The verdict on Solicitor No. 2, incidentally, is 'not proven'.)

But whereas 'the most experienced Queen's Counsel in this field' was happy to write an Opinion that because there was no evidence of negligence, the defendants' offer of £1,000 should be accepted – and ignore the evidence of negligent driving and faulty brakes staring him in the face (which Opinion came within a whisker of sabotaging the child's claim), the present Counsel is of sterner stuff. Shortly after his letter to the Legal Aid Committee the solicitor's clerk has a meeting with Counsel, as the letter envisaged. However, the outcome is rather different to what he expected: Counsel takes the unprecedented step of ordering Solicitor No. 3 off the case, and nominates another firm to take it over.

A few days later Mr. Andrews receives a letter from his new solicitors: 'Mr. Bryan Anns [the Counsel] suggested that we should take over the conduct of the proceedings, relating to the injury to Tessa, from Messrs. [Solicitor No. 3], and we confirm that we should be pleased to do so. Messrs. – have delivered to our offices a bundle of papers which we hope to study during the next few days . . . Meanwhile perhaps you would kindly write to us confirming that you agree to us acting on your behalf.'

This letter is dated 20th April 1967, over five years since Tessa's accident; and Mr. Andrews's hopes of being able to pay for specialist therapy in Switzerland or America – or indeed anywhere – to enable her to reach her full potential are fading. In any case, as the years tick by and Tessa enters adolescence, the chances of successful therapy diminish. Meanwhile the only institution he could get her into was a mental hospital, where her condition deteriorated as she was kept permanently drugged. So he removed her, and once again tried to look after her as best he could at home. As he pointed out, a brain-damaged child is not the same as a mental defective, but can respond to proper treatment. 'But to see the dreadful conditions of many mental hospitals, I will not condemn my child to such a place.'

* * * * * *

In April 1967 Mr. Andrews's Solicitor No. 4 takes over the case. But the first thing he does is to ask the Legal Aid Committee to authorise him to get a further Opinion from a Queen's Counsel. The Legal Aid Committee not only authorizes this, but makes it the subject of a new *condition* which it imposes on Mr. Andrews's legal aid certificate, viz. that no further step shall be taken *until* Queen's Counsel's Opinion is taken and submitted to the Committee – and the Committee decides, in the light of such Opinion, that the case may proceed. At any time while a plaintiff is plodding the musty labyrinthine passages to the Court room, the Legal Aid Committee can impose fresh conditions on his legal aid certificate, or revoke it altogether. The philosophy is that if anything comes to light which casts serious doubts on the plaintiff's chances of winning, public money should not be wasted by continuing to subsidize his case. Plausible as this may sound, it puts the legally-aided plaintiff even more at the mercy of his own legal advisers.

So Solicitor No. 4 submits the papers to a Queen's Counsel (not of course the original one) who, on 27th July 1967, gives a rambling ten-page Opinion. The gist of this Opinion is that the distance of the tyre mark, made by the van's offside wheels, from the kerb at the point of collision (10 feet 4 inches); and the nature of Tessa's injuries; and the evidence of the passer-by that Tessa and the other girl were carefully looking for a place to cross, and cautiously stepped off the kerb between two parked cars as he passed them* – all indicate that Tessa was struck as she merely put her head out from between the parked cars to see if it was safe to cross. Therefore the van was being driven too fast and too near the parked cars.† And Counsel gives his learned conclusion that (a) the case should proceed; (b) the first thing to do is to contact the passer-by and the policeman who made the post-accident report to see whether, after so long a delay, they are still available to give evidence; (c) the Statement of Claim should be amended to include the allegations that the van was being driven too near the parked cars and that its brakes were faulty (see p. 222).

Notice that Queen's Counsel's Opinion does not contain any esoteric *legal* points, but for the most part consists of a reasonably intelligent person's observations on the evidence in front of him – most of which (and a few more besides) had been made by Mr. Andrews to his first solicitor five years previously.

The solicitor sends Queen's Counsel's Opinion to the Legal Aid Committee which requires him to contact the passer-by and the policeman, and then go back to Queen's Counsel for his *further* Opinion. And six months later, 25th January 1968, after the solicitor has contacted the passer-by and policeman – the former's recollection being as clear as ever, the latter's being somewhat dimmed – Queen's Counsel gives his further Opinion. This is basically the same as his earlier one: the evidence is still sufficient to show that 'the van was being driven very close indeed to the line of stationary cars. As I indicated before, I think that this prima facie is a negligent act in such an area at such a time and when going at some speed.'

Now Queen's Counsel knew – because he mentioned it in his

---

* The passer-by had confirmed this in a letter dated 13th June 1964.

† Or, to put it into Counselese: '*I think that the speed combined with the closeness which this van was to the stationary vehicles in combination indicates that the driver by doing what he was really deprived himself of any reasonable opportunity of avoiding this kind of accident which is one which he could readily have foreseen might occur.*'

first Opinion – that Tessa had been holding the hand of another girl when the accident occurred. As this other girl was the only eye-witness to the accident, it is fairly obvious that she should be contacted and asked to make a statement. Yet Queen's Counsel did not suggest this in his first Opinion of July 1967, but rectifies the omission in his second Opinion six months later. The solicitor makes a note of Counsel's advice (at the meeting of January 1968 at which Counsel gives his advice *verbally* before putting it in writing), as follows:

'Counsel advised that I should see the other child and . . . we would need to know that she was being led by the hand by Tessa who led the way between two narrowly parked cars and poked her head out, and the next she knew was that Tessa had been injured.' Three days after making this note, the solicitor writes to Mr. Andrews asking for the address of this other child (explaining that he proposes asking for an interview). Fortunately Mr. Andrews has her current address and a month later, 19th February 1968, *ten months after he was first instructed*, the solicitor does see the child who does make such a statement.

This solicitor is a partner of one of the most eminent firms in the country. Yet notice how he is apparently incapable of working out for himself that the first thing he must do, when acting on behalf of an accident victim, is to interview and get statements from the relevant witnesses, i.e. policeman who made the post-accident report, passer-by, and the other child. But he has to go to *Counsel* to be told. And Counsel advises him (July 1967) to contact and interview the first two witnesses, so he contacts and interviews the first two witnesses; and six months later (January 1968) Counsel advises him to contact and interview the third witness, so he contacts and interviews the third witness.

On the other hand, if it were not an eminent firm of solicitors and a Counsel and a Queen's Counsel dealing with the case on Mr. Andrews's behalf, but someone having the same status, education and common sense as a reasonably alert assistant manager of a suburban chain store – whose clients would not need legal aid to employ him, and who would not need to write windy ten-page opinions to himself – such a person would have probably got these three statements not in ten months but ten days.

Anyway, the solicitor submits Counsel's further Opinion to

the Legal Aid Committee, which at the end of February 1968 authorizes the case to proceed: that is to say, it removes the extra condition which it gratuitously imposed ten months previously when Solicitor No. 4 took over the case. Solicitor No. 4 notifies the defendants' solicitor that, as advised by Queen's Counsel, the case is going to proceed. He replies:

'We are in receipt of your letter. . .and quite frankly we are literary amazed. What our Clients will now decide to do we cannot say, they will probably decide to withdraw any offers and contest the matter to its conclusion and there is only one possible result. We appreciate that you are only carrying out your instructions but it does seem a great pity that the infant should suffer.'

After a few days the defendants' solicitor has sufficiently recovered from his literary amazement to write to Mr. Andrews's solicitor:

'We would like the opportunity of discussing the situation with you because there are considerations here which we feel are of paramount importance to the child, and we would like to put these considerations to you before a certain course is adopted.'

One week later the defendants' solicitor tries again: 'We do not know whether our clients' offer [£1,000 in full settlement] has been made known to the Legal Aid Committee but we would like confirmation of this . . . because we are going to report to our Insurance Company clients who may suggest that we ourselves ought to write to the Legal Aid Committee with regard to this matter because . . . a long time ago this ex gratia offer was made which we honestly feel was in the child's interests, and we would very much regret to see a position created which would mean that the child would *lose the benefit of the generosity of those responsible for our being instructed.*' This is the same threat which was made to Solicitor No. 3's clerk – that unless Mr. Andrews accepted the offer of £1,000, the defendants' solicitor would write to the Legal Aid Committee and get his legal aid revoked, so the child would ultimately get nothing.

Mr. Andrews's Solicitor No. 4, however, merely replies with a curt demand that the defendants' Defence is filed.

The defendants' solicitor tries a different approach: 'We had discussions with [Mr. Andrews's Solicitor No. 1]. We also had discussions with [Mr. Andrews's Solicitor No. 3's clerk]. It seems to us therefore that there can be no possible objection to having a general discussion with you before matters go too far and it is impossible to retract. In the circumstances therefore we would suggest you favour us with an appointment for our representative to call upon you for a general talk with regard to the matter.'

This approach proves more successful, and a meeting takes place between Mr. Andrews's solicitor and the defendants' solicitor on 20th March 1968. As a result, Mr. Andrews's solicitor sends the following letter to the Legal Aid Committee dated 21st March 1968:

> 'We called on the Defendants' Solicitors to serve their clients' Defence but they asked for an opportunity of having a 'without prejudice' discussion with us . . . During the course of our discussion the Solicitors stressed that in their view our Client had no possibility of winning the claim. We stated that we had been advised by Queen's Counsel, and tended to share his view, that although the claim is difficult it is not hopeless. The Solicitors then asked us whether we knew that there was no frontal damage to the car (sic) driven by their Client. They have in their possession a consulting engineer's report which *appears to indicate* that the damage suffered by the car consisted of a double scratch on the nearside lower panel commencing in about the centre of the wheel-base of the vehicle – almost dead centre. Apparently there was hardly any indentation on the side of the car. We take the view that this information is extremely important. It may be that Counsel on the information already available, combined with this later piece of information, will not alter his view that the proceedings should continue, but you may feel it proper to authorize us to place the papers before him once again.'

As with his predecessor's letter to the Legal Aid Committee, the writer's meaning is just beneath the surface, and needs just a little scratching to uncover it, as follows:

We had a discussion with the defendants' solicitors. They consider that our client has no chance of winning the case (i.e. of proving the driver was negligent), and we told them that our Queen's Counsel's opinion was that while our client's case was not hopeless it was not very strong. They have an engineer's report which appears to indicate that there was no damage to the front of the vehicle but that there was a double scratch on the nearside panel between the wheel-base. We take the view that this information is extremely damaging to our client's case (since it indicates that the child came into contact with the side *of the vehicle, in which case the driver could not have seen her and so could not be said to have been negligent). It may be that despite this new piece of information Queen's Counsel will not alter his view that our client's case should proceed, but we invite you to authorize us to take Queen's Counsel's further opinion to see whether this is so, or whether he advises that in view of this information our client's case should not after all proceed, in which case you will presumably cancel his legal aid certificate.*

At the same time the solicitor writes to Mr. Andrews warning him of this new development, and that 'this information makes our case more difficult as it suggests that however careful the driver of the van had been he could not have avoided Tessa. I hope to discuss this evidence with Counsel before long.'

Now although if some evidence comes to light which undoubtedly shows that the defendant had not been negligent (and thus torpedoes the plaintiff's case) it is the duty of the plaintiff's legal advisers to relay it to the Legal Aid Committee, Mr. Andrews's solicitor's letter raises one or two questions.

Bear in mind that the Legal Aid Committee can, at the drop of a hat, put yet more obstacles in Mr. Andrews's path: or it can revoke his legal aid certificate altogether, in which event Mr. Andrews would have to abandon the case. So why does his solicitor write such a potentially ruinous letter to the Committee – and why does he tell Mr. Andrews that 'this information suggests that however careful the driver of the van had been he could not have avoided Tessa' – when:

(1) A scratch on the side of a van, which was five years old at the time of the accident and which is now eleven years old, could have a hundred and one different causes; and in any event is not likely to have been caused by a hard smooth object such as a child's head which (if you recall) was the only part of Tessa which was injured.

(2) The police report – in the solicitor's possession – states 'there was no damage to the van and nothing on it to indicate which part of it came into contact with the injured girl'.

(3) The evidence of the brake mark shows that the driver saw the two girls 30 to 40 feet *before* the collision (as noted in Counsel's July 1967 opinion).

(4) Even if this new information *did* indicate that Tessa was hit by the side of the van, it would not affect the main allegation of negligence (as advised by Counsel in his two opinions) that the

driver was driving too fast and too *close* to the line of stationary cars, so that Tessa was struck as she merely poked her head out to see if it was safe to cross.

(5) If the solicitor really believes that this information so weakens his client's case that he must refer it to the Legal Aid Committee, why does he not ask to *see* – and get a copy of – the report in question, instead of writing such a letter on the mere say-so of the defendants' solicitor?

So both Mr. Andrews's Solicitor No. 3's clerk and his Solicitor No. 4 in turn notify the Legal Aid Committee that they have received evidence which they indicate will probably (Solicitor No. 3's clerk), or might (Solicitor No. 4), cause Counsel to advise that Tessa's claim for compensation should not after all proceed. In the case of Solicitor No. 3's clerk this evidence is certain 'documents' he has received from Mr. Andrews, which turn out to be some copy letters which Mr. Andrews sent him showing the difficulty he was having in placing Tessa in a suitable institution. In the case of Solicitor No. 4, the 'evidence' is scarcely less inconsequential – that he has been told by the defendants' solicitor that he has a report 'which appears to indicate' that an eleven year old van had a scratch on its side. And the reason for the learned gentlemen taking such action is presumably the same in both cases.

But whereas Solicitor No. 3's clerk informed the Legal Aid Committee that he was going to seek Counsel's advice on the 'documents', Solicitor No. 4 is more circumspect, and invites the Committee to authorize him to submit the 'information' to Queen's Counsel for his advice. But this the Legal Aid Committee does not do. Instead it authorizes him to *submit a copy of the engineer's report* to Queen's Counsel for his advice (letter dated 8th April 1968). So on 10th April 1968 Solicitor No. 4 writes to the defendants' solicitor asking for a copy of the report 'for consideration by our Queen's Counsel'. Note that he has not hitherto asked for a copy on his own initiative.

However, although the defendants' solicitor had been so anxious for the meeting to take place in order to disclose these 'considerations of paramount importance', he is rather coy in producing the actual engineer's report. He replies (15th May 1968): 'This is a matter which does require consideration. We suppose we went further than we should have done when we had our discussion with you, but we were anxious that you should appreciate the position. You may rest assured that when we get definite advices we will be in touch with you.' Some weeks later Solicitor No. 4 again asks the defendants' solicitor for the report, adding 'we would have thought that your clients would not object to a copy of the report being sent to us *if it might result in the present proceedings being resolved*' (i.e. by Mr. Andrews's Queen's Counsel advising that the case should not proceed, and the Legal Aid Committee revoking his legal aid certificate, and Mr. Andrews consequently having to accept the defendants' offer of £1,000 in full settlement). But the defendants' solicitor still demurs; and the report, with its 'extremely important information', is quietly forgotten.

Solicitor No. 4's tentative departure from the straight and narrow having come to naught, he resumes his former role of pursuing his client's claim for compensation in the traditional desultory manner. The defendants' solicitor finally serves the *Defence* – in answer to the plaintiff's Statement of Claim served over two years previously; and in June 1968 Solicitor No. 4 places all the papers before Counsel* for his advice on what to do next.

A month later (15th July 1968) Counsel advises that the next step is to *amend the Statement of Claim* along the lines advised by Queen's Counsel a year previously. And he drafts the additions to be made – one line alleging that the defendant 'drove too close to the parked vehicles on his near side', and a few lines alleging that he failed to maintain the van properly in that the brakes did not operate efficiently and/or the tyres were badly worn and/or had incorrect pressures. Again note that the £50,000 a year solicitor is not qualified to draft these amendments himself, but has to go to *Counsel.*

And note the time scale. With solicitor, ordinary Counsel, and Queen's Counsel dealing with Mr. Andrews's case (plus a bit of help from the Legal Aid Committee), it has taken fifteen months since Solicitor No. 4 took over the case to achieve the first procedural step – that is, the drafting of half a dozen lines to be added to the Statement of Claim. Or rather, the first step in the

* This is the ordinary Counsel (Counsel No. 3 see footnote p. 220) who first advised in March 1966, and who is the routine adviser. Queen's Counsel would not be used for routine advice but only if there was a special reason – e.g. if the solicitor considered there was a matter of particular importance, or the Legal Aid Committee specifically required a Queen's Counsel's opinion.

first step. Since it's not a question of simply amending the Statement of Claim. Oh dear me, no. Unless the defendants' solicitor agrees to the amendments (which he doesn't), the question of whether the amendments should be allowed to be made has to be argued by the parties' Counsel (accompanied by their respective instructing solicitors) before a Master – the plaintiff's Counsel arguing that they *should* be allowed, the defendants' Counsel arguing that they *shouldn't*. In other words, a mini trial before a mini judge has to take place to decide this procedural point. Incidentally these mini trials are an important part of High Court procedure; and the Masters' corridor is usually buzzing with solicitors and Counsel waiting to argue procedural points such as whether or not the plaintiff or defendant should be allowed to amend one or other of his 'pleadings', or be allowed further time to take this or that step, or be ordered to disclose this or that document, and so on.

In this instance, in view of the delay, the Master *refuses* permission for Mr. Andrews's Statement of Claim to be amended. So another mini trial takes place, by way of appeal against the Master's decision, before a Judge in Chambers who – on 16th October 1968 – *allows* the amendments to be made.

The amended Statement of Claim and the Defence having now been exchanged, Mr. Andrews's solicitor and the defendants' solicitor serve on each other 'Request for further and better particulars of Defence', and 'Request for further and better particulars of Statement of Claim', respectively. This is standard procedure, the purpose being to make the parties more specific in their allegations or counter allegations, so that each knows precisely what is going to be alleged against him, and therefore what he will have to answer, at the trial. Whereas a request for 'further and better particulars' is necessary if the Statement of Claim or Defence is too widely or vaguely worded, the procedure is usually just another time-wasting routine in which unrealistic (even fatuous) questions are drafted by the parties' Counsel, sent to the other side's solicitor, passed to *his* Counsel, who drafts meaningless non-replies (rather after the manner of the ritual dance which the vendor's and purchaser's solicitors execute in a conveyancing transaction). For instance, in Mr. Andrews's case the amended Statement of Claim alleged that the van's brakes did not operate efficiently, and/or the tyres were badly worn, and/or had incorrect pressures. The defendants' request for further and better particulars asked: 'Precisely what is alleged to have been wrong with the brakes. . .in respect of each tyre state the extent of its wear. . .and state the pressure in each tyre.' This request was answered: 'The Plaintiff is unable to state precisely what was wrong with the brakes. . .The Plaintiff is unable to state in respect of each tyre the extent of its wear. The Plaintiff does not know the pressure in each tyre.'

The Defence denied negligence, and alleged that the accident was caused by the plaintiff who 'moved from between parked vehicles on the nearside of the defendant's van as it was passing and collided with the side of the said van.' The plaintiff's request for further and better particulars asked: 'What part of her body it is alleged the plaintiff moved and. . .from where to where it is alleged that she moved. . .and whether it is alleged that the plaintiff moved. . .before the said van drew level with the plaintiff or as it was level with her.' This was answered: 'The case is sufficiently pleaded.'

This particular quadrille can be relied on to add another six months to the pre-trial delay. In this case the request for further and better particulars of Defence was drafted by Mr. Andrews's Counsel on 15th July 1968 (at the same time as he drafted the amendments to the Statement of Claim), sent to the defendants' solicitor on 2nd August, and replied to on 31st January 1969. In fact this six month delay between receiving the request for further and better particulars and supplying them, is *average* – as found by the Royal Commission on Legal Services (section 10.16).

So *x* months to get Counsel's opinion, *y* months to get this or that witness's statement, *z* months for this or that procedural step – that's how the months before a High Court case comes to trial become years. Not only is the time it took the defendants' solicitor to supply the further and better particulars of the defence average (as found by the Royal Commission), but the time it is taking Mr. Andrews's Solicitor No. 4 to get the case to trial is average as well. If you remember, he took over the case pretty well from scratch in April 1967. Broadly, 1967 was the year in which he took Queen's Counsel's Opinions, and got the witnesses' statements. 1968 was the year in which the Defence was served, the Statement of Claim was amended, and 'further and better particulars' of Statement of Claim and Defence were requested and given. And 1969?

Before a High Court case actually comes to trial it has to be *set down for hearing*. That is, after the procedural documents have been exchanged, and the various steps taken, the case is officially put in the queue of cases waiting for a hearing date: rather like when your papers have been checked at the port office and you are permitted to drive through the barrier, you join the line of cars waiting to be admitted onto the cross-channel ferry – when there's a seamen's strike.

But, if you remember, there was a condition attached to Mr. Andrews's original legal aid certificate: that *before* the case is set down for hearing, Counsel has to assess the evidence and give his final Opinion on the plaintiff's chances of success (i.e. of showing that the accident was caused by the driver's negligence). And the Legal Aid Committee will then, in the light of such Opinion, either permit the case to proceed to trial; or it will revoke the legal aid certificate – in which event the case will have to be abandoned. The plaintiff's position is therefore very precarious at this point; and obviously Counsel's final Opinion, and the solicitor's instructions to Counsel 'to advise on the evidence' – wherein the solicitor summarizes all the facts and evidence on which Counsel bases his Opinion – are extremely delicate documents.

Accordingly, on 24th February 1969 Mr. Andrews's solicitor instructs Counsel to advise on the evidence. But for some reason he seems more concerned to put the *defendants'* case than his own client's:

> 'The Defendants' solicitors stated that in their view the plaintiff had no case at all. They state that their client's position is equivalent to that of a driver driving along quite innocently normally and carefully when someone runs under his front wheels: in such a case the driver cannot avoid the other person who is badly injured but with no liability attaching to the driver. Apparently the Defendants have a mechanical report (although a copy has been sought on a number of occasions by Instructing Solicitors it has not been made available) showing that the damage to their client's car was a mark on the nearside panel in the centre of the wheel base, consisting of two scratches tailing off along one side . . . At the time of the accident the driver was 52 years old and had been driving for approximately thirty three years without any accident. The Defendants might be prepared to increase their

offer but it is unlikely that they will increase it by more than a few hundred pounds.'

The solicitor mentions the defendants' offer on two further separate occasions in these Instructions to Counsel:

'The accident took plaçe on 19th March 1962 and a *without prejudice offer was put forward by the Defendants' Insurance Company on the 11th Jaunary 1963.*'

'Liability on behalf of the Defendants was categorically repudiated but the Insurance Company offered to pay £1,000 purely as an ex gratia payment to express their sympathy for the child's misfortune. . .Counsel has seen Mr. Andrews, the 'next friend', in conference: he is a gentleman of Polish origin and previous solicitors found it difficult to convince him that before the Defendants could be made to pay, they would have to be shown to be negligent. Mr. Andrews was reluctant even to consider accepting the offer of £1,000 and after consultations with Counsel it was decided to proceed with the action.'

The impression to be gained from these passages is that a man aged 52, who has never had any kind of accident since he began driving thirty three years previously, was driving along in his usual careful manner when the child suddenly ran out in front of him, and was badly injured. The driver's insurance company made an offer of £1,000 purely out of sympathy, which the child's father wouldn't even consider, since, being a foreigner, he cannot understand our English legal system whereby you have to prove the driver was negligent before you are entitled to compensation.

Nowhere in these 'Instructions to Counsel to advise on evidence' does the solicitor give an equivalent precis of the evidence supporting his own client's case (see p. 211/212); in fact he never specifically mentions it at all. When it comes to the witnesses, the solicitor says that the policeman's memory has faded. As to the other witness, the passer-by – whose all-important evidence is that he saw the children walking slowly hand in hand looking for a safe place to cross the road, and that as he passed them Tessa cautiously stepped off the kerb – the solicitor says 'Mr. Garber's recollection is also weak.' But this is not true. According to a note in the file which the solicitor himself made: 'A signed statement has been obtained from Mr. Garber *whose recollection is fairly keen notwithstanding the time which has elapsed since the accident.'*

It would seem that Mr. Andrews's solicitor is still angling for the Legal Aid Committee to revoke his client's legal aid certificate.

Nevertheless a month later (March 1969) Counsel gives his advice: that there is sufficient evidence for the case to proceed. Two months after that (May 1969) the Legal Aid Committee gives its permission for the case to be 'set down for hearing' – i.e. proceed to trial – and on 6th August 1969 Mr. Andrews's solicitor writes to him: 'I am glad to say that the case has now been set down for hearing. No hearing date has been fixed and early in November we propose to apply for a date which will be suitable for all our witnesses and Counsel.'

Let me go back to another procedural step which was also taken over the preceding period. Queen's Counsel in his second written opinion, dated January 1968 (which was preceded by a conference), advised that as there had been no mechanical inspection of the van, it would be advisable for ordinary Counsel to draw up 'Interrogatories'. These are written questions delivered to and answered by the defendant *before* the trial, and are sometimes useful to enable matters to be raised at the trial which would otherwise be inadmissible. In his written opinion to the solicitor six months later (15th July 1968), ordinary Counsel states: 'I cannot recall the precise nature of the difficulties we are in over the evidence and I do not quite understand Queen's Counsel's advice on the question of interrogatories. I wonder if Instructing Solicitors made any notes at the conference of 23rd January 1968?' – to which the solicitor replies that he didn't. Ordinary Counsel then suggests that Queen's Counsel should draw up the interrogatories, so the solicitor duly instructs Queen's Counsel; and on 9th June 1969, *a year and a half after they were first suggested,* another conference takes place between solicitor, ordinary Counsel and Queen's Counsel at which Queen's Counsel drafts the interrogatories.

Now at this conference on 9th June 1969, Queen's Counsel also advises that the make and dimensions of the parked cars between which Tessa emerged should be ascertained (from their registration numbers which had been noted on the plan which the *first* Queen's Counsel had initially requested all those years ago); so the solicitor dutifully gets to work to try and trace these cars.* Yet when Queen's Counsel made that suggestion the solicitor had already had the case for over two years, and Queen's Counsel and ordinary Counsel between them had already written half a dozen Opinions. In the same way, you will recall that in January 1968, six months after his initial Opinion, Queen's Counsel advised that the girl whose hand Tessa was holding should be contacted.

Bearing in mind that the time scale from when Solicitor No. 4 took over the case to the trial is *average* (as found by the Royal Commission), this is what happens when the pre-trial work is handled by solicitor and Counsel or – as in this case – solicitor, Counsel and Queen's Counsel. The solicitor sees his role as merely feeding Counsel with information and carrying out his advice. It seems he cannot act on his own initiative. Ordinary Counsel sees his role as a middleman between solicitor and Queen's Counsel – responsible for drafting routine Court documents, but with Queen's Counsel (who will ultimately conduct the case in Court) as the brains of the outfit. Queen's Counsel sees his role as giving overall general directions, but leaving the minutiae to ordinary Counsel and solicitor. Thus no-one takes overall responsibility, and works out at the outset exactly what evidence is required and what has to be done before the trial. But between the three of them – if they have enough conferences, and write enough Instructions and Opinions to each other over a period of two or three years – with any luck all the points which should be thought of will be thought of; and everything which needs to be done will be done.

Whilst this leisurely way of going about things evidently suits the lawyers, it is not only aggravating for their client, the plaintiff, but may easily be fatal to his case. For instance Solicitor No. 4 took over the case in April 1967. Pursuant to Queen's Counsel's initial Opinion of July 1967, he gets a statement from the passer-by in November 1967; pursuant to Queen's Counsel's *second* Opinion of January 1968, he gets a statement from the other girl in February 1968. Fortunately both witnesses were then still traceable, but it could easily have been otherwise.

---

* In his letter of 6th August 1969 he writes to Mr. Andrews 'I am anxious if possible to find out what the cars were between which Tessa *ran*. . . It appears from one of the plans I acquired when I took over this action that Tessa *ran* between a goods van and another car.' (Scarcely a reassuring letter for his client to receive since it is the plaintiff's case that she did not run at all.)

But I digress. It is now August 1969, and the case has been set down for hearing.

After August the days grow shorter, and before you can say 'Master's summons for an order that the defendants' answers to the interrogatories be served on the plaintiff's solicitor', we're into 1970. Come the spring Mr. Andrews's solicitor assures his client: 'So far as the witnesses and evidence are concerned we are ready to go to Court.' Now the problem is that the defendants' medical expert has died. 'Accordingly fresh medical reports had to be obtained, and because both doctors were extremely busy this caused delay.' Well it would, wouldn't it? Six months later (29th September 1970), Mr. Andrews writes to his solicitor pointing out that he has heard nothing further about a date for the trial – 'I cannot sit and wait passively for ever.' His solicitor replies that the recent delay has been caused by the respective doctors' inability to agree on Tessa's present medical condition, but the solicitor now feels that 'it will be in Tessa's interests for the trial to be held as quickly as possible [come, that's a good thing!] to which end it has become necessary to obtain the other side's consent to our applying for an appointment before the Clerk of the Lists to obtain a fixed hearing date.'

Eventually in November 1970 a date for the trial is fixed: 9th February the following year.

So it now seems that the case is definitely going to come to Court. But what would be an appropriate amount of compensation for Tessa if the Court *does* find that the accident was caused by the van driver's negligence? Ah, that is another question. A month before the trial Mr. Andrews's solicitor asks him about his plans for Tessa if he wins the case, adding: 'I understand from several sources that National Health Service Institutions can offer equally good if not better facilities than most private homes. It may be that you will have extreme difficulty in placing Tessa in a private home even though you would be able to pay their fees, because she is so problematical a case.' When Mr. Andrews indignantly refutes this, explaining that had he left Tessa in a NHS institution she would have been so over-drugged that she would by now be little more than a cabbage, the solicitor changes his tack:

'I agree with you that it is generally conceded that National Health Instutitions cannot offer as good facilities as private institutions. However it is possible that so grave have been Tessa's injuries, the superior facilities offered by private institutions may not benefit her any more than the inferior institutions offered by the NHS.'

On the morning of 9th February 1971 the parties, and their solicitors, and their Counsel, and their Queen's Counsel, and their witnesses, and their medical consultants, and their mechanical engineers, and a few supernumeraries besides – all assemble outside the designated Court room in the High Court buildings. Just before the case is due to start the defendants increase their offer to settle out of Court from £1,000 to £5,000. A common ploy, this. Mr. Andrews's Queen's Counsel advises him to accept. Mr. Andrews refuses, and his Queen's Counsel –visibly angry – strides into the Court room.

* * * * * *

The trial takes four days, 9th, 10th, 11th and 12th February 1971. The first day is taken up by the respective doctors' reports, and evidence, as to Tessa's present mental state. Come the second day, the policeman who made the post-accident report, which stated that the tyre mark 10 feet 4 inches from the kerb was made by the van's *offside* wheels, cannot remember – after nine years – what reasoning prompted this conclusion. (One would assume it was the position of the van when it finally stopped.) So most of the second day is taken up with interminable questioning and cross-examination of the expert witnesses as to the make, model and dimensions of the parked cars between which Tessa emerged, and the dimensions of the van (including any protruberances), and whether the tyre mark was made by the van's *offside* wheels – as is contended by the plaintiff's Queen's Counsel – or whether it couldn't have been made by the van's offside wheels, and therefore must have been made by its *nearside* wheels – as is contended by the defendants' Queen's Counsel.*
On the third day the other witnesses give their evidence, that is, the passer-by, the girl whose hand Tessa was holding, and the van driver himself; and Queen's Counsel for both parties make their

---

* You will remember the significance of this point. If this tyre mark, 10 feet 4 inches from the kerb at the point where Tessa was struck, was made by the van's *offside* wheels, it must have been driven dangerously close to the line of parked cars; so that Tessa would have been hit as she merely poked her head out to see if it was safe to cross.

closing speeches. On the fourth day the judge sums up and gives judgment.

In the event, the judge does not accept that the tyre mark was made by the van's offside wheels – because there is no direct evidence to support it – and decides that therefore Tessa was *not* struck as she poked her head out between two parked cars. But the judge accepts the evidence of the girl whose hand Tessa had been holding, and of the passer-by, that Tessa did not *run* into the road. And he accepts that the tyre mark, noted in the police report as commencing at the spot where Tessa had been hit, shows that the van driver saw her well before the collision, *and that he failed to swerve* (see (c) and (d) on p. 212).

As so often happens in a case which takes *x* years to come to Court and costs *y* thousand pounds in legal fees and involves *z* hours of evidence and cross-examination, the outcome was determined by a couple of minutes questioning of the defendant driver on the third day – not as it happened by the plaintiff's Queen's Counsel, but by *the judge himself* after the plaintiff's Queen's Counsel had finished his cross-examination:

Plaintiff's Queen's Counsel: 'Unless your lordship has any further questions?'
Judge: 'Yes. If you had seen one or the other of these children some 30 feet away* . . . you would have had sufficient time to swerve, wouldn't you?'
Van driver: 'Quite, yes, sir.'
Judge: 'You said you did swerve?'
Van driver: 'Yes, sir.'
Judge: 'From the photograph, the van's steering wheel is like a bus's steering wheel.'
Van driver: 'Yes, sir.'
Judge: 'Sitting where you are you can turn that wheel very fast to the nearside or the offside?'
Van driver: 'Yes, sir.'
Judge: 'Have you any explanation as to why in fact you stopped *having only altered course, as far as we can see, about the*

* The judge considers that the driver was 30 feet away when he first saw the children because that is the average 'thinking distance' when travelling at 30 m.p.h. (the admitted speed), bearing in mind that the tyre mark or brake mark *commenced at the point of collision.* Incidentally the judge has not added on any 'build up' distance before the brakes reach maximum efficiency. (See point (c) and footnote on p. 212).

width of your van, 5 feet 8 inches?'
Van driver: 'Yes, sir.'
Judge: 'Why so little?'
Van driver: 'Because I just swerved away from the child. That's all it needed, just to swerve away from her coming out, sir. I couldn't have turned it right around could I, else I would have shot right across the road, sir.'
Judge: 'But you only moved some 5 feet 8 inches to the other side of the road?'
Van driver: 'That's all; I just twisted the thing away, *that is all I had time for.*'
Judge: *'It was just a slight twist?'*
Van driver: *'That's all, yes, sir.'*
Judge: 'I see. Thank you.'

So there we are. The judge decides that Tessa had been *walking* (not running) across the road, and that the van driver was negligent – and must therefore pay her compensation for her injuries – because he was driving too fast (30 m.p.h.); and more particularly because, although he saw the children in plenty of time, he failed to swerve and so avoid the collision.

So even though some of the obvious leads were irretrievably lost due to the five years' inaction of Mr. Andrews's first three solicitors (e.g. the van's brakes were never examined, a signed statement was never obtained from the policeman who made the accident report as to *why* he considered the tyre mark was made by the van's offside wheels), there was still enough evidence of the van driver's negligence to enable Mr. Andrews to win the case when it finally came to Court nine years after the accident.

Of course, Mr. Andrews was lucky in his judge. He could have got one of the less intelligent or patient variety – e.g. one who thinks that if a female hitch-hiker is raped she is guilty of *contributory negligence*, or that a clause in a contract allowing the vendor to take back 10% of the land he has sold is not an unusual clause. It's just another facet of the lottery which decides whether an accident victim gets compensation or not.

And here we may observe two further points which show what a lottery our legal system is. Had the van driver been *more* negligent, in that he had not applied his brakes so hard, there would have been no tyre mark on the road, and therefore no evidence whereby Tessa could have won her case. On the other hand, if he had been *less* negligent, and had not been driving so fast, so that Tessa's injuries had not been quite so catastrophic, the award of damages (compensation) against him would have been far greater. As it was, the judge awarded Tessa £40,000 (£35,000 damages and £5,000 interest), a significantly lesser sum than might have been expected, because in view of her extensive brain damage she has little appreciation of her own dismal condition; and therefore the judge considers that her actual *suffering* is that much less.

Nevertheless, despite all his legal advisers, Mr. Andrews has triumphed. £40,000 was still a considerable sum in 1971.

But that is not the end of the matter. It rarely is, in this business. Two weeks after the trial was concluded, the defendants lodge Notice of Appeal.

An appeal is not the same as a retrial. The witnesses do not attend Court again and no more evidence is given, but the evidence given at the trial is presented to the appeal judges in transcript form. And the plaintiff's and defendants' lawyers (Queen's Counsel attended by ordinary Counsel attended by instructing solicitors) respectively argue that the trial judge was or was not justified in coming to his decision on that evidence. Whereas at the original trial there is one judge, there are *three* judges in the Court of Appeal. If two of those three uphold the defendants' appeal – i.e. consider that the trial judge was *not* justified in deciding as he did – then the defendant wins his appeal, and the original decision of the trial judge is quashed, and the plaintiff gets nothing (except a bill for fifty thousand pounds legal costs if he happens not to be legally-aided).

Thus Mr. Andrews, who for some time prior to the trial had been making plans to place Tessa in a renowned rehabilitation centre in America with the compensation he was confident British Justice would award him, once the case finally came to Court, finds that from the practical point of view it is as if the trial never happened: and whether there *would* be any compensation has to wait on the judgment of the Court of Appeal.

So it's back to the Legal Aid Committee with an application to extend his legal aid certificate to cover the legal costs of defending the appeal, and Solicitor No. 4 instructs Counsel and Queen's Counsel to argue the appeal on Mr. Andrews's behalf, and Mr. Andrews is warned by his lawyers that the outcome is as problematical as that of the original trial, and the case is set down for hearing and put in the list, then taken out of the list, then put back in the list, and in June 1972 – one year four months after the trial, and ten years three months after the accident – the defendant's insurance company offers to settle by paying £30,000 (i.e. £10,000 *less* than the original award by the judge) in full settlement of Tessa's claim and abandon its appeal, which offer this time Mr. Andrews *does* accept, and the money is put in trust for Tessa pursuant to a Court order (as although she is now of age she is mentally incapable of managing her affairs), and that's finally the end of the case.

But it's also pretty well the end of Mr. Andrews. Shortly afterwards he has a stroke. He recovers to a certain extent but is mentally much impaired. He instructs another firm, Solicitor No. 5, to sue Solicitor No. 3 for negligence, which case drags on for a few years until, in view of Mr. Andrews's deteriorating health, it is settled out of Court for an agreed payment of £2,500. Then he has another stroke. Then he dies.

* * * * * *

Four footnotes:

(1) Neither Mr. Andrews, nor his widow, ever got the £2,500 (or any part), being the agreed settlement of his negligence action against Solicitor No. 3. Solicitor No. 3 did pay this sum but decided he could not also afford to pay Solicitor No. 5's costs, that is, Solicitor No. 5's costs for suing Solicitor No. 3 and getting the out of Court settlement of £2,500 – *which costs came to £5,719.* As Mr. Andrews was legally aided for this action (as he had been for the main action) these costs had to be paid by the legal aid fund, which has resource to any compensation recovered by the plaintiff. In other words, any sum the defendant pays is first appropriated to the legal costs, and only when these are satisfied does any surplus go towards meeting the plaintiff's award – no surplus, no compensation.

Incidentally, those journalists and others who so glibly talk about being able to sue your solicitor for negligence, might ponder Solicitor No. 5's bill of nearly £6,000 for a case that did not even go to trial. If you sue your solicitor and lose, and you are not legally aided, it will cost you at least *double* that sum in legal fees – i.e. your own and those of the other side.

(2) Going back to the main case, this was finally settled by the defendants paying the agreed sum, and agreeing to pay the plaintiff's legal costs. As the case had gone to Court, these legal costs have to be 'taxed' (vetted) by a 'taxing master' (Court official). Before costs can be 'taxed' the bill has to be drawn up, separately specifying and charging for each item; and as a High Court action spans four years (on average), the resulting bill is a formidable document. The plaintiff's solicitor normally sends his file to a specialist firm of costs draftsmen to draw it up, which has to go through the mountain of papers which the case has generated. When the bill is drawn up, the plaintiff's solicitor gets an appointment to go before the taxing master. Then a sort of mini trial takes place in which the *defendants'* solicitor tries to whittle the bill down by arguing that certain items have been overcharged or should not be on the bill at all, and the plaintiff's solicitor argues to the contrary, and the taxing master, in the role of judge, decides. Finally the taxing office at the Court issues a certificate embodying the taxing master's decision.

As this mini trial is a 'legal' process, involving the Court office, costs draftsman, and the solicitors acting for the plaintiff and the defendants, the time scale is commensurate with the legal proceedings which gave rise to it. In Mr. Andrews's case, for instance, the taxing master's certificate was issued on 30th January 1976, over three and a half years after the agreed settlement.

This delay in settling the secondary issue of costs means that the legally-aided plaintiff has to suffer an equivalent delay in getting the full amount of his award – because the legal aid fund (to which all monies are initially paid) will not release the total amount until the plaintiff's legal costs have been paid by the defendant, and the defendant cannot pay them until they have been finally determined by the taxing master. But more significant (for reasons we shall shortly examine), it means that when a case goes to Court, the plaintiff's lawyers have to suffer this delay in getting paid, whereas *if the case is settled out of Court the plaintiff's legal costs are normally agreed informally at the same time, and paid at once.*

(3) Tessa did not derive any benefit from the settlement her father achieved on her behalf. Because of his deteriorating health, the plans which Mr. Andrews had been making for her rehabilitation in America came to nothing. In any case by 1972,

when the defendants' appeal was finally abandoned, and Tessa was 18, it would probably have been too late to achieve any significant improvement in her condition. She is now a permanent inmate of a mental institution, which would probably not have been the case had the £30,000 compensation been paid within a year of her accident, instead of ten years after – in accordance with the rules and procedures of British Justice.

(4) If any reader is interested in querying the authenticity of any of the events in the foregoing narrative, and cares to write to me (address on rear cover) enclosing a stamped addressed envelope plus the current cost of photo-copying, I – or in the event of prolonged absence my assistant – will send the relevant copy document(s). Meanwhile a few of them are reproduced in the appendix immediately following.

OUR REF 3/39/A.1300

11th September, 1963

Dear Sir,

re: Your Daughter's Accident

We are in receipt of your letter of the 6th instant.

We are well aware of the seriousness of the injuries to your daughter.

This, however, does not alter the fact that the onus will be upon those representing her to prove that the accident was due wholly or in part to the negligence of the lorry driver and there is no evidence upon which this could be established.

We must point out to you in the clearest possible language that if you commence proceedings we are of the opinion that they will fail. Not only is this our opinion but as you have seen, this is also the opinion of the most experienced Q.C. in this field.

If you lose, not only will there be nothing for the benefit of your daughter but you will become responsible not only for the costs of those acting on behalf of your daughter but also for the costs of the other side and the total sum involved could be very considerable.

On the other hand, if the offer is accepted there will be £1,000. available (which will of course be subject to the control of the Court).

Whilst of course this is not the sort of sum which would be awarded if your daughter were successful in an Action, we are quite certain that it is the best obtainable in the circumstances.

This offer will not be kept open very much longer and we must again urge you to let us have your instructions to accept this subject to the leave of the Court.

Yours faithfully,

INSTRUCTIONS TO COUNSEL TO ADVISE

InstructingSolicitors have commenced proceedings in this matter and delivered a Statement of Claim. The Defendant's Solicitors telephoned us saying that the are unable to understand why the Plaintiff was granted a Civil Aid Certificate in respect of the proceedings. Instructing Solicitors are informed that they made their offer of £1,000 not with an admission of liability but because their Client had some sympathy with the injuries sustained by the child. They feel however, that if it is our Client's intention to persue the claim in this matter they must withdraw the offer of £1,000 and deny liability. They have also stated that they feel they will have to report the matter to the Law Society with a view to having the Legal Aid Certificate in this matter discharged. We informed them that in the circumstances, we would obtain further advice in this matter particularly in view of the fact that it could be prejudicial to the infant.

In the circumstances will Counsel please advise thereon.

MR. BRYAN ANNS.

JW/PV 27th January 1966

JW/LH
1/2/5/5574/G/CM

22nd March, 1967

The Area Secretary,
The Law Society,
No.1. (London) Legal Aid Area,
Area Headquarters,
29/37 Red Lion Street,
London, W.C.1.

Dear Sir,

re: Teresa A (An Infant)

We acknowledge receipt of your letter of the 3rd instant the contents of which we note.

In this matter we have had the opportunity of seeing Counsel on several occasions. The position is that proceedings have been commenced in this matter and a statement of claim has been delivered. The Defendant's Solicitors take the view that the offer of £1000 which was made in this matter before we were instructed is quite adequate, in view of the complete denial of liability in this matter. We have now received a number of documents from Mr. A relating to his daughter and are going back to Counsel to discuss the matter further. Counsel is very concerned as to the offer which has been put forward and in the light of the absence of evidence to show negligence on the part of the moterist. The Defendant's Solicitors are still prepared to pay the sum of £1000 in settlement of any claim on behalf of the infant in this matter which the father of the infant is not prepared to accept. If Counsel advises in the light of the further documents obtained that the offer should be accepted we will refer the matter back to you and in the light of Counsel's Opinion it may be necessary for a summons to be issued to the maters, in view of the fact that Mr. A is not prepared to accept the offer.

We will write to you further when we have obtained Counsel's further advise in this matter.

Yours faithfully,

T/JM/A.1667

4-1/2/4/5574

21st March, 1968.

he Area Secretary,
he Law Society,
o. 13 (London East) Legal Aid Area,
rea Headquarters,
9/37 Red Lion Street,
ondon, W.C.1.

ear Sir,

re: Teresa A________, an Infant

We refer to our correspondence culminating with your etter of the 23rd February.

On receipt of the amended Civil Aid Certificate we called on the Defendants Solicitors to serve their Clients Defence but they asked for an opportunity of aving a "without prejudice" discussion with us. They alled at our offices yesterday and stressed that if the action proceeds their Clients offer to pay £1,000 to Teresa will be withdrawn and will never be repeated. Both ourselves and Counsel and the Legal Aid Committee were aware of this threat which has been made on previous occasions.

During the course of our discussion the Solicitors stressed that in their view our Client had no possibility of winning the claim. We stated that we had been advised by Leading Counsel and tended to share his view that although the claim is difficult it is not hopeless. The Solicitors then asked us whether we knew that there was no frontal damage to the car driven by their Client. They have in their possession a consulting engineers report which appears to indicate that the damage suffered by the car consisted of a double scratch on the near-side lower panel commencing in about the centre of the wheelbase of the vehicle - almost dead centre. Apparently there was hardly any indentation on the side of the car.

We take the view that this information is extremely important. It may be that Counsel on the information already available combined with this later piece of information will not alter his view that the proceedings should continue but you may feel it proper to authorise us to place the papers before him once again.

Yours faithfully,

OUR REF. T/JM/A.1667 2nd April, 1968

Dear Mr. A ,

I have delayed dealing with your letter of the 4th March as a representative from the Solicitors acting for Company Limited wanted to call at these offices to discuss the accident. During our discussion he indicated that a firm of consulting engineers had reported on the damage to the van which consisted of a double scratch on the near-side lower panel commencing in about the centre of the wheelbase of the vehicle - almost dead centre. This information makes our case more difficult as it suggests that however careful the driver of the van had been he could not have avoided Teresa. I hope to discuss this evidence with Counsel before long.

Yours sincerely,

T/JM/A.1667 10th April, 1968.

Dear Sirs,

We write to enquire whether you would be prepared to disclose at this stage a copy of your engineers report for consideration by our Leading Counsel.

Yours faithfully,

YOUR REF: T/JM/A.1667

15th May 1968

Dear Sirs,

We have your letter of the 10th instant, the contents of which we note. This is a matter which does require consideration, we suppose we went further than we should have done when we had our discussion with you but we were anxious that you should appreciate the position. You may rest assured that when we get definite advices we will be in touch with you.

Yours faithfully,

moved to new premises - kept on losing letters from Instructing Solicitors but eventually supplied Mr. Jennings' present address. Unfortunately although he eventually signed the Statement (bundle 11) Counsel will see from the letters annexed to it that he cannot in fact recall many details surrounding the accident. Mr. Garber's recollection is also weak.

A Statement was obtained from the child accompanying Teresa when the

An extract from Solicitor No. 4's 'Instructions to Counsel to Advise on the evidence' – on which advice depends whether the Legal Aid Committee will allow the case to proceed to trial, or whether it will cancel the plaintiff's legal aid certificate.

a detailed statement from former P.C. Sidney Jennings and former Constable (now Serjeant) Cooper. Neither of these gentlemen can recollect the accident. A signed statement has been obtained from Mr. Lewis Garber whose recollection is fairly keen notwithstanding the time which has elapsed since the accident. The ambulance

An extract from Solicitor No. 4's note in the file.

9 *Why the cases of Mr. Perkins, David Johns, and Tessa Andrews are typical*

In the previous section I examined three actual cases where someone, having been injured in an accident, claimed compensation under the rules and procedures of our legal system. David Johns, who was injured at school, settled out of Court just before the trial. Mr. Perkins, who was injured at work, went to Court and lost his case. Tessa Andrews, injured in a road accident, went to Court and won. Between them these three plaintiffs employed a total of eleven firms of solicitors and ten Counsel.

Their cases are not necessarily the worst I have examined. I chose them because I think they tell us most about our legal system and the lawyers who operate it. In short, I think they are typical. My opponents will of course disagree.

The question could have easily been settled by the Royal Commission on Legal Services, or the Consumers' Association (publishers of *Which?*). Either of these bodies could mock up a typical accident – in fact, Tessa's would be ideal. A policeman, a hospital consultant, the two witnesses, the 'father', and a solicitor who would purport to act for the driver and his insurance company, would all play their respective parts. The 'father' would instruct a hundred unsuspecting solicitors (in different parts of the country) to claim compensation on behalf of his brain-damaged child; and after three years the results would be assessed. How many of our hundred solicitors (or their clerks to whom they farmed out the case) had got signed statements from all the witnesses, had got an expert's report on the mechanical condition of the van and the tyre mark on the road, had refused to be deflected by the defendants' solicitor's delaying tactics, and had taken the necessary steps to get the case to Court? Alternatively, how many had done virtually nothing except issue a writ to prevent the claim being statute barred? How many solicitors had put what pressure on the 'father' to settle out of Court for, say, £5,000 plus legal costs (which offer would be put forward by the defendants' solicitor)? How many solicitors and Counsel had succumbed to the offer of a £5,000 bribe (tactfully disguised as exceptionally lucrative business), and had tried to sabotage the father's case? How many Counsel's opinions – which presumably all our solicitors would seek – were competent, concise and comprehensive? How many were *reasonably* competent? How many would just about secure a doubtful pass in a first year law students' examination? How many were not even up to that standard?

As neither the Royal Commission on Legal Services, nor the Consumers' Association, was or is interested in carrying out such a survey – and despite their concern to maintain their members' standards for the protection of the public, I doubt whether the Law Society or the Bar Council would be either – we shall never know.

Nevertheless we can get an inkling from certain findings of some reputable bodies. The cases I have chronicled between them raise three issues: (1) delay, (2) incompetence, (3) corruption. In fact these categories often overlap. Delay is a facet of incompetence; and both delay and apparent incompetence may be due to corruption.

Delay is prejudicial to a plaintiff for two reasons: it increases his stress; and it decreases his chances of winning his case when and if it does eventually get to Court – because his witnesses' memories will tend to fade, and their testimony will be the more easily challenged by the defendant's Counsel. Moreover the evidence itself may disappear.

David Johns's case took four years five months to come to Court (September 1973 to February 1978); Tessa Andrews's case took nearly four years to come to Court from when Solicitor No. 4 took it over – virtually from scratch (April 1967 to February 1971); and Mr. Perkins's case took seven years to come to Court (July 1973 to June 1980). According to the Royal Commission on Legal Services these time scales are typical. I quote: 'The analysis of the time taken to dispose of cases in the Queen's Bench

Division in 1977 [and three quarters of such cases are in respect of personal injuries] shows that the average lapse of time between cause of action and trial was *four years*.' (para 22.25.) And 35% of all Queen's Bench cases which came to Court in 1977 had taken between four and eight years from the accident to the trial (Vol. 2, section 10.5). Therefore the time which David Johns's case, and Tessa Andrews's case (from when Solicitor No. 4 took it over), took to come to trial is *average*; and the time scale of seven years for Mr. Perkins's case is not exceptional.

Not only is the time scale of our three plaintiffs' legal actions typical: their accidents themselves are also typical. A workman is injured while operating a machine in a factory, a child has his eye put out in a school playground, another child is knocked down as she crosses or prepares to cross the road. Accidents, unfortunately, happen all the while; and they happen in the way that Mr. Perkins's, David's and Tessa's accidents happened. Of course how complicated the evidence is whereby negligence may be proved, will vary from accident to accident. In this respect Mr. Perkins's case was probably simpler than average; Tessa's more complicated than average; and David's just about average.

In Mr. Perkins's and David's cases it should have taken no more than two or three days to get the necessary evidence of negligence – photograph of metal table top, and a typical casting in the former; statements from the boys in the playground and the supervisors, plan and photographs of the playground, in the latter. To get the evidence in Tessa's case should have taken perhaps a month to six weeks – police report, statements from policeman and two witnesses, plan of street, expert's report on van and tyre mark in road, details of parked cars. So in the average personal injury case it should take between a few days and a month to get the available evidence of negligence. Neither are the High Court procedural documents in themselves particularly complicated or prolix. In Tessa's case the Statement of Claim was typed on one and a half sides of foolscap, and the Defence on half a side. Neither is the Court administration the chief factor in causing delay. As found by the Royal Commission (section 10.12), 71% of all cases were heard within a year of being 'set down for hearing' (that is, when the parties' solicitors decide they are ready and apply to the Court for a hearing date).

Of course there are endless opportunities for the *defendants'* solicitor to prevaricate and procrastinate – and, as we have seen, it is in his clients' interests that he should do so. Nevertheless there are measures (e.g. Master's summonses) which the plaintiff's solicitor can take to counter his opponent's delaying tactics. Significantly, the Royal Commission found that the average time it took the plaintiff's solicitor to issue the writ – which is the first procedural step in the action, and which needs no co-operation from the defendants' solicitor, was *seventeen months* (section 10.15).

Therefore, even allowing for a nine months wait from when the case is 'set down for hearing' to the trial, and some successful delaying tactics by the defendants' solicitor, a personal injury case should take no more than two years from accident to trial if prosecuted reasonably competently.* That personal injury cases, on average, take *double* that period means that the plaintiffs' lawyers handling them are, on average, *incompetent*.

Another factor common to our three plaintiffs was the pressure to which they were subjected by their own legal advisers to settle out of Court – that is, to accept the defendant's (insurance company's) miserable offer, and withdraw their legal action. Mr. Perkins was offered £500. David was offered £1,000, whereas if negligence was proved in Court he would have been awarded around £15,000. In Tessa's case the offer was £1,000 (whereas the Court actually awarded £40,000). All three plaintiffs were emphatically advised on several occasions by their own lawyers that if they refused the defendants' offer, and insisted on going to Court, they would lose their case and get nothing. Moreover in David's case – where the defendants made their offer only at the last minute – Mrs. Johns was strenuously advised by two firms of solicitors, two ordinary Counsel, and one Queen's Counsel, to abandon her case.

Here again we have some independent findings which indicate that such pressure is typical, and that our three plaintiffs were unusual only in the way they withstood it.

According to the Pearson Report† 'less than 2% of cases in which an *attempt* was made to recover damages for personal

---

* In fact this is the average time for a *libel* case to come to trial (as found by the Royal Commission, section 10.5) – libel being a more complicated branch of law, in respect of which the plaintiff will invariably consult specialist advisers.

† Royal Commission on Civil Liability and Compensation for Personal Injury. Chairman, Lord Pearson (1978).

injury reached the stage of a hearing in Court.' (para. 394.)

The Cantley Report* came to a similar conclusion: 'In any given year approximately 9,000 personal injury writs are issued in London; of these only about 300 go to judgment after a full trial' – i.e. slightly over 3%.

The Pearson Report also concluded that only 6.5% of injured people get any compensation for their injuries (para 78); which means that 93.5% of injured people do *not* get any compensation. This latter figure on its own does not tell us very much, because Pearson did not break it down into those who took legal advice and those who did not. However he gives us more revealing statistics as to the amount of compensation which the successful 6.5% did obtain:

> 'Most settlements are small. About 60% of them amount to £500 or less; 3% over £5,000; and 1% over £10,000' (para. 80).†

In other words, only a tiny minority of injured people who commence legal proceedings (2% or 3%) actually take their case to Court. The remaining 98% or 97% either abandon their action, or accept the defendant's (insurance company's) offer, and settle out of Court. The majority of such settlements are small; and only in a tiny proportion (3%) is a *significant* sum obtained. As to *why* the majority of plaintiffs settle out of Court, Pearson has this to say:

> 'Where a settlement had been reached, informants were asked why they had accepted the offer instead of trying to obtain more [i.e. by going to Court]. *Most had acted on the advice of a solicitor* or trade union.' (para. 401.)

Now injuries which give rise to legal proceedings fall into three categories: (1) those which are not serious; (2) those in respect of which there is less than a reasonable chance of proving negligence in Court; (3) those which *are* serious and in respect of which there *is* a reasonable chance of proving negligence in Court. In the case of the first two categories, the advice of the

---

* Personal Injuries Litigation Procedure Working Party. Chairman, Mr. Justice Cantley (1979).

† These findings are broadly corroborated by another survey *Compensation and Support for Illness and Injury* (OUP), which found that only in 11% of the cases which were settled out of Court did the amounts exceed £2000.

plaintiff's lawyer to settle out of Court for an insubstantial sum is perfectly sound. But what of the third category? Assuming as a rule of thumb that the three categories are numerically roughly equal, it would seem from the conclusions in the Pearson and Cantley Reports that the majority of seriously injured people either abandon their action or settle out of Court for insubstantial sums, on the advice of their lawyers, *even when they have a reasonable chance of winning their case in Court.* In other words, the advice given to Mr. Perkins, Mrs. Johns, and Mr. Andrews to accept the defendants' nominal or insubstantial offer, and settle out of Court, is that given by the majority of lawyers in similar cases.

To this evidence we may add our empirical findings. If our three plaintiffs had each had one incompetent or corrupt lawyer, their experiences would be inconsequential. But they didn't. Mr. Perkins instructed *five different solicitors in succession*, who between them instructed three Counsel (ignoring the Counsel who accepted the brief but sent a substitute). All five solicitors and all three Counsel were hopelessly incompetent. Mrs. Johns instructed two firms of solicitors in succession, who between them instructed two ordinary Counsel and one Queen's Counsel. In her first firm her case was dealt with by the two partners in turn. The first ordinary Counsel and the Queen's Counsel were incompetent. The three solicitors, and the second ordinary Counsel, were corrupt. Mr. Andrews instructed four solicitors in succession, who between them instructed two ordinary Counsel and two Queen's Counsel. In this case the stakes were the highest of any personal injury litigation. At least three and quite possibly four of his four solicitors (or in the case of Solicitor No. 3, his clerk) were corrupt; the first Queen's Counsel was corrupt; the two ordinary Counsel were incompetent; the second Queen's Counsel was barely competent.

You would have to toss a coin an awful lot of times before it landed heads *eight* times in succession; and you would have to wait quite a long time before it landed heads *four* times in succession. These three plaintiffs could not have had the experiences they did; neither would all but a tiny minority of personal injury claims be abandoned or settled out of Court for nominal or insubstantial sums; neither would those personal injury claims which *do* come to Court take (on average) four years to get there – if the majority of lawyers who handle this sort of work were not either incompetent or corrupt.

Let's look at the reasons *why* they are.

10 *Why the majority of lawyers dealing with these cases are either incompetent or corrupt (1) Corruption*

As I tried to show in the first part of this book, a solicitor or Counsel (or any professional) is morally no different to any other person. Anyone who thinks he is should ask himself *why* he thinks he is, and will find the reasons written on the vapour of his own wishful thinking. Therefore as every calling will have the same percentage of potentially corrupt operators, it will not be the morality of the operators which varies from one calling to another, *but their opportunities for corruption.* The reason why car mechanics have a worse reputation for dishonesty than clergymen is not that they are any more dishonest, but because under their current conditions of work they have greater scope for dishonesty. In medieval times, when folk were so naive and superstitious that they could be sold pardons and holy relics, and vehicles were less complicated, the situation was reversed – and the clergy presumably had a worse reputation for dishonesty amongst the intelligentsia than, say, wheelwrights.

The reason that hardly a week – sometimes hardly a day – goes by without some newspaper item on police corruption, is not that the police are intrinsically any more corrupt than any other calling; but that having enormous powers over gentlemen with large amounts of loose cash, they have more *opportunities* for corruption than any other calling.

Except lawyers. Unless they are acting for an exceptionally stubborn plaintiff like Mr. Andrews, the plaintiff's lawyers have the power to decide whether their client's personal injury claim shall come to Court, or whether it shall be settled out of Court; that is to say, in the case of a serious injury they have the power to decide whether the defendant's insurance company will have to pay their client a substantial sum by way of compensation, or whether it can get away with an out of Court settlement of, say, a couple of thousand pounds. Lawyers therefore have as much opportunity for corruption as the police.

But lawyers have a couple of advantages. First, unlike a corrupt policeman who has to keep his illicit riches stashed under the floorboards, the corrupt lawyer can enjoy his, since a successful lawyer is expected to be wealthy. Second, the corrupt policeman has to do some sort of obviously shady deal involving several untrustworthy people, and money has to change hands; so there is always the risk of exposure – hence all the newspaper items. The corrupt lawyer has no such problem. For him no shady deals, no cryptic conversations in crowded pubs, no bundles of £5 notes changing hands. For him all that is needed is an urbane exchange, perhaps something on the following lines.

In a smart restaurant two men are dallying over the last course of a lavish business lunch. One tells the other that one of his companies is taking a headlease of an office block which it will then underlet in 46 different units, all legal fees (probable total £30,000) to be met by the respective underlessees. Would he like the legal work? It seems that the other, who is a partner in a large firm of solicitors, *would* like the legal work. Says the first gentleman, as if by way of afterthought: 'I see you're acting for that unfortunate child who got knocked down by one of our reinsured's drivers. Of course no question of negligence on the part of the driver as far as I can see. Didn't stand a chance. Child ran straight into him. If anyone should be sued it's the parents, if you ask me. We might be able to make an ex gratia offer of £1,000, and your costs of course, but certainly no more.' 'Well,' replies the solicitor, 'my managing clerk is dealing with that one. I did see the father at the outset but I must confess I don't know the up to date details. I rather thought he might have a case.' 'Well, you'll obviously do what you think best for your client, but I can't see him getting a negligence case off the ground. Of course as you haven't worked for us before, my co-directors will have to approve your appointment to handle the leases, but I think I can persuade them if necessary.'

The meal is finished. Then the handshake. Perhaps a bit of

pressure with the old thumb.

A few days later the defendants make an ex gratia offer of £1,000 over the telephone. The solicitor looks in on his clerk. 'What's the position on that running down case – you know, the injured child? The defendants have made an offer of £1,000 with no admission of liability.'

'Well', replies the clerk, 'we've got the accident report from the police, but as far as I can see it doesn't really help us as no one saw the accident. I've interviewed the two bystanders mentioned in the police report but unfortunately they didn't see anything either. The father has suggested some possibilities. Perhaps we could check the actual vehicle if we could find out where it is, and it seems she was holding the hand of another girl –.'

'Yes, I saw that letter. These people who think they know it all and start telling us how to do our job. No, you'd better shoot everything you've got down to Counsel for an opinion. There's some urgency here because the defendants say they won't keep this offer open very long. Let me see your instructions before they go. Use Mr. *X* Q.C. on this one, because frankly I think it will be a question of having to persuade the father to accept. £1,000 may not be much but it's a lot better than nothing. Anyway, we'll see what Counsel says. Trouble is in this game you just can't get into these people's heads that they've got to prove *negligence.* You know it and I know it, but these people think that just because they're injured they're automatically entitled to compensation.'

'Yes, sir,' replies dummy clerk, and does what he is told. (Every solicitors' office has at least one dummy clerk, and often he is the firm's most valuable asset.)

Meanwhile the solicitor has a little chat with his chum Mr. *X* Q.C. whose opinion, when it eventually comes, conveniently ignores the evidence of negligent driving and faulty brakes in the police report; and concludes that *as there is no evidence to prove negligence on the part of the driver* the defendants' offer of £1,000 should be accepted. The solicitor tells his clerk to send the client a copy of Queen's Counsel's Opinion with a letter urging him to accept the offer before it is withdrawn.

Such a plan is almost bound to succeed. Most people will accept their solicitor's advice – albeit with a shrug and a sigh – particularly when it is backed up by Counsel's Opinion. After all, they are the experts. But even if a plaintiff was not disposed to accept such advice, he would normally be powerless to take his case further *because once Counsel has given his learned opinion that the defendants' offer should – in all the circumstances – be accepted, the Legal Aid Committee will refuse legal aid, and that will usually be the end of the matter.* Even if the plaintiff was minded to finance the case himself, the solicitor will warn him that he will almost certainly lose the action, and end up not only with nothing but having to pay thousands of pounds in his own and the other side's legal costs. Even if the plaintiff is still undeterred, he will have to go to *another* solicitor (because it will be evident that the first one is not interested in pursuing the case); and he will have difficulty in finding a second firm to take his case seriously when there is an adverse Counsel's Opinion on the file. In any event it will now be a year and a half since the accident, and the evidence needed to prove the defendant's negligence as like as not will have disappeared. Mr. Andrews, it is true, did manage to withstand such pressure, got the legal aid refusal reversed, and won his case. But then he was a wholly exceptional person, and moreover in his case the most important piece of evidence (the tyre mark) was fortunately fixed for all time in the police report. Even then the struggle killed him.

So in the vast majority of cases, whether an accident victim can take his case to Court, or whether he is forced to accept the defendants' nominal or insubstantial offer and settle out of Court, will turn on what his own Counsel writes in his Opinion. And what Counsel writes in his Opinion will turn on how the solicitor frames his 'Instructions to Counsel' – which are always in writing, but no doubt may be supplemented verbally in appropriate cases. Neither is it only the initial Counsel's Opinion which decides whether the plaintiff's action shall proceed. If you remember, even when the plaintiff has been granted legal aid and the case is under way, the legal aid can be withdrawn at any time if new evidence comes to light (e.g. a scratch on the side of an eleven year old van) which the plaintiff's legal advisers consider seriously weakens their client's case; or if the defendant makes an offer *which in the circumstances the plaintiff's legal advisers consider reasonable.* In such cases it is the plaintiff's solicitor's duty to report the position to the Legal Aid Committee,* which will then discharge the plaintiff's legal aid certificate.

Therefore in the vast majority of personal injury cases it is as

* Legal Aid Handbook 1983. Notes for Guidance issued by the Law Society.

easy as falling off a log for the plaintiff's solicitor and Counsel, acting in unison, to sabotage their client's case.

And as safe. Suppose the client complains to the Law Society (as Mr. Andrews did) that his solicitor is not carrying out his instructions, but is putting undue pressure on him to accept the defendants' derisory offer? No worries. The solicitor merely tells the Law Society how he (or his managing clerk) consulted one of the most experienced Counsel in this field who, after considering all the papers, advised that the defendants' offer should be accepted in view of the lack of evidence to show negligence. And the Law Society will merely pass the solicitor's letter on to the client, perhaps adding its own comment (as it did in Mr. Andrews's case) that as Counsel has advised that the defendants' offer is reasonable in the circumstances '*we do not understand why you are not willing to accept it*'. Suppose that the client *understands* what has happened (as Mrs. Johns did), and complains to her Member of Parliament that her solicitor has withheld vital evidence in his Instructions to Counsel, and as a result of Counsel's consequent unfavourable opinion she has lost her legal aid? Still no worries. The M.P., after getting the solicitor's version, will reply that whether evidence is relevant or not is a *legal* matter which must be left to the lawyers. In other words, no one in authority would dream of properly investigating the client's complaint. So even if the client tries to complain about his lawyers, he will find himself caught in the 'professional trap' – that is, where he realizes the professional is up to some jiggery-pokery, but there is nothing he can do about it.

If there is no intrinsic difference between the morality of one calling and another, but the amount of corruption in any calling is commensurate with the *opportunities* for corruption, there will be as much corruption in the legal profession as in the police. And if (as is reasonable to suppose) the amount of corruption in any calling is also inversely proportionate to the risk of exposure, it follows that there will be *more* corruption in the legal profession than in the police.

I have shown how a solicitor and Counsel, acting in unison, can easily and safely sabotage their client's case. On the other hand, if the plaintiff's solicitor is uncertain of getting a complaisant Counsel, a less sophisticated but still effective way of sabotaging his client's case is for the solicitor simply to do nothing. In theory, of course, his client can always dismiss him and instruct a more energetic one, but in practice it is not so easy. The layman, whose only knowledge of the subject is that legal cases take a long time, will have no idea of what his solicitor is supposed to be doing on his behalf; and will therefore be readily fobbed off with such assurances as 'We're in the process of submitting a case for the Opinion of Counsel', 'We will shortly be issuing a writ to protect your interests', and so on. By the time he realizes that his case is getting nowhere, and neither is it likely to in the hands of his present advisers, a couple of years will have elapsed since the accident. So by the time he does get round to instructing another solicitor, the evidence to prove his case will probably have disappeared. In theory he can sue the first solicitor; but again in practice this presents insuperable difficulties, because he will have to prove not only that his solicitor was dilatory, but that the delay has ruined his case – for which he needs to prove that he had a valid case to ruin in the first place, so he's back where he started.

I have given an example of how I think a reinsurance company might try to mitigate the size of a higher than average claim against it. But a bribe can take many different forms. The defendants' offer to settle out of Court invariably includes, in addition, payment of the plaintiff's solicitor's costs, so the plaintiff gets the offer *net*. Now when a case goes to Court the plaintiff's solicitor's costs are vetted ('taxed') by a Court official; but when the case is settled out of Court, the costs are usually agreed informally between the parties' solicitors. Therefore what is to prevent a canny insurance company lacing a parsimonious offer to settle the plaintiff's claim out of Court with a rather more generous offer in respect of his solicitor's costs?

Even without any deliberate loading of his costs, *the plaintiff's solicitor is always better off when a case is settled out of Court.* Firstly, because when a case is settled (and the costs agreed informally) the solicitor gets his costs immediately; whereas if the case goes to Court, his costs are 'taxed' – which is almost as lengthy a procedure as the actual litigation itself. Secondly, whereas litigation which goes to Court is one of the less profitable areas of solicitors' work, litigation which is settled is as lucrative as conveyancing. This is especially so when the settlement is made early on in the proceedings. In such cases the defendant's insurance company is unlikely to quibble over a bill for a few hundred pounds, whereas the plaintiff's solicitor will probably have only done a few hours work, viz. a bit of correspondence, taking Counsel's Opinion and perhaps issuing a writ. So on being settled out of Court, a potentially bothersome and unprofitable case is suddenly transformed into a straightforward profitable one.

As we have seen, in 97% of all personal injury cases in respect of which writs have been issued, the plaintiff, on the advice of his solicitor, either abandons his case or else settles out of Court. But as the solicitor almost invariably stands to benefit financially, one way or another, from such advice being taken, how do we know whether in giving it he is putting his client's or his own interests first?

Nor is direct financial gain the only motive for corruption. Personal injury cases invariably involve the individual fighting a large and powerful institution – the local Council or Education Authority, the local industrial magnate, and in any event their Insurance Company. Now lawyers are fond of proclaiming their independence, and how they can be relied on to stand up for the little man. But can they? The plaintiff will usually instruct a *local* solicitor. And that solicitor's most rewarding business will *not* be personal injury work – which will be a 'one off' job – but commercial conveyancing and company work. If the solicitor is reasonably ambitious he will also have his fingers in other lucrative pies – directorships, insurance company agencies, etc. – and as like as not he will be an aspiring member of his local Rotary group and masonic lodge. In other words, in his business and social life the solicitor will be hobnobbing with the same sort of people, and on some occasions no doubt the very same people, whose slovenly or underhand practices the little man is employing him to expose. Which is yet another reason why you may find your friendly local solicitor, although ready enough to take your case, prosecutes it so half-heartedly thereafter; and why if, on your insistence, it does go to Court, it will take four years to get there.

Let's go back to that figure of 97% of all personal injury claims in respect of which writs are issued, which are either abandoned or settled out of Court. Most legal commentators merely repeat this (or a similar) statistic without apparently attaching any significance to it. The legal profession itself sees it as a cause for self-congratulation: how the plaintiff's solicitor's experience and negotiating skill gets his client the best possible offer without the hassle of having to go to Court – e.g. 'If you are a victim of an accident a Solicitor has the skill and knowledge . . . to negotiate with an Insurance Company so that you receive the maximum compensation *and* legal costs.' (Law Society pamphlet *Had an accident? See a Solicitor.* The Law Society's italics, incidentally.) It never occurs to anyone to wonder whether there may be any reasons for that revealing little statistic other than the plaintiff's solicitor's negotiating skill, or the defendant's insurers' generosity.

On the other hand, there has been some useful research, *Negotiated Justice*,* into the practice of *criminal* cases being 'settled out of Court'. The way this happens is that just before the trial Counsel for the prosecution and Counsel for the defence do a deal whereby the defendant (here meaning someone accused of a crime) agrees to plead guilty, in return for the assurance of a significantly reduced sentence. This practice of 'plea bargaining' (as it's called) is quite widespread, although officially unrecognized. And the authors' main conclusion from their survey is that a significant proportion of defendants, who would probably have been acquitted if their case had gone to full trial, *were subjected to pressure by their own Counsel to plead guilty*, to which they succumbed and were consequently convicted and imprisoned.

The authors are rather coy as to the reasons they suggest *why* the defendants' Counsel should subject their clients to this pressure,† and tactfully refrain from mentioning the obvious one: that if the defendant pleads guilty instead of not guilty, the case takes ten minutes instead of the whole day; and Counsel (having agreed his fee beforehand which is not reducible however quickly the case is disposed of) can then take another case and earn himself another fee. Indeed his clerk may have actually booked him for another case in the hope that the previous one *will* settle: 'The clerks overload their principals with engagements in the hope that where two cases conflict one will

* *Negotiated Justice* by Baldwin and McConville, published by Martin Robertson.

† Counsel frequently has had inadequate time to study his brief and does not want to expose his lack of preparation by trying to fight the case; Counsel is concerned to promote the administrative efficiency of the system of which he is part (p. 111).

settle or go short, so that the barrister will still be able to do both cases and collect two fees instead of one.' (*The Bar on Trial* p.120). Even if Counsel has not got another available case, he can profitably use the bonus time to catch up on paper work.

So the authors of *Negotiated Justice* say that in criminal cases Counsel frequently put pressure on their clients, who would not otherwise have been convicted, to plead guilty. And the reason they do (say I) is that they have a *financial interest* in their clients so doing.

In other words, when an adviser – whether Counsel acting for the accused in a criminal case, or a solicitor acting for the plaintiff in a personal injury case – has a financial interest in his advice being taken, his advice is suspect; the greater the financial interest, the more suspect the advice. And a system whereby that adviser is in a position to exert such pressure on his client that the client has virtually no option but to accept his advice, is going to be abused. If a defendant in a criminal case is liable to be pressured by his own lawyer to 'settle out of Court' against his interests, how much more vulnerable is a plaintiff in a personal injury case – where there are even less checks on the lawyer's advice and the manner in which it is given, and where the lawyer may stand to gain far more than just the fee of another case.

11 *Why the majority of lawyers dealing with these cases are either incompetent or corrupt (2) Incompetence*

As stated with uncharacteristic candour, on the front page of the Law Society's Gazette (April 30 1980):

'We may identify three types of litigation solicitor. First, those with great expertise in a particular field, such as acting for insurance companies or trade unions. They run rings round the rest of us. Then there is the average competent practitioner. Finally, there are those (few) solicitors who should not be allowed within 100 yards of a law Court.'

As stated in the Cantley Report, about 97% of personal injury claims, in respect of which writs are issued, do not actually go to Court; but are either abandoned or else settled out of Court by the plaintiff accepting the defendants' offer. And as found by the Pearson Report, the vast majority of settlements – a proportion of which must inevitably be in respect of serious injuries, where there is a reasonable chance of proving negligence – are for nominal or insubstantial amounts. In the last chapter I suggested a reason for this: that the plaintiff's solicitor, having in whatever degree a personal financial interest in the matter, often puts pressure – sometimes well nigh irresistible pressure – on his client to accept the defendants' inadequate offer.

In this chapter I suggest another reason: that the plaintiff's solicitor will fall into either the second or more probably the third category mentioned in the above quotation. That is, the plaintiff's solicitor will either be an average practitioner, who, although described as competent, will nevertheless (as the writer admits) have rings run round him by the defendant's insurance company's solicitor; or else he will be so incompetent that he 'should not be allowed within 100 yards of a law Court.' His client will therefore eventually either have to abandon his case, or else accept whatever derisory sum the defendant's insurance company offers.

The writer of the article thinks that only a few litigation solicitors acting for the plaintiff fall into this latter category. I, on the other hand, think that many – possibly the majority – do. He gives no reasons for his view. Let me give some for mine.

First of all the training. As with many other callings, the job the solicitor is trained to do is not the job he does. He gets an *academic* training, learning all about the law and, in this context, the law of negligence, with all its wondrous academic ramifications – e.g. whether Mrs. Moo, who suffers nervous shock when Alf, a scaffolding contractor, drops a pole onto the top of a bus which after being carried 50 yards falls off upsetting a workman's brazier which causes her child's dress to catch fire, can sue Alf.*

But as we know, in real life *it isn't the solicitor who advises Mrs. Moo.* If he was consulted by her he would go straight to *Counsel.* Most accidents do not entail any such complicated chain of events so beloved by university lecturers – in fact they involve little or no academic law at all. Nevertheless, whatever the facts of a case, before legal proceedings are set in motion the solicitor almost invariably instructs Counsel to advise. Counsel also drafts the various Court documents,† decides the strategy, and finally argues the case in Court. Even the Master's summonses, which settle preliminary procedural disputes, are usually argued by Counsel, with the solicitor sitting behind him.

What, then, is the plaintiff's solicitor's job? Does he *have* any job, other than to act as an intermediary between his client and Counsel, and as a post office between Counsel and the other side's solicitors? In fact he does. The legal profession has been divided into Counsel and solicitors; and in personal injury cases it is Counsel who advises on the law, decides on strategy, drafts all

---

* This was a question in the Cambridge law exam. Another question, which I vividly remember, asked the candidate to advise a circus midget as to his rights of action in respect of the loss of his wife's company, when his wife (also a midget) was injured by a performing elephant overbalancing off his stool.

† In High Court actions it is normal to use Counsel for all the paper work – *Criminal and Civil Litigation*, Raymond.

the Court documents, and finally argues the case in Court. This leaves only one material job for the solicitor, and that is to get the *evidence* – the evidence, that is, whereby Counsel will be able to argue in Court that his client's injuries were caused by the defendant's fault. In other words, Counsel is the lawyer and the solicitor is the *enquiry agent*. Thus the plaintiff's solicitor, in Mr. Perkins's case, should have inspected and photographed the metal table top (with its alleged holes) which Mr. Perkins was working on, and collected a typical casting. In Mrs. Johns's case he should have photographed and drawn up a plan of the school playground, and taken statements from the two playground supervisors, and the children in the playground who might have seen the accident. In Mr. Andrews's case he should have got statements from the witnesses, arranged a mechanical inspection of the van, got details of the parked cars between which Tessa emerged, and so on.

But this is not the job a solicitor has been trained to do. He has learned all about the origins of the Court of Common Pleas in the 14th century, but he has had no instruction on how to use a camera. However, the trouble isn't so much that the solicitor has not been trained to be an enquiry agent, but that the training he *has* had, and his status thereafter, militate against him being an *efficient* enquiry agent.

A good enquiry agent is prepared to work unsocial hours, and he is mobile. In fact most of his work will be done *outside* his office. So within a couple of days of being consulted by Mr. Perkins he would have called at the factory to photograph the table top. When Mrs. Johns tells him about David's accident he knows that he must interview and get statements from the other children, if not that evening at any rate the next – i.e. before the school contacts them. As soon as Mr. Andrews leaves his office he gets on to a mechanic he knows and makes arrangements for him to inspect the van and its brakes. *In other words, apart from being able to use a camera, an enquiry agent's only qualification is common sense.*

But a solicitor has been to university where he has obsessively learned about such things as the law of perpetuities, and the Settled Land Act, and the legal formalities for freeing slaves in the Roman Empire, and whether Mrs. Moo can sue Alf for the nervous shock she suffered when Alf set off a complicated chain of events which culminated in her child's dress catching fire, and what rights the circus midget has against the owner of the performing elephant which overbalanced and injured his equally diminutive wife, and a thousand and one equally useless things besides. And the reason the solicitor has his head stuffed full of these academic legal conundrums over a period of three years, is to make him see his client's accident as a complex *legal* problem, rather than as a prosaic event requiring him to spend a couple of days getting a bit of straightforward evidence – just as he must see the house his client is buying as something involving myriad *legal* implications, rather than as a physical thing about which there are a few simple points to be checked. *Because only if he sees his client's accident, or his client's house, in such terms can he justify his professional status*, and esoteric procedures to match. In other words, the purpose of the solicitor's training is not to develop, but to *atrophy* his common sense; so that he can convince himself – and everybody else – that in sending out his printed forms of nonsensical questions which make up the basis of domestic conveyancing, or in 'instructing Counsel to Advise' in a routine personal injury case, he is giving his clients a skilled and *professional* service.

So the one qualification which the plaintiff's solicitor needs for his job – common sense – is the one qualification which the experts responsible for his training will have done their best to ensure he does not possess.

Moreover, his professional status after his training further militates against him doing his job properly. An enquiry agent should have no status but be prepared, at the drop of a hat, to get into his car and drive to the factory, the playground, the address where the van is being kept, or wherever, to pick up the evidence before it disappears. But the solicitor is a professional man who has passed law examinations. And a professional man who has passed law examinations *doesn't* go round to a factory in the outskirts of the town and photograph a metal table top, or spend an afternoon going to some suburban address with a mechanic to check a van's brakes, or spend his evening interviewing children in the hope that they can tell him something about a playground accident. Instead, he sits behind his great big desk, dictating his letters and his 'Instructions to Counsel' to his secretary. And if he does tumble to the fact – or if he is advised by Counsel – that some evidence needs to be collected outside his office, he will generally get someone *else* (his clerk or an outside agent) to do it.

In short, the able solicitor will not generally be found doing personal injury work, because he realizes that he can never be anything more than Counsel's enquiry agent. The less able solicitor, who does do it, will have been successfully *protected* from the uncomfortable realization that he is nothing more than Counsel's enquiry agent by devices which will tend to make him a *ludicrously inefficient* enquiry agent.

Thus Mr. Perkins's first two solicitors, who had the case for one and a half years, and six months, respectively, never inspected the table top to see whether it had holes in it. His third solicitor arranged an inspection fifteen months after taking over the case, and did not inspect it himself but instructed a *consulting engineer* – by which time the original table top had disappeared. Mrs. Johns's three solicitors never inspected the playground or interviewed the children. Mr. Andrews's first three solicitors never took statements from any witnesses or arranged a mechanical inspection of the van. His fourth solicitor took ten months to get statements from the three witnesses, and two and a half years before he set about trying to trace the make and model of the parked cars between which Tessa emerged; and he took those steps only after Counsel had advised them. It is true that I suggested that incompetence might not be the sole explanation for Mrs. Johns's and Mr. Andrews's solicitors' apparent ineptitude. But that the manner in which our three plaintiffs' various solicitors* went about getting the evidence to prove their clients' case is typical, is indicated by the findings of the Royal Commission on Legal Services which I previously quoted: the average time from accident to the issue of a writ (i.e. the *first* step in a legal action) is seventeen months; the average time from accident to trial is four years; and in 35% of all cases, the time from accident to trial is *between four and eight years*.

Then there is a revealing little passage in a book, *Checklists for Solicitors* (on sale in most legal bookshops), which outlines the steps which a solicitor should take when acting for a plaintiff in a personal injury case (p. 142):

---

* In fact the plaintiff's solicitor is often a solicitor's *clerk*, and one might think from the foregoing that a clerk would be more adept at his job than a solicitor. But as we saw from our three plaintiffs' chronicles, it seems to make little difference to the quality of the work whether it is done by the one or the other. This is because the clerk, being subservient to the solicitor (and getting an appropriately low salary), automatically adopts the practice and *ethos* of the profession. (The previous paragraph, in any case, applies to both solicitor and solicitor's clerk.)

'1. Take statement from client and advise if there is a prima facie case.
2. If there is. . .help client complete application for legal aid.
3. *Upon receipt of. . .legal aid certificate,* inspect the scene of accident and make a sketch plan.
[4.–7. Write letters to defendant, surgeon, doctor, police.]
8. Interview witnesses and take statements.'

As it usually takes a couple of months for the Legal Aid Committee to process an application for legal aid, and as the plaintiff's solicitor usually supports his client's application with Counsel's Opinion (especially in serious cases), we may assume that a legal aid certificate will be granted four or five months after the accident in those cases where the plaintiff's solicitor has been reasonably expeditious. And double that period is probably the norm, which would tally with the Royal Commission's finding that seventeen months is the average time between the accident and the issue of a writ. So if the plaintiff's solicitor waits for the legal aid certificate before he sets about trying to get the evidence – which apparently is the recommended procedure – then he will not start trying to get the evidence until four to ten months *after* the accident. Any self-respecting enquiry agent would realize that this is unacceptable; and that as the evidence to prove the plaintiff's case is liable to disappear at any time (either of its own accord or with a little assistance from the other side), it should be obtained within *days* not months of him being instructed. The legal profession seems not to have twigged this rather crucial fact.

The public is told that one of the characteristics of a profession is that its members have to observe higher standards than the law demands of an ordinary tradesman. In the case of the legal profession, this claim is bogus. As stated in the quotation with which I opened this chapter, there are those solicitors 'who should not be allowed within 100 yards of a law Court' – just as there are those central heating contractors who should not be allowed within 100 yards of a radiator, and those builders who should not be allowed within 100 yards of a building site. But whereas you have some remedies against the latter group, you have virtually none against the former. If water starts leaking out of your radiators after the contractor has installed them, you have some means of redress. You can withold payment, or sue him in the County Court; but more important, you know at once that he is incompetent and so you can dismiss him. Similarly if the builder you have engaged to build an extension digs a couple of trenches in the first week, and then doesn't turn up but keeps making excuses, you know he is unreliable, so you dismiss him and get another. Not so in the case of an incompetent or unreliable lawyer, *whose competence or reliability the client has no means of assessing*.

How do you know whether your solicitor is taking the necessary steps to bring your case to Court when you have no idea what those steps are? You will have heard that legal actions take a long time, but as the months tick by, how do you know whether your solicitor is busy beavering away on your behalf, or whether the file is lying forgotten in his filing cabinet? Maybe you will eventually tumble to the fact that your legal action is getting nowhere because of your solicitor's incompetence or indifference (if such is the case), but it will be a couple of years before you do. And even then there is nothing you can do about it. Complain to the Law Society? A waste of a postage stamp. Sue the solicitor for negligence? A waste of £5,000. In short, the solicitor can be almost as incompetent or dilatory as he pleases, but he risks virtually no sanctions. You won't even be able to withhold payment of his bill, because he will refuse to release the file to your new solicitor until his costs are paid.

The public is also told that a professional man takes more *responsibility* than a tradesman – a claim which in this context has an even more hollow ring.

You, who have been seriously injured in an accident, instruct a solicitor to sue for compensation. Who has responsibility for the conduct of your case? The solicitor? But after the initial interview he handed the matter to his trusted and experienced managing clerk, and took no further part in it. The trusted and experienced managing clerk? But he went to Counsel at every turn and acted only as Counsel advised. Counsel? But he can only give such advice as he is asked for, and besides he can only go on such facts as he is given in his instructions (which incidentally you are not permitted to see). Queen's Counsel, who argues the case in Court? But you can't sue him however badly he does it, or even if he doesn't turn up at all, but sends along a substitute who picked up the papers for the first time half an hour before the trial. In any case, you have no contact with your Counsel, and may not even *speak* to him direct.

As we saw, Mr. Andrews's Solicitor No. 4 contacted the third witness (the girl whose hand Tessa had been holding at the time of the accident) ten months after he took over the case. If by that time she could no longer be traced, he would reply to any accusation of negligence that he had taken Counsel's opinion seven months previously; and in that opinion Counsel had advised him to contact the policeman and the passer-by, but had *not* mentioned the girl. Counsel, if accused, would argue that it is not his job to do *all* the thinking, but to give an overall opinion and outline the general strategy. So if necessary each can shelter behind the other.

Another consequence of splitting the plaintiff's legal adviser into solicitor and Counsel is that crucial facts can easily get lost, either falling through the gap between them, or remaining buried under the mounds of paper which they shunt backwards and forwards to each other. It is easy enough for the plaintiff's solicitor (especially as he will tend to be one of the less ambitious of his species) to think that all he need do is relay everything his client has told him about the accident, and leave it to Counsel to decide what is relevant – i.e. let Counsel do all the *thinking*. It is equally easy for an overworked Counsel to assume that the solicitor will have brought anything important to his attention, and therefore not look beyond his Instructions. Thus Queen's Counsel, in his Opinion in Mrs. Johns's case, wrote: 'It seems to me that the system of supervision must be conceded to have been adequate.' He assumes this because he has been told that there was a supervisor present, and no question of a *single supervisor being inadequate* had been raised in the solicitor's Instructions to Advise. On the other hand, the solicitor did not raise the point presumably because he left it to Counsel (who had a plan of the playground, with dimensions) to decide. So the crucial question – whether a single supervisor was or was not adequate for that playground, for those children – was never considered either by solicitor or Counsel but, as it were, fell through the gap between them.

Of course it is true, as advocates of the system are forever pointing out, that the client *can* sue his solicitor for negligence. But unless the negligence consists of a straightforward procedural slip (e.g. failing to issue the writ in time), such a course is even more hazardous than the original litigation. For a start, the client has to engage *another* solicitor and Counsel – who may turn out to be just as incompetent as the original pair. Moreover, having already wasted four years on the original case, the prospect of another four years on another lawsuit, with the possibility of ending up with nothing but a bill for £12,000 in legal fees (if Mr. Andrews's Solicitor No. 5's fees are typical, see p. 245), would surely deter all but the most masochistic.

We are told that the professional man has to observe higher standards, and take more responsibility, than the law demands of the ordinary tradesman. In the case of the lawyer the opposite is true. Because there are virtually no sanctions against him, and because of his masterstroke of splitting himself amoeba-like into solicitor and Counsel, the lawyer can get away with lower standards, and take less responsibility, than any car mechanic, jobbing builder, or central heating contractor. Which is why the plaintiff stands a better chance of having his car competently repaired or his extension competently built or his central heating competently installed, than he does of having his personal injury case competently handled.

To make matters worse for him, rather different considerations apply to the solicitor acting for his opponent, who in effect will invariably be an insurance company.

The insurance company is in business to make money for its shareholders (and directors), and the money it makes is the amount by which the premiums exceed the claims. Therefore the insurance company's solicitor's job is to get those claims which he considers have a chance of being successfully contested, one way or another, settled at the minimum figure. And whereas the plaintiff will usually instruct a local solicitor, who will tend to be a jack of all trades – deriving most of his income from conveyancing, probate and divorce, but taking on personal injury cases when occasion demands – the insurance company's solicitor will be a specialist. And unlike the average plaintiff's solicitor, he will be expert at his job – because if he wasn't, he wouldn't be doing it. As succinctly stated in the quotation from the Law Society's Gazette, with which I opened this chapter, he will 'run rings round the rest of us'.

Adjusting his tactics to the particular degree of ineptitude of the plaintiff's solicitor, the insurance company's solicitor will know when simply to ignore his letters; when to dangle the offer of a meeting in front of him (which somehow always gets postponed); when to indicate that he is waiting for a doctor's report or whatever, 'on receipt of which we will be in touch with you' (which somehow always gets delayed). He will know how to exploit the procedural processes to the full. For instance, we saw that in Mr. Andrews's case it took the defendants' solicitor *six months* to supply the 'further and better particulars of defence' requested by Solicitor No. 4 (date of request 2nd August 1968, date supplied 31st January 1969). *In fact this is the average time it takes the defendants' solicitor to supply such particulars, as found by the Royal Commission* (section 10.15).

In short, the defendants' solicitor will know how to string along his opponent, in the happy knowledge that each half year's delay he can achieve increases the plaintiff's psychological strain, and so makes him more amenable to settling out of Court; and also makes his case more difficult to prove if it *does* eventually go to Court.

12 *The system itself*

In the last two chapters I suggested two reasons why the vast majority of claims for compensation in respect of personal injuries are unsuccessful, being either abandoned or settled out of Court for nominal or insubstantial sums: viz. that the majority of the plaintiffs' solicitors are either corrupt or incompetent.

Now let's recap on the system itself.

Under English law, someone who is injured in an accident (plaintiff) is entitled to compensation for his injuries only if they were caused by someone else's (defendant's) fault. This is decided by legal battle. The plaintiff's legal champions try to show in Court that their client's accident *was* caused by the defendant's fault, and so get their client adequate compensation; the defendant's (insurance company's) legal champions try to show that it *wasn't*, and so exonerate their client from paying compensation. Accident of course means any accident, not just a road accident. The battle proceeds as follows:

The plaintiff consults a solicitor and gives him the facts of the accident as he understands them. The solicitor (or clerk to whom he delegates the matter) sends a summary of those facts to Counsel, and asks Counsel to give his *opinion*. If Counsel's Opinion is that the plaintiff has a reasonable chance of winning his case in Court, the solicitor will – if the plaintiff is eligible – submit an application for legal aid supported by Counsel's Opinion, and a couple of months thereafter legal aid will be granted (either unconditionally, or limited to one step or series of steps, after which the Legal Aid Committee will reassess the position). Then the case gets under way. Plaintiff's solicitor instructs Counsel to draft writ and Statement of Claim which, when drafted, is sent to the defendant's solicitor. Defendant's solicitor sends Statement of Claim to *his* Counsel with instructions to draft Defence which, when drafted, is sent to the plaintiff's solicitor. The parties' solicitors then serve on each other 'request for further and better particulars' of the Defence and Statement of Claim respectively, which requests will have been drafted by their respective Counsel, who in due course will draft the 'further and better particulars' requested.

Somewhere along the line there will be one or more Master's summonses. These are mini trials at which the parties' lawyers argue disputed procedural points – e.g. whether the plaintiff should be allowed to amend his Statement of Claim, whether the defendant should be ordered to supply fuller 'further and better particulars' of his defence. Then when all the 'pleadings' have been settled there is 'discovery of documents', when the parties' solicitors exchange lists of documents in their clients' possession, stating which they are prepared to disclose, which they claim are privileged. Then the parties' solicitors instruct their respective Counsel to 'Advise on Evidence'. Then there is a 'Summons for Directions', at which the Master gives directions on any procedural points which are still outstanding, and decides on the number of expert witnesses which each party shall be allowed to call at the trial. Finally, when there are no further documents to be exchanged and no further procedural points outstanding, the case is 'set down for hearing' – that is, officially put in the queue of cases awaiting trial. Then a date will be given by the 'Clerk of the lists'.

As we have seen, that little lot, on average, takes *four years*.

Thus it is not so much a battle as a war of attrition; and 97% of plaintiffs who initiate actions do not stay the course, but either accept the defendants' offer and settle out of Court, or else abandon their claim.

The tiny minority who fight on will have their day (or three or four days) in Court. The plaintiff's solicitor will send Counsel Instructions to argue the case in Court. And when the day of the trial finally arrives (usually about nine months after the case is 'set down for hearing'), the parties and their solicitors and their Counsel and their witnesses and their expert witnesses will arrive at the Court; and the plaintiff's Counsel will try to show that the accident which happened four years previously was the defendant's fault, and the defendant's Counsel will try to show that it wasn't.

If the plaintiff's claim is in respect of a serious injury he will probably be advised to have a Queen's Counsel, in which case it will be Queen's Counsel who presents the case in Court. Behind him will sit the ordinary Counsel, who will have advised throughout and drafted the procedural documents. Behind him will sit the solicitor, who will have fed the facts to Counsel. Behind him will sit the plaintiff, who will have fed the facts to the solicitor. At the other end of the same benches will sit the equivalent legal team representing the defendant. In due course the witnesses, in answer to questions from Counsel, will relate what they remember seeing of the accident. And depending on how they, and the parties themselves, give their evidence and stand up to cross-examination by the opposing Counsel, and any other evidence produced by the parties' Counsel, the judge will decide either that the plaintiff's Counsel *has* shown that the plaintiff's injuries were caused by the defendant's fault (in which case he will order the defendant to pay the plaintiff an appropriate sum of compensation); or that he *hasn't* (in which case the plaintiff gets nothing).

If all goes well for the plaintiff – if he has a good Counsel, a good solicitor, good witnesses who are still available, a good judge, and assuming he also has a good case – he will win his case, and get compensation for his injuries. But what a lottery it is!

Suppose he has a competent Counsel but an indifferent solicitor (who perhaps failed to relay some crucial fact); or a good solicitor but an incompetent Counsel, or one who was substituted at the last minute because the original one was detained on a case elsewhere; or a competent solicitor and a competent Counsel, but the key witnesses were no longer available or, if available, they became hopelessly confused when cross-examined by the defendant's Counsel as to what they remembered seeing of the accident – possibly in a split second – four years previously; or a competent solicitor and Counsel and unshakeable witnesses, but an incompetent and unsympathetic judge? In the event of any of these permutations the plaintiff, even if he has a good case, will probably lose. And not only will he get no compensation for his injuries, but (if not legally-aided) he will have to meet all the legal costs himself – his own and those of the defendant.

Having looked at the delay, and some other aspects of the system, let's now take a look at these costs.

Everyone knows that High Court cases are expensive, but no-one knows exactly *how* expensive. Surprisingly, there have been no surveys on the subject. The published figures for average legal aid costs do not distinguish between those cases which are settled out of Court, and those which go to trial. The Royal Commission on Legal Services told us the average *time* it takes a High Court case to come to trial, and the average cost of a *conveyancing* transaction, but not the average cost of a High Court case which goes to trial. Neither did the Pearson Commission, or anyone else. So we will have to try and work it out for ourselves.

The going rate for a Queen's Counsel (whose services a seriously injured plaintiff would be advised to engage) to argue the case in Court, is currently about £1,000 for the first *day* of the trial, plus about £500 for each day thereafter.* The mute ordinary Counsel, who sits behind him, is generally paid at the rate of half the Q.C.'s fee. And for good measure there is a fee payable to Counsel's *clerk* – usually 10% of Counsel's fees. Thus for a four day trial with a Q.C. – normal for a serious case where liability and amount are contested – the plaintiff's Counsel's fees for the actual trial, overall, will be about £4,000. (A Court day, incidentally, is only 5 hours – 10.30 a.m. to 4.30 p.m., with an hour for lunch.)

The legal fees for the pre-trial work are more variable. A costs draftsman told me that the plaintiff's solicitor's profit costs (i.e. excluding Counsel's fees) for this sort of litigation would normally be between £5,000 and £7,500;† and that in the last bill he drew up, which was in respect of a serious personal injury case which took four years to come to Court, culminating in a two day trial, the plaintiff's solicitor's profit costs came to £6,000. So

* A Sunday Times article ('The Huge Cost of going to Law' by Bruce Page and Phillip Knightley), dated *10th November 1974*, put a Q.C.'s fee in a personal injury trial at £800 for the first day plus £150 per day thereafter; and although the Law Society subsequently wrote contesting the article's conclusions, it did not dispute the actual *figures*.

† This would tally with some of the figures of actual bills previously mentioned – e.g. the overall bill for the defendants' legal costs in Mr. Perkins's case, which entailed a *one* day trial and *no* Q.C., came to £3,331. Mr. Andrews's Solicitor No. 5's bill for suing Solicitor No. 3 (which case was settled out of Court) came to £5,719.

assuming an average bill of £6,000 for the pre-trial work in a serious personal injury case coming to trial in 1983, and average Counsel's brief fees of £4,000, the plaintiff's legal costs will be in the region of £10,000. Multiply by two to include the *defendants'* legal costs, and it seems that a plaintiff who does not qualify for legal aid will have to pay £20,000 in legal costs if he loses the case.

This, I maintain, is the average overall sum for legal costs in a serious personal injury case in which both parties employ a Queen's Counsel – that is, when eight lawyers (or hangers on) have to be paid: solicitor, ordinary Counsel, Queen's Counsel, Counsel's clerk, times two. Some such cases will no doubt cost less. Equally, other cases, which seem to turn on questions of no more than average complexity – e.g. in trying to deliver Stuart Whitehouse with forceps, did Dr. Jordan pull too hard and too long before abandoning the attempt? – will cost significantly more. As we saw (p. 62), to decide that particular question in the negative, and that therefore Mrs. Whitehouse was not entitled to any compensation for her brain-damaged child, cost over £150,000 in legal fees.

What sort of justice is this which gives an injured person, who wins his case, compensation only after a four year war of attrition – when he has just suffered at best a calamity, at worst a tragedy, and is therefore emotionally in the worst position to wage it? Alternatively, what sort of justice is this which makes an injured person, who loses his case, pay some £20,000 for the judge's decision that he is *not* entitled to any compensation?

Even then, the lawyers' fees which the losing party has to pay are by no means the only costs of the case. There is an army of other people to be paid – judges, masters, Court officials, clerks, legal aid personnel, office cleaners etc. – all of whom receive state salaries. In effect, the plaintiff in bringing his case to Court is enjoying a hefty subsidy from the taxpayer. For a judge to preside over a four day case costs £1,000 (Court sits approximately 190 days a year, judge's salary £50,000 p.a.). The cost of the rest of the assorted crew and amenities, apportioned to the plaintiff's case might be in the region of £4,000.

So when someone is seriously injured in an accident, the Court's decision whether his injury was or was not someone else's fault, and therefore whether or not that someone else's insurance company has to pay him compensation, costs – on average – £25,000. Of this, £20,000 is paid by the losing party or, if he is legally-aided, the taxpayer; and £5,000 is paid by the taxpayer in any event.

Now these disproportionate costs have even drawn some comment from some of the dignitaries of the legal profession – e.g. Lord Goodman: 'Who would embark on litigation confronted with the possibility of paying these mammoth and terrifying amounts? . . . What a reproach on the legal system that we have costed it out of use.' (Law Society's Annual Conference, 1974.) And from a former President of the Law Society: 'There is no point in having the *world's greatest system* if it is so expensive as to be unavailable for a significant percentage of the population . . . Our legal system is like a finely tuned Rolls-Royce. It operates superbly for the few who can afford it.' (Law Society's Conference 1982.)

As to the President's quotation, it is an old sales trick to equate expense with excellence, and compare dubious but highly priced services to a Rolls-Royce. In this case the analogy is false. A truer motoring analogy is that the more money a taxi driver wishes to make out of his customer, the less efficiently will he drive him to his destination. Under the present system his only scope for inefficiency is to take a circuitous route. But if over the past two hundred years cab-drivers had been allowed to *design their own system*, they would have designed a system whereby the customer not only *has* to travel by taxi in the towns, but employ *four* taxi drivers (or associates) as well – driver, senior driver, navigator, and negotiator. The resulting system would not only be incredibly expensive, but ludicrously inefficient. We understand this correlation between expense and inefficiency well enough when it comes to the unions: not quite so well when it comes to the legal profession.

Because over the years lawyers have been allowed to design their own system, and because they love money as much as anyone else, they have designed a system whereby an injured person (plaintiff) is entitled to compensation for his injuries only if they were caused by someone else's (defendant's) fault; and only they are competent to determine whether it was or not. This they do by two or three lawyers in the plaintiff's team, and two or three lawyers in the defendant's team, performing a complicated ritual dance culminating in a trial, at which one of the lawyers in the plaintiff's team (who will not have had any direct contact with the plaintiff, but will have had the facts of the accident filtered to him through the other lawyers in the team) will try to show that the accident, which occurred four years previously, was the defendant's fault; and one of the lawyers in the defendant's team will try to show that it wasn't; and the judge, god-like, will decide the truth. Not only does this procedure take four years and cost some £25,000, but in many cases the lawyers might just as well be arguing how many angels can dance on the top of a pin as discover the truth about the plaintiff's accident under such ludicrous conditions.

13 *Why a team of lawyers is the worst equipped unit for the job – but why should the job have to be done at all?*

Because personal injury cases are decided in a Court of Law, and argued by lawyers dressed up in wigs and gowns, who have performed an esoteric ritual and speak in a strange language scarcely intelligible to outsiders, it is assumed that *therefore* they must involve questions of law which only lawyers may comprehend. But this is a fallacy. Of course it is possible that a mother might suffer nervous shock after a scaffolding contractor inadvertently sets off a complicated chain of events culminating in her child's dress catching fire. But although such situations are the staple fare of law students, the vast majority of accidents don't happen that way. The vast majority of accidents – in factories, in schools, on the roads, or wherever – happen in the way that our three plaintiffs' accidents happened.

Mr. Perkins, a bandsaw operator, was injured by a metal casting he was trimming flying up and hitting him on the jaw. David Johns had his eye put out by one of his playmates larking about in the school playground with a bit of broken car aerial. Tessa Andrews was knocked down as she was crossing, or preparing to cross, the road.

Now these cases did not involve any complicated points of law, or indeed any legal points at all. They merely involved questions of *evidence* – evidence, that is, as to whether or not the plaintiff's accident was the defendant's fault. Mr. Perkins's case turned on whether or not there were holes in the metal table top in front of the blade, in which the bits of surplus metal on the casting he was trimming would catch, and so cause it to jam. David's case turned on how long before the accident Ian had been larking about flicking his playmates with mud with the bit of broken aerial; and therefore whether a reasonably vigilant supervisor should have been alert to the potential danger in time to prevent the accident. Tessa's case turned on whether she had proceeded cautiously, or had bolted into the road; how near the van was being driven to the line of parked cars between which she emerged; when the driver first saw her, and whether he had swerved; whether his brakes were faulty, and so on.

And just as these three cases, despite the mountains of ritualistic candy-floss, did not involve any questions of law, but only questions of evidence, so it is with the vast majority of personal injury cases.

Now a team of professionals operating an elaborate and complicated system is the best unit for some jobs, and the worst unit for others. As we have seen, Mr. Perkins's case took *seven years* to come to Court; David Johns's case was settled out of Court nearly *four and a half years* after the accident; Tessa Andrew's case took *four years* to come to Court from when Solicitor No. 4 took it over. And as we have also seen, these time scales are typical for High Court actions. Moreover by the time the plaintiff's lawyers actually got round to trying to get the evidence, in Mr. Perkins's case it had disappeared, and in Tessa's case a vital part (the policeman's notebook) had disappeared. Here again this would seem to be typical, judging from the tiny percentage of personal injury actions which result in the plaintiff getting significant compensation.

In the course of chronicling Mr. Perkins's and David's cases, I indicated how a single layman (RAMS),* with no qualifications other than common sense and the ability to use a camera, would have gone about the job. How he would have got the necessary evidence, not in two or three years but in *two or three days*. And how such a person would be quite competent to argue the plaintiffs' cases in Court, because the argument in the vast majority of personal injury cases does not turn on any complex legal points but, again, is a matter of common sense.

In Mr. Perkins's case, the plaintiff's argument is that the holes in the metal table made such an accident likely, having regard to the nature of the work; and that his employers, in providing such a machine, were therefore to blame for the accident. In David's

* See p. 153.

case his argument is that Ian (aged 8) had been chasing his playmates, and flicking them with mud with a bit of broken car aerial, for long enough for a reasonably alert playground supervisor to have noticed what he was doing, and to have intervened to prevent the accident; and the fact that no supervisor *did* intervene was the fault either of the school or Education Authority in failing to provide sufficient supervisors for that playground, or of the supervisor who went indoors, or of the supervisor who remained outside.

Tessa's case is more complicated than the other two. Yet here again, assembling and presenting the evidence to show that her accident was the van driver's fault is only a matter of common sense. It is common sense that if a passer-by volunteers the information that he noticed the two girls hand in hand carefully looking for a place to cross the road, and that as he passed them the elder one *cautiously* stepped off the kerb, that obviously helps show that Tessa did not suddenly bolt in front of the van giving the driver no chance to avoid her. It is common sense that if the van's offside wheels were 10 feet 4" from the nearside kerb at the point of impact, then (given the width of the parked cars and the van itself) the van must have been driven dangerously close to the parked cars, so that Tessa *would* have been struck by it had she merely poked her head out to see if it was safe to cross. It is common sense that if there was only *one* continuous tyre mark on the road, that indicates that the brakes on the opposite wheels might have been faulty, and so on. If you remember, the most telling point against the driver at the trial was that because the tyre or brake mark *commenced at the actual point of impact*, he must have seen Tessa well *before* he hit her, and therefore he had time to swerve. But it does not need a Queen's Counsel in wig and silken gown at £1,000 a day, attended by ordinary Counsel in wig and ordinary gown at £500 a day, instructed by a solicitor at £250 a day, to make this point. Anyone who picks up a copy of the Highway Code will see, on the back cover, that at 30 m.p.h. the thinking distance (i.e. the distance a car will have travelled between the time an average driver *sees* something to make him brake, and when he actually *starts* braking) is 30 feet. In any case, it was not the plaintiff's Queen's Counsel who *did* ask the driver the crucial questions which elicited that he had not swerved, but the judge, after learned Counsel had concluded his cross-examination (see p. 242).

I am not saying that in RAMS's hands our three plaintiffs would necessarily have *won* their cases, which would depend on various imponderables (how the witnesses gave their evidence, what view the judge took, etc). Nor am I saying that there would not be any incompetent RAMSs around. I am saying that because RAMS does not need to take Counsel's Opinion at every turn, or get legal aid, and because he does this work full time, and because he does the whole job himself, and because he is mobile and has a camera and has no status – he can do in two or three days what it takes a team of lawyers two or three years. He is therefore the best equipped unit to do the job of getting the evidence, and presenting the plaintiff's case in Court. And a team of lawyers – shunting the papers backwards and forwards one to another, with their windy instructions and counter-instructions,and their formalistic nonsense under which, as like as not, the crucial issues of the case will lie forever buried – is, in my humble submission, the worst.

* * * * * *

But why should the job have to be done at all?

Any system which requires the injured party to prove negligence before he is entitled to compensation will always have three fundamental defects, whatever procedural reforms are made, and however competently the plaintiff's case is presented.

Firstly, whether or not the plaintiff has proved his case – i.e. has shown that his injuries were caused by the defendant's fault – must always depend on the decision of a *judge*. Now we may treat the judge as a God, address him as 'my lord', attire him in imposing raiment, stand up and bow each time he enters and leaves the Court room, but unfortunately he remains a human being for all that. And judges being human beings, a similar proportion of them will be as incompetent, prejudiced, or downright dishonest, as in any other group of human beings. The dishonesty, of course, will be intellectual rather than financial, and I have given some examples in Chapter 2.

But even if we could somehow breed a race of competent and impartial human beings to preside over our judicial proceedings, there can never be any absolute criteria for determining so broad a question as whether or not the plaintiff's accident was the defendant's fault. We think that if we pay £25,000 into the legal machine we will somehow get the truth. But in this context there is no such thing as 'the truth' – only one man's, the judge's, *opinion.* Thus after carefully listening to the evidence, Judge X decides that the obstetrician, in attempting to deliver baby Whitehouse by forceps, pulled too hard and too long, and must therefore pay him £100,000 damages to compensate him for his permanent and disastrous brain damage. Judge Y, on the other hand, after carefully listening to that same evidence, comes to the conclusion that it has *not* been shown that the obstetrician pulled too hard and too long, and that therefore Stuart Whitehouse is *not* entitled to any compensation. Judge X, after carefully listening to the evidence in Tessa Andrews's case, concludes that the accident was the van driver's fault, and awards her £40,000 damages. Had it been Judge Y on duty, he might well have concluded that the accident had *not* been shown to be the van driver's fault, and would have awarded her nothing.

So if one sunny morning you are mown down by a motor car and crippled for life, whether you get compensation for your injuries, or whether you get no compensation but have yourself to pay an equivalent sum in legal costs for bringing your case to Court, may well depend on whether it is Judge X or Judge Y who happens to be assigned to your case – *or even whether it is Judge X who is the trial judge and Judge Y who sits in the Court of Appeal, or vice versa.*

The second defect is that the plaintiff has to prove (on the 'balance of probabilities') that his injuries were caused by the defendant's fault. That is, he needs *evidence* to prove it.

Sometimes this evidence will be static (e.g. the metal table top, with its alleged holes, which Mr. Perkins was working on). But more often, and especially in the case of road accidents, the evidence will be the testimony of eye-witnesses.

Now as a result of several people having been wrongfully convicted on identification evidence, it has finally been recognized that it is unsafe to convict a defendant in a criminal case on eye-witnesses' testimony alone. To demonstrate the point, Nationwide once mocked up a crime (a man stealing a picture and running out of a building) in front of an unsuspecting coach party, who were then asked to identify the 'criminal' in an identity parade. Out of twelve people, seven said they did not know, two identified the right man, and three identified the *wrong* man. If eye-witnesses are an unreliable source of evidence in criminal cases, they must be even more unreliable in personal injury cases, where they are asked to recount what they saw *four years after* the accident; and where, in the case of road accidents, the subject of their testimony will be motor vehicles, which move faster than criminals. Therefore to prove his case in perhaps the majority of instances, the plaintiff has to rely on evidence which by its nature is suspect, and therefore the more easily impugned by the defendant's Counsel.

Moreover there are several danger areas in which it is unlikely that there will be *any* forthcoming witnesses, or other evidence, to show how an accident occurred. A road accident at night, the streets are deserted: how, then, is the injured party to prove that the accident was the other driver's fault? A steering defect in a car causes a serious crash; the car in question is a write-off: how, then, can the injured party prove how the accident happened? After a road accident, the unconscious injured party is taken to hospital: how, then, is he expected to get the evidence to prove that the accident was the other driver's fault? A drug has disastrous side effects: how can the victim prove that the drug company was at fault? An accident at work – the only witnesses are the defendant's employees, who don't want to lose their jobs. A booboo in a hospital – the only witnesses are the colleagues of the doctor who perpetrated it. And so on, and so on.

Ironically, as accident victims go, Mr. Perkins, David Johns and Tessa Andrews were the *lucky* ones – those whose accidents happened in such a way that there was a good chance of proving that they were caused by someone else's fault. But those same accidents, while still being the defendants' fault, could just as easily have happened in circumstances which gave them *no* chance of proving it. In short, whether or not you get compensation for your accident depends on whether or not you can prove the defendant was at fault; and whether or not there is any evidence around to prove it, is just the luck of the draw.

The third fundamental defect of any system which requires an accident victim to prove negligence before being entitled to compensation, is that accidents can happen *without anyone being negligent*. David Johns lost his eye in a playground accident at school. Tessa Andrews suffered permanent brain damage after she was knocked down by a van. As it happened, their accidents were caused by someone else's negligence. But those same injuries could just as easily have occurred without anyone being at fault. It seems that Ian had been chasing his playmates, and flicking them with mud with a bit of broken car aerial, for several minutes before the accident. Thus had the playground been properly supervised, a reasonably vigilant supervisor would have been alerted, and would have intervened to prevent the accident. But Ian could just as easily have suddenly picked up the implement off the ground and lunged at David, giving a playground supervisor no chance of preventing the accident, however vigilant she was. There would then be no question of negligence on the part of the school or its staff, and therefore no question of any compensation for David. But David has still lost his eye.

Suppose Tessa *had* bolted in front of the van, giving the driver no chance to avoid her. No negligence on the part of the van driver, and so no compensation. But Tessa is still brain-damaged, and her need for compensation is in no way diminished because her accident happens not to have been anyone else's fault. One sunny morning you are mown down by a motor car, and crippled for life. If the accident was caused by the driver not looking where he was going, you are entitled to compensation. If it was caused by unaccountable brake failure, you are entitled to nothing.

So whatever procedural reforms and improvements are made to the system, and even if we *could* breed a race of superior beings of unquestioned competence and probity to operate it, as long as it requires an injured person to prove that his injuries were caused by someone else's fault as a condition to being entitled to compensation, it can never be more than a lottery.

The system may have been more appropriate for the age in which it came into being – the early part of the 19th century – when there were no such things as motor cars or factories or multi-national drug companies, and when a man was hanged for stealing a sheep. But it seems to have outlived its usefulness – except, of course, for the lawyers who make such vast sums out of it.

So what to do? Well, the answer is obvious. Give injured people compensation automatically, in accordance with the severity of their injuries and their future needs, without requiring them to prove that their injuries were caused by anyone else's fault. This is not a new idea. It was suggested for *road accidents* by the Pearson Royal Commission in 1978; and in New Zealand it is actually being put into practice for accidents generally. Pearson suggested that his scheme should be financed by a levy on petrol. In New Zealand the necessary finance comes out of the general rates and taxes.

But I have a scheme to raise the necessary finance to give every accident victim (or in the case of a fatal accident, his dependants) immediate, automatic and generous compensation, which would not require a levy on petrol or anything else; and which would not only entail no additional cost, but would leave the rate-payers significantly *better* off.

14 *The Solution*

Each year approximately one million houses in England and Wales change hands.

In almost every case, for each of these houses which change hands the seller will have appointed an estate agent, and both seller and purchaser will have instructed separate solicitors to do the conveyancing. The purchaser's building society will also have instructed a solicitor and a surveyor.

Assuming that the average house sells at £35,000, the estate agent's fee will be £700 (2%). The solicitors acting for the seller and purchaser will each charge, on average, £350. The purchaser's building society's solicitor charges a further £50 to £150* – and its surveyor charges £50 to £100 (the two latter fees being paid by the purchaser/borrower).

So for each house that changes hands the seller and purchaser together pay some £1,600 in fees; which multiplied by a million *equals a national total of £1,600,000,000 paid in house transfer fees every year.*

As in the personal injury scenario, most of the work for which these fees are charged is useless or worse than useless; and that small proportion which does have some use could be done far more efficiently at a fraction of the cost. Let's have a look.

(1) Estate Agents

The estate agent's bill is the biggest single item. The work the

---

* The building society usually instructs the purchaser's solicitor, who therefore acts in a dual capacity and collects *two* lots of fees.

estate agent does falls into the latter category, i.e. it is useful in that the estate agent introduces the purchaser to the seller. But how inefficiently he does it; and how grossly he overcharges for what he does.

Suppose after a lifetime of devoted service to my profession I wish to retire to a reasonably pleasant suburb in, say, North London. I visit the half dozen estate agents in the area I have chosen, and spend a couple of hours wading through the particulars of houses they have given me. I then spend two or three days visiting the more likely sounding ones; and discover that lawyers are not the only people who have cultivated a secret language designed to conceal, rather than reveal, their meaning – 'wealth of exposed beams', 'laid mainly to lawn', 'period cottage in need of some modernisation', 'desirable family residence in much sought-after area', 'early inspection recommended', and so on. How can I tell the good stuff from the rubbish? I can't. How can I get to know of *all* the houses for sale in the area? I can't. In fact whether I find the house I'm looking for is as much a lottery as whether I get compensation if I'm injured.

How could it be done more efficiently?

Every area has a public library assigned to it. It will be obligatory for the seller of a house in that area to supply the librarian with four photographs of the house (front, back, and outlooks therefrom), and information confined to address, price, number and dimensions of rooms, and size of garden. These photographs and particulars are displayed on a board or boards in the public library; cheapest houses on the left, more expensive on the right. Detailed map of area is also displayed. Library opens 9 a.m., shuts 8 p.m.

Result: seller saves £700 in estate agent's fees; purchaser is saved innumerable wild goose chases, and has a better chance of finding the house he wants.

(Incidental result: the environment is improved, as the only 'For Sale' boards permitted are those of modest dimensions, supplied by the librarian.)

(2) Seller's Solicitor

When solicitors attempt to justify their conveyancing charges, they invariably refer to the *purchase*. Even solicitors cannot make out much of a case for the *sale* conveyancing, which entails:

(a) drawing up a simple contract (name and address of seller, buyer, address of house, price, and half a dozen standard conditions); (b) answering the purchaser's solicitor's printed form of questions with some standard rhythmic inanities ('the deeds are silent but inspection may reveal', 'we know of none but the property is sold subject to any there may be' etc.), which give away no information at all; (c) liaising with the purchaser's solicitor and seller's building society. For this the solicitor charges £350 – which represents a rate of over £100 an hour for what is in effect low-grade clerical work.

How could it be done more efficiently?

The seller does his own sale conveyancing with assistance (if required) from the librarian, who will supply him with the necessary contract form, and a simple guide – in the same way that most people can find their way round the formalities entailed in getting a *passport*, but there is an enquiries office available if they get stuck.

Result: seller saves £350 in solicitors' fees.

(Incidental result: falls in love with librarian.)

(3) Purchaser's Solicitor

This is the work which is not only useless but *worse* than useless. It is useless because the solicitor's job (now that he no longer has to investigate the seller's title in the case of registered houses) is primarily to check that the house has no quasi-legal defects – e.g. that it has direct mains services, that there are no disputes with the neighbours, that there are no imminent developments of the adjoining land, etc. But the way the solicitor checks these things is by sending printed forms of questions to the seller's solicitor and to the local Council, which have almost no chance of getting any useful information. After all, it would be an absurd mechanic who checked a second-hand car, on behalf of a potential purchaser, by sending the seller a list of questions: 'please confirm the clutch is working properly' etc.

The solicitor's work is *worse* than useless because the purchaser is led to believe that his solicitor is checking that everything about the house is 'all right'; therefore the purchaser will not himself bother to check the commonsense points which should be checked by a brief inspection of the house, and by personally asking a few questions at the Council offices.

Consequently neither the purchaser *nor* his solicitor checks them, but they are simply left to chance – occasionally with disastrous results.

Furthermore, although the purchaser using common sense has a better chance of checking the various points than the solicitor with his printed forms of questions, there are many grey areas – due to the haphazard nature of the conveyancing system, and the fact that the few bits of quasi-legal information about a house are either imperfectly recorded in several different places, or else they are not recorded anywhere at all.

How could it be done more efficiently?

We already have the basis for an efficient system – the Land Registry, which now covers three-quarters of all houses in England and Wales. When a house is registered, the Land Registry issues a 'Land Certificate' for that house (which supersedes the previous title deeds), and which sets out the name of the owner, current mortgages, and contains a plan. Transferring the house from seller to purchaser is done by a simple form. In fact, the Land Registry was set up at the beginning of this century for the very purpose of simplifying the system, and so enabling people to do their own conveyancing.

Unfortunately something went wrong; and that is that the Land Registry did only half the job. It has simplified or cut out the work traditionally done by the purchaser's solicitor *after* exchange of contracts (i.e. investigating the seller's 'title' to the house); but because the Land Registry omits the fixed information which the purchaser needs to know, it has left untouched the solicitor's pre-contract procedures. Consequently the purchaser's solicitor makes a great song and dance about all the complicated things which he has to check *before* exchange of contracts. Moreover, in creating his smokescreen the solicitor has been greatly assisted by the Land Registry's practice of slavishly copying onto the Land Certificate perplexing, often voluminous, but generally *obsolete and unenforceable* restrictive covenants.

Therefore to make the system efficient, and achieve the original aim in setting up the Land Registry, all that is needed is to erase the latter and insert the former. Clear off all the obsolete and unenforceable restrictive covenants, and other verbal rubbish, which clutters up practically every Land Certificate; and in its place insert the few bits of relevant fixed information about the house which the purchaser needs to know – i.e. whether the road is a public highway, whether mains water and drainage are directly connected, whether planning permission was granted and so on.

Similarly, instead of the purchaser's solicitor sending to the local Council a six-page printed form crammed with complicated questions about umpteen Acts of Parliament under which the local Council *might* have issued a Notice or have a proposal affecting the house – the Council simply exhibits a comprehensive map on which it marks those houses and areas in respect of which it *has* issued a Notice or *does* have a proposal, or *has* received a planning application. This map, of course, is displayed next to the 'houses for sale' board at the library.

So after agreeing the price of the house with the seller, the purchaser is given a copy of the Land Certificate (which sets out all the fixed information he needs about the house); and he then checks on the Council map that the house and adjoining land are not shaded in red or spotted in green or whatever, and therefore that the Council has no designs on it.

The purchaser then completes the remaining enquiries and formalities himself, with a printed guide and with assistance, if necessary, from the librarian.

Result: purchaser saves £350 in solicitors' fees; purchaser is able to check in a few minutes the things he needs to know about the house, which under the existing system his solicitor spends four to eight weeks *failing* to check. Therefore purchaser runs *less* risk of finding anything untoward (e.g. a new road, an unsightly development, a troublesome neighbour etc.) after moving in.*

(Incidental result: the time scale of the transaction would depend solely on the parties, not their solicitors' conveyancing formalities. So if the parties wanted to complete within a week, they would be able to do so.)

(4) Building Society's Solicitor and Surveyor

The purchaser's building society employs these gentlemen – surveyor to survey the house, solicitor to check all the legal documents – because if the purchaser/borrower subsequently

---

* Incidentally the Government's widely publicized pledge to break the solicitors' conveyancing monopoly does not include any proposals to alter the conveyancing *system*, and is therefore an irrelevance. If work is useless, or worse than useless, it makes little difference whether it is done by a solicitor for £350 or a 'licensed conveyancer' for £250.

defaults on his mortgage repayments, the building society might have to sell the house to recoup the amount of its loan. Therefore the building society must know that the house has no legal or physical defect which might prevent it from being able to do so. This is the theory. In practice, the risk of (a) a defaulting borrower coinciding with (b) the building society finding that, for whatever reason, it could not sell his house *for the amount of the loan then outstanding*, is infinitesimal.

How could it be done more efficiently?

Building societies to dispense with the services of solicitor and surveyor (although the purchaser/borrower, of course, still hands over the signed printed form of mortgage and Land Certificate to the building society's clerk on completion). In the event of a borrower defaulting, and the building society, for any reason, *not* being able to recoup itself by selling the house for the amount of its loan and interest then outstanding (e.g. if an Abbey National borrower defaulted owing £20,000, and Abbey National found that it could only sell his house for £15,000), then it would recover its loss from a central compensation fund set up for that purpose. As three-quarters of a million building society mortgages are granted each year, it would only need each borrower in any one year to contribute £1 to finance the fund for the next decade or so.

Result: purchaser is saved some £200 in building society's professional fees; conveyancing processes are greatly speeded up. It would, of course, be up to the purchaser to decide whether to have his *own* survey.

(Incidental result: building societies would be *better* protected, since employing a solicitor or surveyor does *not* guarantee that a house has no legal or physical defect.)

Therefore by rationalizing the house transfer system, the house buyer and seller are each saved a total of £1,600 every time they move house. But they will still pay *half* of it – though not into the pockets of the estate agents and solicitors, *but into a personal injury compensation fund.*

It is logical that house-owners should subsidize this fund. Firstly, having over the years stoically subsidized a rather dubious cause, they should not object if instead they now subsidize a more worthy one – especially as it will be to the extent of only half the previous levy. Secondly, they are the better off members of the community, and enjoy considerable tax concessions by virtue of their house ownership. Thirdly, they will henceforth get the benefit of an efficient system of house transfer, in place of a ludicrously inefficient one.

Also available to be channelled into this compensation fund is the £30 million a year which the Legal Aid fund currently pays out to provide lawyers to argue the cases of those plaintiffs who are eligible for legal aid; and whose over-priced services will now no longer be necessary. In other words, instead of £75,000 of tax-payers' money going to provide a team of lawyers to argue (in vain as it happened) that Stuart Whitehouse's brain damage was due to the negligence of the obstetrician who delivered him, and that therefore the obstetrician should pay him compensation for his injury, that £75,000 will go to swell the fund from which he will be compensated automatically.

Result: without anyone having to pay an extra penny, we have a yearly personal injury compensation fund of £830 *million*, from which victims of every sort of accident (or their dependants) will be automatically compensated in accordance with the severity of their injuries, and their future needs – without having to prove that their injuries were caused by anyone's negligence; and without having to go anywhere near a lawyer.

Incidental result: having consigned two pockets of pernicious professionalism (personal injury compensation and house transfer) to the refuse heap, where they undoubtedly belong, the long-suffering British public might finally shake itself out of its apathy, and take a more critical look at some of the others.

Further reading

My other book, *The Conveyancing Fraud*, tells you how, even under the existing system, you can do your own house purchase and sale *without* a solicitor; and how, by following my detailed instructions, you are bound to do the job better than the professional.

Incidentally, the Government's widely publicized pledge to break the solicitors' conveyancing monopoly, by allowing other suitably qualified people to do conveyancing, is an irrelevance. There are no proposals to alter the conveyancing *system* in any fundamental way; and if work is useless or worse than useless it makes little difference whether it is done by a solicitor or a 'licensed conveyancer'. Equally, if work is useless, the customer is being overcharged whether he pays £700 to the former or £200 to the latter.

Some press notices:

A refreshing book and a useful one – *Observer*.

The book is easily understood and a 'must' for anyone about to buy or sell a house and who wants to save a lot of money – *Kentish Independent*.

Mr. Joseph gives step by step instructions on how to go about selling and buying. He has worked as a conveyancing solicitor so he should know what he is about. . .There is little, if any, aspect left out – *Daily Telegraph*.

However much one may dislike the author's tone, it is quite clear from his book that he is a highly competent man – *Solicitors' Journal*.

A rattling good yarn – *Private Eye*.

This book is dynamite for the legal profession – *Guardian*.

Mr. Joseph's book is excellent – *Financial Times*.

Required reading – *Daily Mail*.

The Conveyancing Fraud is available from me direct (address on rear cover), price, during 1985, £3.95 post free.

Barrister: lawyer who argues the case in the High Court and advises his 'instructing solicitor' when requested to do so, as the action proceeds. May not see or contact the client direct, but only through his instructing solicitor.

Civil Law: body of rules transgressing which is a wrong against the *individual* and which gives that individual a right to compensation; as distinct from **criminal law**, which is a body of rules transgressing which is a wrong against the State, which *punishes* the transgressor.

Counsel: synonymous with Barrister.

Court: civil cases are dealt with in two types of court: the *High* Court, which is where the vast majority of personal injury cases are heard or initiated; and the *County* Court (which has jurisdiction up to £5,000), which normally hears breach of contract and neighbours' disputes etc. In this book 'Court' invariably means the High Court. (Both types of Court have branches in the major towns.)

Court Hearing: *see* **Trial**

Damages: compensation which the Court (if it finds in favour of the plaintiff) orders the defendant to pay the plaintiff.

Defendant: the person against whom a legal action is brought. In personal injury cases, although the nominal defendant is the person who actually caused the injury (or his employer), the real defendant will be his *insurance company*, which will have to pay any compensation awarded. It is the insurance company which instructs solicitors to contest the claim on the defendant's behalf, and negotiates any settlement. If someone is negligent in the course of his employment, his employer is also liable *vicariously*. Thus David Johns's action would be against the playground supervisors *and* the Education Authority, their employers.

Legal Aid: a scheme whereby people whose income and capital are below a certain limit, and who have a reasonable chance of winning their case, can bring their case to Court, and their legal fees will be paid by the *State*. Applications for legal aid are decided by the **Legal Aid Committee**, (actually the **Area Committee**). An applicant who is granted legal aid gets a **Legal Aid Certificate**, which may be *conditional* (e.g. Counsel's Opinion might have to be taken before the case goes to trial, and only if favourable will the case be allowed to proceed); or *limited* to one or more steps after which the Legal Aid Committee will reassess the position.

Litigation: the process of bringing a civil case to Court.

Negligence: to win his case and get compensation, the plaintiff has to prove that his injury was caused by the defendant's negligence. There are various definitions of negligence but they all boil down to the defendant being at fault.

Next Friend: when the person bringing a legal action is a minor, he has to bring the action through his 'next friend' (usually one of his parents), who instructs a solicitor, and makes the decisions on the infant's behalf.

Personal Injury Litigation: where the plaintiff's legal action is in respect of **personal injuries**, i.e. injuries to his person, and he is claiming compensation (damages) from the defendant. To succeed he has to 'prove' that his injuries were caused by the defendant's **negligence** (fault).

Plaintiff: the person who is bringing a civil action.

Prove: to show 'on the balance of probabilities'.

Queen's Counsel (or **Leading Counsel** or **'Silk'**): member of an elite body of Counsel appointed by the Lord Chancellor. Generally employed to handle serious cases. Commands substantially increased fees, and has to be attended by an *ordinary* Counsel throughout the trial.

Settled out of Court: where at any time prior to the trial the defendant makes an offer to the plaintiff, which the plaintiff accepts in full settlement of his claim, and discontinues his legal action. The offer invariably includes, in addition, payment of the plaintiff's legal costs incurred to date, so that the plaintiff gets the offer *net*. If the plaintiff refuses the offer and the case goes to Court, the offer is, of course, automatically withdrawn. 97% of all personal injury cases in which writs are issued are either abandoned or settled out of Court.

Solicitor: lawyer who deals with a wide variety of matters e.g. conveyancing, probate, wills, etc. When he is consulted in a personal injury case involving a Court action he will invariably instruct a Counsel to advise, and draft the procedural documents, and it is Counsel who presents the case in Court. The solicitor may be compared to the general practitioner, and Counsel to the Consultant.

Statement of Claim: *see* **Writ**

Subpoena: Order requiring a witness's attendance at Court.

Trial or **Court Hearing:** the culmination of a civil case. If it is a negligence case in respect of personal injuries, the plaintiff's Counsel produces evidence to show, and argues, that the plaintiff's injuries *were* caused by the defendant's negligence; and the defendant's Counsel produces evidence, and argues, to the contrary; and the Judge decides which version he accepts. If the Judge accepts the plaintiff's version, he will decide on the amount of compensation the defendant must pay him. The losing party has to pay all the costs. So if the Judge decides that the plaintiff hasn't 'proved' his case, the plaintiff not only gets no compensation but has to pay his own and his opponent's legal costs.

Writ and Statement of Claim: the legal document which initiates the Court action; the latter sets out the detailed facts whereby the plaintiff is alleging that his accident was caused by the defendant's negligence.